If you want to learn the ways of decentralized disciple-m[...]
for you. In this manifesto on multiplication, Rob and L[...]
work for how to see movement happen. Rob and Lance [...]
as practitioners. If you want to grow, be challenged, and practice unleashing the
potential of raising up leaders, then pick up a copy of *The Starfish and the Spirit*.

Myron Pierce, author, lead pastor of Mission Church,
founder and president of Every Inner City

As a church planter in the West, I often have "yes, but how?" questions about
disciple-making movements and microchurch multiplication. In this book, Rob and
Lance have crammed eye-opening insights into every page, along with practical
tools for every leader to reimagine the future of the church. If you're passionate
about catalyzing every member of your church to effectively help others find their
way back to God, get reading.

Emma Jeffery, regional director of NewThing Western
Europe, Soulcity Church, United Kingdom

Like a cool rain after a decade of drought, *The Starfish and the Spirit* delivers relief,
respite, and a total rethink on what it means to follow Jesus in this remarkable
mission field we call life! Bravo to Rob and Lance for following and inviting us to
join them.

Hugh Halter, author of *The Tangible Kingdom*, *FLESH*, and *Happy Hour*

This book is a game changer. Get this down, and church multiplication becomes easy.
I've led starfish churches throughout my adult life. I loved and use Ori Brafman's
book, but this one explicitly addresses church leaders and the tensions that keep
us from the simplicity of church multiplication. My advice: read *The Starfish and
the Spirit* in concert with your key leaders to unlock a Great Commission future for
your team.

Ralph Moore, Hope Chapel

The Starfish and the Spirit is a handbook for movement making. My friends Rob
Wegner and Lance Ford brilliantly offer us a simple and scalable framework that
allows the Spirit to move and in so doing turns disciples of Jesus into an unstoppable
missional force. If you have a growing sense that God meant more for his church,
read this book and discover what's missing!

Dave Ferguson, lead visionary of NewThing, author of *B.L.E.S.S.:*
5 Everyday Ways to Love Your Neighbor and Change the World

A question much on my mind is this: Will there be church in the twenty-first century that matters? This quite remarkable book argues for what is necessary for the recovery, the re-creation, and the reality of Christian faith to make Jesus visible and evident today. Feast on this, and live into God's starfish communion and mission. This would be church that matters!

Mark Labberton, president of Fuller Theological Seminary

It's been nearly fifteen years since the release of *The Starfish and the Spider*, a groundbreaking book on the genius of decentralized systems and the limitations of hierarchical command-and-control structures. Now Lance Ford and Rob Wegner take that prism for understanding the patterns and potential of self-organizing systems and apply it to apostolic movements to brilliant effect. I kept asking myself, Why hasn't anyone done this before? But I'm glad no one has. I can't imagine anyone doing it better than these guys.

Michael Frost, Morling College, Sydney

There is no doubt that the world is changing, and we are in need of voices who not only see the future with hope and imagination but have the courage to live it out in their lives and leadership. *Authenticity is key.* Fortunately, we've been given just that in the gift of this book. *The Starfish and the Spirit* is not only a map toward authentic Christian leadership but also a guide for how to live out Jesus-practices, in community, in the brave new world we find ourselves in. With passion, insight, and great verve, Rob Wegner and Lance Ford unpack the operation system of how we currently "do church" and reconstruct a way forward that will not only inspire you but also call you to action. Get a copy, buy your friends and leadership team a copy, and go on the journey together!

Doug Paul, author of *Ready or Not: Kingdom Innovation for a Brave New World*

Yes! I love how these guys think and how they make me rethink. So incredibly refreshing. And timely too. We better dream and plan and grow in our vision now, because changes are coming, ready or not.

Brant Hansen, radio host, author of *Unoffendable*, *Blessed Are the Misfits*, and *The Truth about Us*

This book is a compendium for cutting-edge ideas. Rob and Lance have distilled and curated some of the most important thinking and timely tactics for the church in the twenty-first century. I could recommend twenty good books . . . or you could just read this one.

Brian Sanders, founder of the Underground Network, author of *Microchurches: A Smaller Way*

THE
STARFISH
AND THE
SPIRIT

THE STARFISH AND THE SPIRIT

Unleashing the Leadership Potential
of Churches and Organizations

Lance Ford | Rob Wegner
Alan Hirsch

ZONDERVAN REFLECTIVE

The Starfish and the Spirit
Copyright © 2021 by Lance Ford, Rob Wegner, and Alan Hirsch

Requests for information should be addressed to:
Zondervan, *3900 Sparks Dr. SE, Grand Rapids, Michigan 49546*

Zondervan titles may be purchased in bulk for educational, business, fundraising, or sales promotional use. For information, please email SpecialMarkets@Zondervan.com.

ISBN 978-0-310-10899-3 (audio)

Library of Congress Cataloging-in-Publication Data

Names: Ford, Lance, 1964- author. | Wegner, Rob, 1970- author. | Hirsch, Alan, 1959 October 24- author.
Title: The starfish and the Spirit : unleashing the leadership potential of churches and organizations / Lance Ford, Rob Wegner, Alan Hirsch.
Description: Grand Rapids : Zondervan, 2021.
Identifiers: LCCN 2020052530 (print) | LCCN 2020052531 (ebook) | ISBN 9780310098379 (paperback) | ISBN 9780310098393 (ebook)
Subjects: LCSH: Christian leadership. | Mission of the church. | Leadership—Religious aspects—Christianity.
Classification: LCC BV652.1 .F585 2021 (print) | LCC BV652.1 (ebook) | DDC 253--dc23
LC record available at https://lccn.loc.gov/2020052530
LC ebook record available at https://lccn.loc.gov/2020052531

---

21 22 23 24 25 /LSC/ 10 9 8 7 6 5 4 3 2

To the missionaries and microchurch leaders
of the Kansas City Underground

You're the most heart-deep, surrendered-to-Jesus community
of servant leaders Michelle and I have ever been part of. It's
an honor to lay our lives down next to yours. Let's continue
straight ahead toegther until this city we love so much is
filled with the beauty, justice, and good news of Jesus! You
are the heart, muscle, and backbone behind this book.

Rob Wegner

————————————

To John and Chris Knox, my and Sherri's
yokefellows for going on three decades

You both epitomize the joy of living on a kingdom
mission as a true team. You two are God's gift to the
church and one of his best gifts in our lives.

Lance Ford

Contents

Section 3: A Culture for Multiplying Disciples

Foreword

Run toward Your Fears

Ori Brafman

I got the call from my mom a little after eleven o'clock one night in early 2018. My dad had fallen, the untreated skin cancer on his face was bleeding profusely, and he had lost so much blood that he had passed out.

Over the past few years, my brother and I had pled with our dad to go see a doctor, but the response was always a litany of reasons why the medical "establishment" couldn't be trusted. He refused to seek medical attention and instead tried to find a cure through a variety of "alternative" and home-brewed treatments.

First was the switch to an all-raw-meat diet. He had to force himself to eat raw steak, raw liver, raw kidneys, raw eggs, even raw cuts of fat—all doused in cayenne pepper to mask the taste. It would have been almost funny if not for the fact that he had been vegan for the previous thirty years.

Then came his experiments with enzymes. He ordered huge bottles of pills from overseas and popped up to seventy a day. Meanwhile, the tumor on his face grew at an alarming rate. In the span of a single year, it had grown from the size of a nickel to the size of a dollar bill. It covered one whole cheek and was encroaching on his eye and ear.

Eventually he turned to cannabis to cure his ills—this from a man who has never even been drunk in his life. Visiting my parents was like a nightmarish variation of a Cheech and Chong movie: my dad was so stoned that he was barely coherent, dying before our eyes.

Wash, rinse, repeat the conversation about getting help. But to my dad, this fate was preferable to seeing a doctor. He lectured us about chemotherapy being poison and radiation a form of torture.

When a hospice nurse showed up one morning and left a bottle of morphine, I explained to my mom that they don't give self-serve, all-you-can-drink morphine to someone who has a chance of surviving. My mom finally understood the end was near. And she got on board with taking him to the hospital.

Another day passed, filled with discussions and debates about the merits of modern medicine. My brother and I tried everything to convince him. Finally, I put on a hoodie, went outside, and tapped on Dad's window with a long stick. Inside, my brother told Dad, "Look, it's the angel of death. He's here for you." That bit of twisted levity finally got him to agree to get help.

My brother picked up the phone and called 911, and an hour later we went from medicine circa 1500 AD to an emergency room where doctors gave him fluids, IV antibiotics, and three blood transfusions.

"We're here to help you," the hospitalist told him.

My dad had lost so much blood that he was out of it. Asked what year it was, he answered, "Nineteen ninety-two." "Where are you?" "An amusement park."

"At least he's young and having fun," we quipped.

The next day, the antibiotics and blood transfusions were starting to do their thing, and my dad was feeling better by the minute. But he was still confused.

"What is this place," he asked my mom, "where they're so nice and are taking such good care of us?"

"You're in the hospital," she told him. He looked at her with amazement.

Over the next few days, he continued to marvel at the kindness and care he received. He even said at one point that he felt like he was in a resort on a relaxing vacation.

Now, had he gone to see a doctor a few years earlier, the cure would have been a simple ten-minute procedure. But in fearing doctors so much, my dad got himself into such a dire state that he had to be hospitalized. In trying to avoid his biggest fear, he manifested it. But when that happened, it was a joyous occasion.

The news from the doctors was initially mixed. The prognosis for a cancer this advanced wasn't good, but we were able to enroll my dad in a clinical study. Regardless, we now had Dad 2.0, who recognized how much doctors had helped him and, in an ironic twist of fate, was trying as hard as he could to *stay* in the hospital. This new version of my dad was even more appreciative of my mom and even more glad to be alive.

Now more joyful and having faced his fears, he continued the experimental treatment. And then, the truly unexpected happened. Slowly but surely, the treatment worked—to the point where the massive tumor was so diminished that it was no longer visible.

How many of us can say we've confronted our greatest fears? Isn't it strange that doing so can bring such joy?

I started thinking about my own fear: What am I running away from? How can I instead run toward it?

I share this story because the level of fear in our world seems to be rising by the day—not just fear of a virus, but fear of each other.

If I had a time machine and could interview my thirty-year-old self, the one who coauthored *The Starfish and the Spider* in 2006, and ask him what he feared most, he wouldn't have hesitated long.

First, I feared the military. I've been a lifelong vegetarian and founded a vegan nonprofit when I was in college. Nonviolence has been part of my core identity. Never in a million years did I expect that my book would end up being read by our nation's top generals. Never did I imagine I would get to know them. Never could I have believed I would become friends with them. Yes, in many instances we had to put our policy and political differences aside, but what genuinely surprised me was how many members of the military shared my belief in avoiding violence.

My second fear brings us to this book. I was born in Israel and raised in a secular environment, only to move to El Paso, Texas, when I was nine. I'll never forget when a kid named Jason at the local playground asked me in all seriousness whether I had horns.

"Why should I have horns?" I asked in my newly acquired English, with my Israeli-Texan accent.

"Because you're from Israel," he said earnestly, "and my parents say Jews have horns."

I don't think Jason was necessarily brought up to hate Jews. But he certainly was brought up to fear us. And that was when I began fearing religions that seemed to fear *me*. Indeed, here in San Francisco, it's not uncommon to hear people tell how they felt feared and judged by members of their faiths growing up.

And thus, just as I never imagined I would ever set foot in the Pentagon, I never expected I would become friends with Lance Ford and Rob Wegner. What could I possibly have in common with two evangelicals?

As with my friends in the military, I've found that there are issues where our views differ. But Lance and Rob have illuminated for me, in the most beautiful way, something very important: Who cares about the multitude of things that might divide us? Aren't our souls, as humans, the same?

I've slowly experienced the joy of disentangling politics, institutions, and the spiritual.

Often the more afraid we are, the more control we try to exert. Lance and Rob show there's another, more effective way: to let go of control and instead focus on empowerment, service-oriented leadership, and trust. I've learned from Lance and Rob, and I trust them. I encourage you to trust them too. In this time of fear, may we be courageous and open to new discoveries, new friends, and new solutions!

Politics may be divisive, and some institutions may have chiseled away at our trust, but the soul and the spirit will always unite us.

Reimagining Church

CHAPTER 1

Arachnophobia and Spider Bites

The greatest danger in times of turbulence is not the turbulence—
it is to act with yesterday's logic.

—often attributed to Peter Drucker

Jesus called them to him and said, "You know that the rulers
of the Gentiles lord it over them, and their great ones exercise
authority over them. It shall not be so among you."

—Matthew 20:25–26 ESV

When I (Rob) was a boy, I had a terrifying experience that left me with a lifelong fear. Have you had such an experience? A moment where fear paralyzed you, and even now, it gives you the creeps just thinking about it?

It was a sleepy summer afternoon, and I was six. After a rousing morning of outdoor play, I slipped into an accidental nap on my bed. Upon waking, I fluttered my eyes open. Something I couldn't quite make out was floating above me. My vision, still blurred from grogginess, took a few seconds to focus. Suddenly, the blurry image became crystal clear.

I froze.

A large spider, which looked to be the size of a tarantula to my little mind, was hanging on a web six inches above my nose. Fear paralyzed me. I held my breath and couldn't speak. With what I knew was sinister intent, the spider was waiting to drop on my face and bite me.

That was the beginning of a lifelong struggle with arachnophobia, the fear of

Figure 1.1

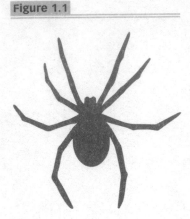

spiders. If you've seen *Raiders of the Lost Ark*, you know Indy's trigger is snakes: "Snakes. Why did it have to be snakes?" For me it is, "Spiders. Why did it have to be spiders?"

It felt like an old Western standoff, but only one of us had a gun. After what seemed like an eternity, I finally yelled, "Mom!" Like a gunslinger, Mom walked in, saw the spider, came back with a tissue, crushed that sucker, and said, "You're fine."

Yet the fear of spiders and spider bites has stayed with me. Lance won't want me to out him, but he's a scaredy-cat too when it comes to spiders.

Imagine our surprise when we both enjoyed a book about spiders. By God's providence, it was life-changing for both of us. The year was 2006. The book was *The Starfish and the Spider: The Unstoppable Power of Leaderless Organizations* by Ori Brafman and Rod A. Beckstrom. Here is what the book proposes:

Consider two types of organizations, one like a spider and the other like a starfish. Spiders and starfish look similar. They both have central bodies with legs that sprout radially from the center. But there are big differences between these two organisms.

If you cut off the head of a spider, you kill the entire organism. Spider organizations, by extension, are standard hierarchies where a "central brain" or

Figure 1.2

decision-making body regulates the actions of the organization in a centralized, direct fashion. If something bad happens to that decision-making body, the entire organization dies.

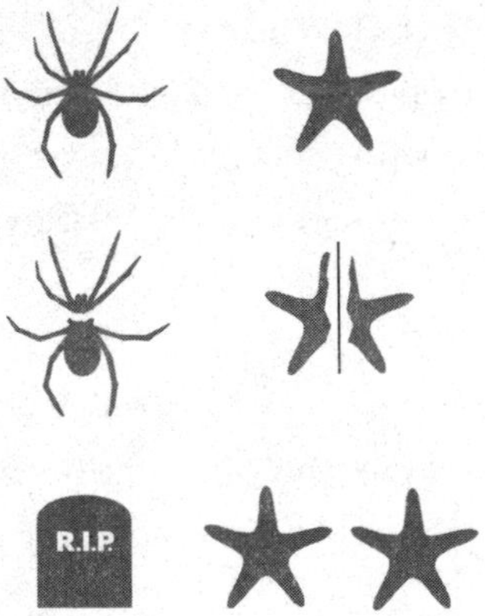

Starfish don't have that problem. If you cut a starfish in half and fling each half to opposite ends of the world, what happens? You get two starfish. A starfish has in each of its cells all that it needs to regenerate a whole new starfish. Every cell of a starfish organization, unlike spider organizations, has everything it needs to reproduce.

Alan Hirsch: The metaphor of the spider and the starfish offers us an important insight into the nature of what we can call "fragile systems" of organization. The more one focuses intelligence and power in the few, the more fragile is that system. This is different from "antifragile" systems, where power and function are dispersed as widely as possible. When the church is viewed through the lenses of fragility and antifragility, it's quite simple to discern the primary form that the New Testament church took.

Back to spider bites.

Have you ever walked into a spider web or been bitten by a spider? Most likely you didn't notice the web until you were already entangled. Or you didn't feel the bite at first and only later discovered a sore or infected spot on some part of your body. Only then did you realize an arachnid had bitten you.

That spider experience has become far too common in the church.

The morning news feed opens with yet another story of a high-profile pastor or faith-based leader caught up in a swirl of accusation. Patterns of sustained abuse of one sort or another, such as bullying, misuse of position, sexual harassment, or just plain burnout from the weight of leading, have come to light. Pastor "Smith" of "Well-Known Church" has resigned, been fired, or is fending off allegations.

When the downfall of famed leadership expert and pastor Bill Hybels came to fruition, the church world was shocked and dismayed. As more and more credible witnesses came forth, a pattern of decades-long positional leveraging and abuse came to light. Arguably the most influential shaper of evangelical church leadership over the last fifty years had tumbled. And it was the very web of leadership systems he had purveyed all along that served to camouflage his actions along the way.

Upon hearing each story, we wonder, "Why does this keep happening? And who will be next?" The stories have become predictably familiar: unhealthy and ungodly patterns and habits bud and build under the cloak of leadership power, rank, privilege, or the stress of responsibility overload. Though we are always saddened at such news, we are becoming less and less surprised. We are usually just disappointed and dismayed that it was *that* person. But spiderwebs are like that. They are most often invisible until you get close to them.

This book is here to help clear out the cobwebs.

As you might have already guessed by the title, the analogy of the spider and the starfish will be central to this book. As we begin, you should know that this book is written differently from most books.

First, a blessing from Ori Brafman, an Israeli-Berkley-leadership guru and coauthor of *The Starfish and the Spider*, to the authors of this book to extend the ideas of said book to the church. Three of us—a South African–born, Australian transplant missional leadership guru; a native Texan; and a Midwestern All-American—have come together to share our stories, experiences, and findings with a goal of helping churches and faith-based leaders move past spidery experiences so they can grow flourishing cultures to help them and their teams fulfill the purpose and mission of their organizations.

Ori's book was a *New York Times* bestseller, and its influence has spread far beyond the marketplace, causing not just Fortune 500 companies but even the US military to rethink leadership. Why? During the era of the Cold War, two equal and opposite armies could potentially meet on the field of battle: land, sea, or air. Modern warfare is radically different. Only one dominant military superpower is in the world today.

If you're ISIS, Al Qaeda, or Russia, how do you fight a superpower? You don't meet on the field of battle but through what military theorists call dirty war or a disinformation campaign. The KGB literally coined the term *disinformation*. You flood the internet with lies, you hack, you release emails, you capitalize on fake news, you foment anger of one group toward another, you fuel fear. Russia has troll farms with bots and algorithms that can work out—based on big data, people's Google search history, and social media habits—what people are afraid of. They can learn people's emotional cartography to pinpoint the time of day they are most susceptible to emotional manipulation and drop an article or tweet in their feed to do so. It's asymmetrical warfare, decentralized. In his book *War in 140 Characters*, on the effect of Twitter on modern warfare, David Patrikarakos makes the point that war is no longer about territory; it's about ideology.[1]

This, of course, has required a major pivot on the part of the US military to rethink its strategy and how it trains its leaders. Ori was hired to help. Eventually, that relationship led to the book *Radical Inclusion*, which Ori cowrote with Martin Dempsey, the former chairman for the Joint Chiefs of Staff.

Ori's is just one voice in a much larger body of work that has emerged over the last fifteen years on the topic of decentralized leadership, the kind of leadership required to lead a movement. There has been a repeated emphasis toward decentralized leadership in the business world, represented by books like *Servant Leadership* by Robert K. Greenleaf, *Leading Self-Directed Work Teams* by Kimball Fisher, *Holocracy: The New Management System for a Rapidly Changing World* by Brian J. Robertson, *Reinventing Organizations* by Frederic Laloux, *Leadership and the New Science* by Margaret J. Wheatley, and so forth. Companies like Visa, Zappos, 3M, and Google have demonstrated how viable and necessary the switch to this leadership model is.

As we (Lance and Rob) have watched this conversation unfold, these books have sounded like prophetic voices, speaking not just to the marketplace and military but also to the church. We believe the origin point in history for this form of leadership is Jesus himself. It's time for the church to return in repentance to our founder's example. In Christian literature, authors like Lawrence O. Richards in *A Theology of Church Leadership*, Alvin Lindgren in *Let My People Go*, Keith Miller in *The Taste of New Wine*, Robert E. Coleman in *Dry Bones Can Live Again*, and many more have been calling us back to decentralized forms of leadership that are required if the church is to become the people movement Jesus designed it to be.

With four combined decades of service as pastors in large successful churches and as trainers to thousands of pastors, we (Rob and Lance) agree with these voices: something is amiss in church leadership. Our journeys within the local church have broken our hearts over the spider bites—the wounds of hierarchical, complicated, and heavy-handed leadership—that millions have experienced. And we admit up front that we've been spider-men ourselves at different times.

Hard work is to be expected, but the busyness of church seems to have supplanted the business of church, and there's an increasing reliance on human power in lieu of heavenly power. Those crises sent us searching for ways of leading that ring truer to the character of our spiritual leader, Christ, and the things he said about leadership.

In that journey, Alan Hirsch has been a big brother, mentor, and dear friend to both of us. It is by no means an overstatement to declare that his influence thoroughly changed our lives and ministries. Through his writing and speaking, Alan has effected positive changes like no other since the turn of the new millennium through his insight into the contemporary church. He calls us to return to an understanding of the church as a movement.

Movements require a new culture and a new language that are mostly foreign to church as we know it in the West. Like anyone seeking to understand a new language, we've recognized a need to find someone who could speak "church-as-movement-ese" and translate that to those of us who speak "church-as-institution-ese."

A number of years back, when my wife, Michelle, and I (Rob) took our entire family to India for the first time, we planned a two-day layover in London to help break up the lengthy and grueling trip for our girls. While there, we had the joy of visiting the world-renowned British Museum, one of the largest gatherings of priceless historic artifacts from every continent and almost every area of human civilization. Admission is free, which is good since the Brits "borrowed" many of the items during colonization and never gave them back.

During our tour, I had a moment of wonder as we stood in front of the Rosetta Stone. This ancient stone unlocked the voice of the Egyptian culture, which had been "unhearable" for centuries. Before the Rosetta Stone, no one was able to decipher Egyptian hieroglyphics. The decree inscribed appears in three scripts simultaneously: ancient Egyptian hieroglyphs, a demotic script, and ancient Greek. This overlapping of languages was the key to unlocking four thousand years of an ancient written culture. This stone is now an icon of all attempts to understand a culture on its own terms.

We found a "Rosetta stone" that overlapped the language of institutional church and movemental church, deciphering for us our experience of church as movement in places outside the West, like India and China, showing us the way to speak that language and create that culture here in the West. That "Rosetta stone" was *The Forgotten Ways* by Alan Hirsch, which came out in 2006, the same year as *The Starfish and the Spider*. The combination of those books changed the trajectory of our lives.

In *The Forgotten Ways*, Alan argues that all God's people have everything within them needed to rediscover church as a movement. Readers are asked to think of this as latent or dormant potential that needs to be rediscovered and then activated. That's why all throughout church history, and even at this present moment, we can *always* find examples of church as movement. The possibility of apostolic movement is always there, resident within us, waiting to be activated and unleashed. When we see even a glimpse of it or read the stories of movement, something inside us cries out, "That's it!"

Alan introduces six elements of movement DNA, or mDNA for short. Together they form the genetic coding of church as a missional movement—the church we see in the New Testament, in past revivals, and currently in places such as China and India. These elements of mDNA, although they have huge ramifications in term of methodology, are first paradigms or cornerstone concepts that change the way we understand the form and function of the church. In our humble opinion, these elements provide the clearest snapshot and most cohesive understanding of church as movement we've encountered.[2] You'll find the mDNA elements throughout this book.[3]

---

mDNA: Elements of Apostolic Movements

Jesus Is Lord: At the center of every significant Jesus movement there exists a simple confession: the claim of one God in and through Jesus, over every aspect of every life, and the response of his people to that claim (Deut. 6:4–6). This was expressed in the New Testament simply as "Jesus Is Lord!"

Discipleship and Disciple-Making: Essentially, discipleship involves the irreplaceable and lifelong task of becoming like Jesus by embodying his message. On the other hand, disciple-making means ensuring that the church or organization is focused on this core purpose.

Missional-Incarnational Impulse: The twin impulses of God's redemptive mission are the dynamic outward thrust toward unreached people (missional) and the related downward impulse into culture (incarnational). Together they seed and embed the gospel into different cultures and people groups.

APEST Culture: The Ephesians 4 ministry and leadership matrix required to both initiate and sustain Jesus movement: the apostolic, prophetic, evangelistic, shepherding, and teaching functions together equip the church for growth, maturity, and unity.

Organic Systems: Phenomenal Jesus movements grow precisely because they don't have centralized institutions that block growth through control. Jesus movements have the culture of a movement and the structure of a network and spread like viruses.

Communitas: The vigorous form of community that thrives in adverse conditions in the context of mission, risk, and challenge (liminality).

We asked Alan to step into this book project to provide his comments on our thoughts, so expect him to pop up now and again to substantiate or challenge our thinking.

Our aim and hope for you as you read this book is to convey a more joyful and productive—and less costly at the human level—leadership ethos that will help you develop a culture that reflects these thoughts:

1. The idea that Jesus provided his leadership model as one that, rather than rising by creating an ascending pyramid to elevate himself, was a descending form that empowered others. His initial circle reproduced similar circles, filling culture with humble servants who also led courageously by making heroes of others, empowering and equipping them to be all God made them to be.

2. The primary forms of leadership we have been using continue to produce an unnecessary human cost. Alan often says, "We are perfectly designed to produce what we are currently producing." What we are seeing should not surprise us. Rather, we should redesign the system to produce different outcomes. As we embark on the third decade of the new millennium, the entertainment industry, corporate business world, and church and faith community have been rocked by a succession of leaders who have been brought down in disgraceful fashion for patterns of behavior linked to bullying, domineering, and abuse of different kinds. On the faith front, several high-profile leaders have resigned their posts solely out of exhaustion or for slipping into self-destructive patterns. Some of these leaders were just plain worn out from the weight of carrying a church or organization on one set of shoulders.

3. Our primary leadership models have emerged from the Industrial Revolution and the Renaissance, which produced singular charismatic hero types. The influence of these eras has had an enormous shaping impact on our current leadership ways and means. Much of what emerges from such concepts runs counter to the culture God advocates for the church and faith-based leadership at large.

4. We are at a junction in church and faith leadership where credibility and integrity are justly being doubted. We need to ask some uneasy questions about ourselves. The answers we will find can lead us not only to truth but to the truth that will set us free to be all that God has designed us to be personally, professionally, and for the sake of the world around us.

5. Most churches and faith groups, large or small, already have the inherent competency and capacity to flourish. What is needed is an understanding of how to unleash the latent wisdom, understanding, talents, and joy that will fuel their tasks and journey.

We (Rob and Lance) will occasionally share our own firsthand spider-bite experiences throughout the book. The goal is not to shame anyone but to demonstrate how serious the problem is, how common the problem is, and how toxic the wrong form of leadership can be. But, in this transparency, please don't read a blanket condemnation of the church in its centralized form. In nature, spiders have their place. We believe Jesus is working in and through the spider (highly centralized) expressions of the church in profound ways. We have both spent many years leading in centralized forms of the church, seeing the Spirit do amazing things in the lives of those congregations, along with countless thousands of other such churches. God's Spirit enlivens and empowers the church, regardless of form. Yet this book is a clear call toward the movemental, decentralized form of church and the pursuant form of leadership required, which Alan and Ori have so clearly articulated and which we hope to make practical with this book.

As you already know, another option lies open before us: the starfish.

Not long after Ori's book *The Starfish and the Spider* came out, copies landed in our (Lance's and Rob's) mailboxes. This agnostic professor from one of the most secular universities in America, through his research, had rediscovered a generous, open, service-oriented, empowering form of leadership. Over time, by providence and blessing, Lance and Ori met at a conference at which they were both speaking. They hit it off. Rob was friends with Lance and a superfan of Ori's work, so Lance introduced them. Conversations ensued. Friendships deepened. We are grateful to Ori for his blessing to extend and reinterpret the starfish concept for the church context. (Check out *The Starfish and the Spirit* podcast, where Ori is a regular contributor.)

From our perspective, as mentioned earlier, Jesus is the origin point of starfish leadership. Over the last fifteen years, we have found Ori's "outside" perspective both prophetic and incredibly helpful in reapplying Jesus' leadership ethos back to the church. What has developed is a series or system of "starfish" that we hope will help church leaders rediscover Jesus' leadership in a fresh and practical way, within a more fluid expression of church.

Again, our end goal is to see the church as movement reactivated, where all six of the mDNA elements can be cultivated and catalyzed. In *The Permanent Revolution*, Alan describes it this way:

> In short, apostolic [missional] movement involves a radical community of disciples, centered on the lordship of Jesus, empowered by the Spirit, built squarely on a fivefold ministry, organized around mission where everyone (not

just professionals) is considered an empowered agent, and tends to be decentralized in organizational structure. . . . Apostolic movements require that we see church beyond its more institutional forms—as a movement of the whole people of God active in every sphere and domain of society. Seen through the lens of institution, the church will be conceived of as being primarily made up of its external forms and not its inner nature—as being made up of the combination of theological preferences, professional clergy, elaborate rituals, denominational templates, distinctive buildings, and the like. Clearly this is not what the New Testament itself means by ecclesia, and although it can be included within more movemental understandings, it is not what we mean by apostolic movement.[4]

Over the course of this book, we will unpack seven starfish, each one carrying five points relating to one key area required to become a missional movement, or what we like to call a starfish movement. We hope to reinvigorate church leadership with the vision, values, and practices to rediscover not only Jesus' leadership ethos and practice but also the outcome of a more movemental expression of the church. Here are the seven starfish we'll cover:

The Movement Starfish: Reimagining the Church as a Missional Movement
The Light-Load Leader Starfish: Equipping Others and Distributing the Weight
The Structure Starfish: Thinking Outside Pyramids and Creating Circles
The Self-Management Starfish: Unleashing Freedom and Facilitating Order
The Disciple-Making Ingredients Starfish: Creating Environments and
    Mixing Ingredients
The Disciple-Making Ecosystem Starfish: Balancing Elements and
    Cultivating an Ecosystem
The Collective Intelligence Starfish: Embedding Simple Processes and
    Becoming a Learning System

Alan Hirsch: The idea of organization has been described as "the mobilization of bias."[5] In other words, every organization is formed to achieve certain outcomes that can't be achieved individually. It is important for leadership to take responsibility for the re-biasing of the organization or church to achieve the outcomes that Jesus intended for it.

This book is organized into three sections: Reimagining Church, A Culture for Multiplying Leaders, and A Culture for Multiplying Disciples. "Culture eats strategy for breakfast," often attributed to Peter Drucker, applies here. The starfish exist for this purpose, creating a robust culture for the emergence of multiplying disciples and leaders. While this categorical organization is helpful for the structure and logic of this book, it does not reflect the actual journey of how a leader and faith community will make their way toward an apostolic movement. At the conclusion of the book, we will share with you a map of the starfish journey, which is about sequence and phases. If you can't wait to see the map, jump to page 291 to take a look now.

Along the way, please know the critique of the current, prevailing church leadership approach is not blind negativity. Most pastors are doing their best to lead faithfully. Yet we can't ignore the crisis. We want to stand on "the edge of the inside" and provide a hopeful critique we pray will lead to a faithful return to what Jesus has in mind for his church.

People who truly, deeply love something have earned the right to critique and help make it truer to its deepest vision. We've both given our entire adult lives to serving the organized church. These things of which we write have been worked out in blood, sweat, prayer, and tears.

One unique aspect of our Scriptures that differs greatly from the other world religions is that our prophets—voices like Isaiah and Jeremiah in the Old Testament and James and Paul in the New Testament—are free to both deeply love the tradition and profoundly criticize it at the same time. Their love demands that they do so. If we didn't love the organized church and her leaders so much, we wouldn't have bothered to write this book. Jesus offered his faithful critique masterfully and with mercy as his motivation. We seek to follow his example in these pages.

As you read, we hope you feel our deep love for the church and its leaders. We also hope you feel us poking you in the chest.

Let's begin. It's time to let the good things run wild!

CHAPTER 2

Good Things Running Wild

The more I considered Christianity, the more I found that while it has established a rule and order, the chief aim of that order was to give room for good things to run wild.

—G. K. Chesterton, *Orthodoxy*

"We gave you strict orders not to teach in this name," he said. "Yet you have filled Jerusalem with your teaching."

—Acts 5:28

The year was 1984. It was a time of huge bangs on young ladies, mullets on young men, jam shorts, ripped jeans, Michael Jackson, and hair metal bands. Obviously, the American culture had reached a place of unrivaled refinement. A missionary kid turned youth pastor, Dan Gute, looked at a Ferris Bueller wannabe—fourteen-year-old me (Rob)—and saw someone who could be a catalyst for something more than high jinks and practical jokes. He invited a ragtag group of teenagers, about twelve of us, oddly enough, and invited us to become disciples who could make disciples. We were young enough to believe we could do it. Over the next years, Jesus walked among us, transformed lives, and turned that youth group of a sleepy, insular Baptist church into a little movement of sorts.

The holy rumpus erupted in us as we experienced Jesus personally, hearing his voice and seeing his face. Good things ran wild through the halls of our schools as we shared our faith. The primal drumbeat of eternal life—not just a length of life but quality of life only Jesus offers—pounded in us as we gathered around hidden firepits in the forest to pray and worship. We knew something ancient and original was happening: a holy rumpus, anchored and deeply rooted yet unhinged and fresh. We read the book of Acts as a script we could be actors in and exclaimed to ourselves, "This is real. Jesus is actually doing this stuff today, here and now!"

The whole thing felt dangerous and unpredictable. The missional, incarnational impulse had been awakened in us. We knew the Holy Spirit had put a foot in our backs, sending us out to our peers who didn't yet know how much they mattered to God. The mall, the arcade, and the high school cafeteria were our mission field. Simultaneously, we shared the good news incarnationally, using the language of our peers (words like *dude*, *radical*, *sweet*, and *gnarly*) and the idioms of our time (shredded jeans with homemade graffiti, mullets, and '80s metal) to give us credibility that we were "one of" and could be trusted.

> **Alan Hirsch:** It's amazing that almost every revolution (cultural or political) seems to be accomplished by young people. Martin Luther King Jr. noted that the true revolutionary is a person who has nothing to lose. The church would be wise to rely more on its youthful revolutionaries and organize around them.

A couple of years into that awakening, the number of teenagers gathered one evening in the old sanctuary was equal to the number of adults in the entire congregation. More than forty of our friends decided to follow Jesus that night. Sure, looking back I can see the baggage we unknowingly carried. Our suitcases were stuffed with things like a radically reduced, wafer-thin, fire-insurance version of the gospel; a young arrogance; a deep dualism that created walls between us and the whimsical, transforming, comprehensive holiness of God that is everywhere; identities wrapped up in our religious performance; and more. But none of that canceled out the essence of what was happening. The old "order" had given room for "good things to run wild."

In the afterglow of that evening, I remarked to Dan, "I'm kind of surprised all the older folks are okay with us using the sanctuary for our stuff. This was kind of a crazy night." With a mischievous glint in his eyes, he grinned and replied, "Some of them know. They've been praying for us. But I want you to remember something, Rob. Sometimes it's easier to ask forgiveness than permission."

Amid the tension between the old order, spiderlike and standing still, and the new order of starfish, decentralized expression of church, I discovered my calling to lead.

What about your calling to lead? Did it come to you amid good things running wild? I bet so. You responded to that call to empower and release more good things to run wild in and through a faith community, nonprofit, marketplace endeavor, or wherever you make your contribution.

Early in my story, I had an experience inside the old order of the church, where good things ran wild in me, and the Spirit set my soul on fire. That experience created a deep longing in me that made me say, "Let the wild, holy rumpus start!" I bet you felt that too.

Yet I also wager that somewhere along the line, you've felt the old order constricting the wild, good things to the point where they were no longer able to run wild. In most churches and organizations, *the order* is the only goal. In those cases, any wild things have to be domesticated. Eventually, one day, you realized you were running a machine built to keep the order. In quiet moments of desperation, you thought, "I didn't sign up for this. Where did all the wild things go? I signed up to help fuel a Jesus movement, but now I feel like I'm running a machine."

On this tension, Alan notes in his book with Dave Ferguson, *On the Verge,*

> With the rise of the Christendom church (the institutional paradigm)—resulting from Emperor Constantine's marriage of the church to the state—the prevailing idea or conception of church became fundamentally *nonmissional.* Historically, the reason for this, of course, is that all who were born within the geographical realm of the Christendom civilization were considered Christian. In the American expression, Christianity was not married to the state (as in Europe) but is nonetheless seen to be an inextricable part of American culture and identity; until the last thirty years or so, if you were an American, you were a Christian, with few exceptions (Native Americans, Jews, and so on). But the net result of either hard (state-mandated) or soft (cultural) Christendom is to effectively create a domesticated civil religion which no longer challenges and transforms society but rather is co-opted by it.[1]

Many church leaders find themselves exhausted and disillusioned leading a form of church that is nonmissional yet demanding of them as the resident "expert" and "professional." Close to 1,500 pastors leave the ministry every month. If they were given the opportunity to make a similar salary doing something else, most pastors surveyed said they'd jump at it.[2] The lingering effects of the COVID-19 pandemic will only make the ministry more challenging and the longing to jump out of ministry even more intense.

Many of us are weary of being keepers of the order.

My youth pastor Dan used that wild moment to help me see the embodiment of G. K. Chesterton's essential point in the quote that started this chapter: the centralized expression of the faith community exists to empower and release the decentralized expression of the faith community so good things can run wild.

The center exists to empower the margins, not the other way around.

That is the main thrust of this book: *the restoration of the running-wild, decentralized expression of the church and the empowerment of the pursuant form of leadership that can and will release it.* In other words, you don't have to ask permission from "the order." Jesus has already ordained and commissioned the good things to run wild. You can find your sacred mojo again.

In this chapter, we begin with a review of the most common understanding of the organized church (spider) and then reimagine faith communities as flourishing, reproducing networks of reproducing disciples, transforming the world by way of good things running wild (starfish). We will also explore the hybrids that exist between these ends of the continuum.

In *The Starfish and the Spider*, Ori refers to this blending as the "Combo Special: The Hybrid Organization." Rather than seeing it as an either/or, spider or starfish, many can go the way of both/and. What kind of creature would that be? You can splice those genes in one of two ways. You have either a spiderfish or a starder. Let's examine the current expression of church in the West through this lens.

The spider, the spiderfish, the starder, and starfish exist on a continuum, moving from centralization to decentralization. Although we celebrate that the Spirit is at

Figure 2.1

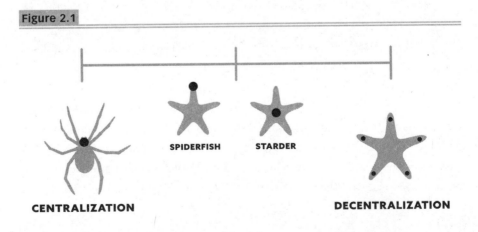

SPIDERFISH   STARDER

CENTRALIZATION   DECENTRALIZATION

work in all forms of the church, our goal is to advocate for movement toward the right end of the continuum. For now, as a way of marking the beginning of the journey, consider the following four marker points, and ask yourself, "Where is our church on the journey toward movement?" More importantly, pay attention to power dynamics. As we move down the continuum, power and authority are pushed further and further out. Where is the locus of power in your church? How does the power work?

The power dynamics are a central issue. High control with centralized power will shut down the possibilities of movement. On this, using the Wesleyan movement as an example, Alan notes,

> Something happens when we try to control things too much that serves to lock up the power of multiplication, and the movement moves on to addition and then on to subtraction. This is exactly what happened in Wesley's revolutionary movement, for instance. Wesleyanism was at its most influential when it was a people movement that was reproducing like mad. It eventually centralized, and as people sought to control what was happening, it lost much of its power to really change the world.[3]

It's not so much the form of church we invite you to examine in this continuum at this point, as it is the form of power. As you read, ask yourself, "Which of these best describes the power dynamics in our church?"

Figure 2.2

The spider expression of church is a centralized form where it is oriented around one location, one congregation, and one gathering under the authority of one leadership head, usually a senior leader or pastor working with a board or council. The locus of power is centralized in that head (represented by the blackened circle). This is the prevailing model in the American church, with more than half of US churches having one location, one service, and one leadership head.[4]

Figure 2.3

The spider's locus of power works like a strand of Christmas lights. If the bulb at the top (the centralized locus of power in the senior pastor) goes out on the single string, so does every bulb below it. The pastor and the board or staff emanate the current (direction, programs, and more) that the congregants connect into. The power also works like currency, with an individual or small group of people "holding" the power.

Figure 2.4

SPIDERFISH

The spiderfish expression of church still has power in a head, usually either a single leader or a small leadership team, with different departments (or arms) of the church expanding the "reach" into different demographics, usually children, students, men, women, and others. In this expression, the church typically has multiple services or venues. The spiderfish expression may also include multiple locations, where one church is cloned in multiple locations that are supported by video streaming. Or there may be a slightly higher level of autonomy where teaching teams work in syncopation, teaching the same series simultaneously in each location. The goal is to create the same experience in multiple places under the oversight of a centralized leadership team that still has a relatively high level of control over each location.

Remember, on the surface, spiders and starfish can look similar in appearance. It's what's happening beneath the surface in terms of the locus of power that marks the difference between a spider church and a starfish church. In denominations and franchise multisites (those that clone the original site with tight control on branding, decision making, and teaching), the locus of power is like a hub and spokes. Unlike with a wheel, the spokes in this diagram flow only one direction: down. The power from the hub flows out and down along the spokes. If the hub is removed, the network disappears.

Figure 2.5

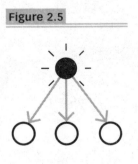

If the main church, or "mothership," in the franchise multisite network were to turn off, the entire network would disappear. Similarly, in many denominations, churches agree on common theological and philosophical distinctives and choose to relate under a centralized authority. Denominations have credentialing processes, dedicated educational institutions, mission agencies, and an agreed-upon hierarchy. If somehow an entire denominational head were removed in one moment, the denomination would either disperse or they would need to immediately appoint a new head. We know of one major denomination that currently has several new heads developing in backroom conversations because of a theological controversy.

They want to be ready to have a new hub and spoke network in place when it comes time to pull out of the old one.

Figure 2.6

The starder expression of church has now shifted the power from the head at the top to a shared leadership model, where leaders from multiple locations come together at the center to empower the margins. No longer is there a senior pastor or a leadership team at one location calling the shots for all the locations. This may look like one church with multiple congregations in multiple locations or a collection of churches collaborating as one church. Now there is a team made up of equals who maintain a high level of independence at the local level while cooperating together on a shared mission in a city or region.

> **Alan Hirsch:** I have always loved the term *chaordic* to describe authentic movemental ways of organizing. As the word suggests, every organization needs enough order (structure) to provide stability and continuity and needs to engage enough chaos to remain creative. Too much order, the organization dies. Too much chaos, the organization dies. Chaordic is where the balance between order and chaos is struck.

Figure 2.7

The starfish is a decentralized expression of the church oriented around multiple locations, multiple congregations, multiple gatherings, and multiple leaders. Imagine the church as a decentralized network of multiplying disciples, missional leaders, and microchurches, the smallest and most essential expression of church. Unlike a denomination or association of churches, which confers ordination and provides general accountability to church leaders through centralized structure, a starfish movement is apostolic—organized around mission breaking through in new contexts—and organizes as a network of networks, made up of families of churches with a common focus, minus the restrictive structures of a denomination.[5]

Remember, if you cut the starfish in half, the animal doesn't die; it reproduces. Now you have two starfish. A group called Order of the Underwater Coral Heroes

(OUCH) discovered this the hard way. OUCH, a group of rogue divers launched in the late 1990s, existed to defend the Great Barrier Reef in Australia. The starfish were growing so numerous that they were beginning to destroy the coral. Taking matters into their own hands, members of OUCH would dive with their knives and then cut the starfish in half to kill them. But the halves regenerated into new starfish—a two for one starfish special! How does that happen? According to Ori Brafman, "They can achieve this magical regeneration because in reality, a starfish is a neural network—basically a network of cells. Instead of having a head, like a spider, the starfish functions as a decentralized network."[6]

In the starfish expression, we see that every member contains within them a church, and every church contains within it a movement. Here in the West, we have a hard time conceiving of this possibility of power being so decentralized. Yet outside the Western world, this view is quite normal. The starfish is best represented by the viral spread of the underground organic church movements in China, India, and many other places around the world.

One of the greatest privileges of my (Rob's) life is the honor of serving indigenous church planting movements in India, Thailand, Laos, Myanmar, and South Africa. The starfish leaders in those countries are among my most treasured friends, mentors, and co-laborers. Experiencing these starfish movements firsthand has changed my sense of what is possible for the church.

For example, in a ten-year window in southern India, what started with a handful of like-minded leaders training a cohort of about thirty ordinary folks (we might call them bivocational pastors) multiplied into a movement of more than 2,000 churches including over 180,000 people. Those thirty people made disciples who made disciples who formed microchurches that reproduced microchurches among unreached people in previously unreached villages. There was hardly a paid professional pastor among the whole movement.

One woman who was very dear to Michelle and me was Martha, a stay-at-home mom. Martha's village was near the interstate, with a high rate of sex trafficking due to its location. Each day while her kids were in school, she began to befriend the prostitutes, living like a missionary among them. New disciples emerged, then a microchurch, then a network of microchurches made up of former prostitutes and their families. Together they opened up a tailoring business to employ the women as seamstresses. Even in a patriarchal society like India, Martha emerged as a leader of a network of microchurches in a couple of years. Modern stories like this from around the world are multiplied in the hundreds of thousands.

It's breathtakingly beautiful.

Returning home to help lead the modern evangelical megachurch I pastored gave me a feeling of whiplash. One Sunday I was watching the good things run wild, a viral movement of reproducing disciples and microchurches sweeping the land. The next Sunday I was back to "church as usual": services timed to the second, tracked in real time with software; bands with lightshows and hazers; "killer" video; church programs for this and that; the next great relevant, catchy weekend series; and more.

Don't misunderstand me. The Spirit was using these means to draw people to himself and then move them into meaningful relationship with Jesus and the church. Yet against the backdrop of this disciple-making movement in India, by comparison, so few were being empowered to their maximum influence. People had to settle for being a "volunteer." We were growing by addition, yet few were making new disciples. One needed to bring them to a building for service or a program designed by a paid professional who could do the heavy lifting for them.

By God's grace, I had enough experience to know that responding like an angry adolescent and screaming, "Burn it down!" would be a waste. That posture would have caused me to miss the point of what the Spirit was saying. What was the Spirit saying to me? "Rob, why not here? Why not now?"

He is still saying that to me—daily, hourly, moment by moment. It has gripped my soul.

How about you?

Starfish organizations don't just happen "over there." Here in the States, our friend Brian Sanders and a handful of starfish leaders have been the spark for a similar movement in Tampa, Florida, called the Tampa Underground Network, which has now reproduced more than three hundred microchurches. That has spanned new microchurch movements in twenty-one other cities, including the Kansas City Underground, the family of microchurches I (Rob) serve. Or consider another one of my coaches, Jeff Vanderstelt, and the Soma family of churches. What started as a handful of missional communities in Tacoma, Washington, has become a network of hundreds of missional communities gathering in congregations in forty-eight cities. How about the amazing movement Jesus has unleashed through Hope Chapel and the servant leadership of Ralph Moore? Forty-five years ago, God called a young pastor named Ralph and his wife, Ruby, to take over a vacant church building in Manhattan Beach. What began as a vision for multiplying disciples and multiplying churches has now become a movement of more than 2,300 churches and counting.

These expressions of church are growing not just by addition but by multiplication. No matter how fast you hit the addition button, you can't keep up with the impact of multiplication.

The Exponential church planting network has created and titled this expression of church as level 5: multiplying. At this level, churches are multiplying on multiple strands out to at least the fourth generation. In comparison, level 1 churches are subtracting, and level 2 churches are plateaued. Currently, 70 percent of the churches in America are at levels 1 and 2.[7] Level 3 churches are growing by addition, finding and solving the problems that limit growth. This growth happens mostly through innovating on the methods of the church growth movement, scaling through multiple venues or multisite. Currently, 23 percent of the churches in America are growing by addition.[8] Level 4 churches are reproducing. This is largely represented by the massive growth of church planting. At level 4, leaders are no longer thinking only about putting more trees in their orchard through multisite. Rather, they are interested in planting new orchards by planting churches that plant churches. Approximately 7 percent of US churches are growing by reproduction.[9]

Figure 2.8

Levels 1, 2, 3, 4 and 5

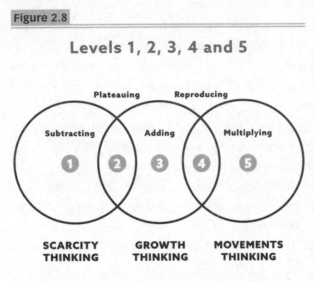

Against that backdrop, level 5 multipliers see multiplying disciples, leaders, microchurches, large churches, and networks as normal. They plan for gospel saturation in a city or region. Their scorecard no longer reads "how many have accumulated at the center" but instead reads "how many have been sent to the margins to multiply disciples and churches." Level 5 is represented by less than .005 percent of US churches.[10]

At levels 1 and 2, the message is "Please stay."

At levels 3 and 4, the message is "Please come."

At level 5, the faith community is a launchpad saying, "Please go!"

Maybe you're wondering, "Isn't level 5 just another denomination? Or what about a church with a larger number of multisites, like Life.Church?[11] Isn't that level 5? Aren't those considered starfish?"

Remember the power dynamics.

In the starfish expression, the locus of power is spread throughout the network in many locations, leaders, and teams. What starts as one starfish will multiply to many, creating a starfish network. The power doesn't reside in one starfish but in multiple star-fish that operate like nodes throughout the network. The power and information move in multiple directions, depending on the usage and need within the network. The goal is to multiply and connect disciples, leaders, teams, churches, and networks in interdependent ways. Within the network, there are multiple points of power. Multiple leadership teams work interdependently with the goal of gospel saturation in a city, region, or country.

Figure 2.9

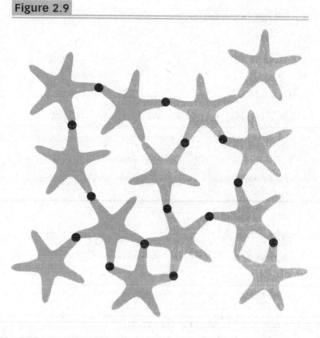

In the *Harvard Business Review* article "Understanding 'New Power,'" authors Jeremy Heimans and Henry Timms make the following distinction between "old power," what we call the spider, and "new power," what we call starfish:

> *Old power* works like a currency. It is held by few. Once gained, it is jealously guarded, and the powerful have a substantial store of it to spend. It is closed, inaccessible, and leader-driven. It downloads, and it captures.
>
> *New power* operates differently, like a current. It is made by many. It is open, participatory, and peer-driven. It uploads, and it distributes. Like water or electricity, it's most forceful when it surges. The goal with new power is not to hoard it but to channel it.[12]

> **Alan Hirsch:** In every group of people—and this is particularly true of God's people, the body of Christ—intelligence is not focused in one or two people but is laced throughout the organization (e.g., 1 Cor. 12:12–27; Eph. 4:1–16). Every part has a role to play in the success and maturity of the whole. This is called distributed intelligence. I invite you to compare your church with that of the New Testament, and be willing to rethink your own structures in the light of Jesus' original design.

New power gains influence from growing other's capacity and increasing their influence to move beyond consumption and join in as cocreators. God's design for the Body is clearly one of new power:

From whom the whole body, joined and held together by every joint with which it is equipped, when each part is working properly, makes the body grow so that it builds itself up in love. (Eph. 4:16 ESV)

As in one body we have many members, and the members do not all have the same function, so we, though many, are one body in Christ, and individually members one of another. (Rom. 12:4–5 ESV)

Just as the body is one and has many members, and all the members of the body, though many, are one body, so it is with Christ. For in one Spirit we were all baptized into one body—Jews or Greeks, slaves or free—and all were made to drink of one Spirit.

For the body does not consist of one member but of many. If the foot should say, "Because I am not a hand, I do not belong to the body," that would not make it any less a part of the body. (1 Cor. 12:12–15 ESV)

He told them another parable: "The kingdom of heaven is like a mustard seed, which a man took and planted in his field. Though it is the smallest of all seeds, yet when it grows, it is the largest of garden plants and becomes a tree, so that the birds come and perch in its branches."

He told them still another parable: "The kingdom of heaven is like yeast that a woman took and mixed into about sixty pounds of flour until it worked all through the dough." (Matt. 13:31–33)

Don't you know that you yourselves are God's temple and that God's Spirit dwells in your midst? (1 Cor. 3:16)

I am the vine; you are the branches. If you remain in me and I in you, you will bear much fruit; apart from me you can do nothing. (John 15:5)

These passages provide fertile biblical ground for the power dynamics of the church. We aren't designed for old power, which is built on institutional hierarchy, but new power, which flows and feels like organic systems: a body, yeast, seeds, trees, living temples, and vines.

Let's consider again the old power models. Heimans and Timms describe it this way:

> Old power models tend to require little more than consumption. . . . But new power taps into people's growing capacity—and desire—to participate in ways that go beyond consumption. These behaviors, laid out in the exhibit "The Participation Scale," include sharing (taking other people's content and sharing it with audiences), shaping (remixing or adapting existing content or assets with a new message or flavor), funding (endorsing with money), producing (creating content or delivering products and services within a peer community such as YouTube, Etsy, or Airbnb), and co-owning (as seen in models like Wikipedia and open source software).[13]

The battle between old and new power is a defining feature of the church at this hour. Consider this as a continuum, with old power at one end and new power at the other. Most of the church's power dynamics have been built around the consuming and sharing end of the continuum, with the power in the hands of a few who design the religious goods and services for the rest to consume and share with others.

New power models are about cocreating and co-owning. This is now the new normal in America. For example, more than five hundred million people now share and shape Facebook with thirty billion pieces of content each month.[14] Etsy has created a platform for countless artists and craftspeople to shine and connect with

Figure 2.10

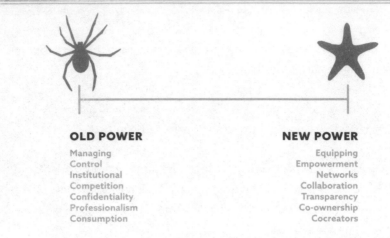

OLD POWER

Managing
Control
Institutional
Competition
Confidentiality
Professionalism
Consumption

NEW POWER

Equipping
Empowerment
Networks
Collaboration
Transparency
Co-ownership
Cocreators

others. Or consider the millions of projects and initiatives that have been launched through Kickstarter.

These new power models see everyone as artists, creatives, entrepreneurs, and investors. In the biblical framework, we call that the *imago Dei*. The church is designed to be a parade of diversity and creativity, where each person can live out the fullness of their God-given uniqueness as a spiritual entrepreneur in the kingdom. With the coming of the Holy Spirit, everyone receives this same power and same commissioning from heaven.

The old power model—where a small number of people are the decision-makers, creatives, and designers for everyone—is still common. But the careful observer can also see a massive transition toward new power models emerging all around us, in every domain of society. Moisés Naím, in his eye-opening book *The End of Power*, describes it this way: "The decoupling of power from size, and thus the decoupling of the capacity to use power effectively from the control of . . . bureaucracy, is changing the world."[15] He cites the current era as one where "micropowers: small, unknown, or once-negligible actors . . . have found ways to undermine, fence in, or thwart the megaplayers, the large bureaucratic organizations that previously controlled their fields. . . . Their advantage is precisely that they are not burdened by the size, scale, asset and resource portfolio, centralization, and hierarchy that the megaplayers have deployed and spent so much time and effort nurturing and managing. . . . The implications are breathtaking."[16] One can't help but think of the story of the early church, a reproducing micropower, eventually helping to topple the Roman Empire.

And yet too often the church operates, almost unconsciously, on old power models where it begins to feel like an assimilating ant colony; everyone gets in line and follow the same instructions: "Go to church, volunteer, go to a small group, give a tithe, invite a friend, rinse, and repeat." As Alan notes,

> When we allow the apostolic movemental way of thinking to reshape our idea of church, we begin to see the sheer transformational power of the church that Jesus designed—a church where each part in the system, be it individual disciple or community, has the full potential of the whole and therefore is intrinsically empowered to achieve what Jesus has set out for us to achieve. We begin to realize that, at least potentially, every believer ought to be considered a church planter and every church should be thought of as a church-planting church. Just as there is the full potential of a forest in every seed, so too is the task of leadership to help every disciple to be a movement in the making.[17]

In this book, we will explore how the church can be reimagined as a mission agency that exists to empower and equip people to live at the producing and co-owning end of the continuum, living fully as missionaries where they live, work, learn, and play, making disciples and leading simple forms of church. In the Jesus movement, everyone follows and everyone leads. In the Jesus movement, every disciple is called to make disciples, find their calling, and own mission fully.

Heimans and Timms also describe a shift from old power values to new power values. New power relies on a networked approach to governance and decision-making. Leaders don't and can't depend on positions or titles for influence any longer, but on transparency and integrity alone. Alan describes this shift as the move from institutional to inspirational leadership:

> In institutional power, it is the human institution that confers the power to an individual to perform a certain task. It is therefore primarily an external source of power that drives the role. Not so with inspirational leadership. Inspirational leadership involves a relationship between leaders and followers in which each influences the other to pursue common objectives, with the aim of transforming followers into leaders in their own right. It does this by appealing to values and calling without offering material incentives. It is based largely on moral power and is therefore primarily internal.[18]

Then inspirational leaders, with new power models and values, give their platform to others to develop and launch them out on mission. The focus shifts from developing your own leadership to multiplying and developing the influence of others, decentralizing the power and authority out to them while activating their gifts, their dreams, and their kingdom assignments.

Consider the following matrix as another way of visualizing how these various expressions of society and the church accumulate and wield power according to old and new models and old and new values.

Under the old power models and values, the idea was to build a castle and rule as a benevolent king over the people, using the old models and old values to grow larger while consolidating power. Under new power models and values, "our platform" exists for the mobilization of others into their mission and calling, their influence for the kingdom, turning the crowd into an apostolic movement.

Figure 2.11

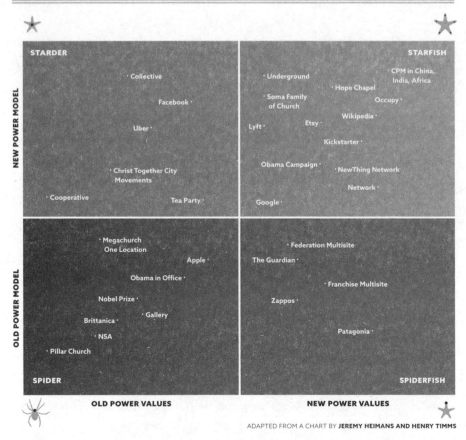

ADAPTED FROM A CHART BY **JEREMY HEIMANS AND HENRY TIMMS**

To bring a little more clarity to the various expressions of church and how the locus of power functions within them according to the new and old power models and values, consider the multisite spectrum introduced in the book *MultiChurch* by Brad House and Gregg Allison.

There are seven models along their spectrum:

Pillar: one church with a single service
Gallery: one church expanded to multiple services or venues
Franchise: one church cloned to multiple sites
Federation: one church contextualized in multiple locations
Cooperative: one church made up of multiple interdependent churches
Collective: a collection of churches collaborating as one church
Network: individual churches joining together for a common goal and support

You can see in the previous chart where we plot out these various hybrids. Pillar and gallery churches land in the spider quadrant. Franchise multisite lands in the spiderfish quadrant, as does federation multisite, which moves a little closer to the starfish quadrant. Collectives and cooperatives land in the starder quadrant. Multiplicative networks like the church planting movements (CPMs) in China, India, and Africa, along with movements like the Underground Network, the Soma family of churches, and the Hope Chapel movement, live in the starfish quadrant.

In the starfish quadrant, movemental-type leadership recognizes that everyone plays and everyone has the seed of a movement within. As Paul said in Colossians 1:27, "Christ in you, the hope of glory." God's people just need awakening, clearance, and equipping to live into that truth. A missional movement requires that power and function flow away from the center to the outermost margins. As Darin Land states in *The Diffusion of Ecclesiastical Authority*, the leaders in the book of Acts were "consistently sharing their authority with others, these leaders allowed the diffusion of authority to new individuals rather than the concentration of authority in the hands of the few. . . . They were able to do this because their authority was based on deference and mutual honor, not only on legal rights. Thus, the diffusion of ecclesiastical authority resulted in a net increase of authority, which in turn propelled the growth of the church."[19]

Long live the starfish!

In closing, let's review by comparing the two extreme ends of the continuum. In the next chapter we will look at the example of the early church for deeper insight.

Table 2.1*—A Comparison of Power Dynamics

QUESTION	SPIDER	STARFISH
Is there someone in charge?	Yes. Depends on hierarchy. One leader/board locally, often with another larger hierarchy denominationally. Pyramids with a few leaders at the top.	No. Flat structure. Relies on influence rather than control. Multiplies leaders and leadership teams. Reproduces circles of leaders.
Is there a headquarters?	Yes. The church or faith community is strongly associated with one leader with centralized programs at a building. Church is an activity, building, or event, so we "go to church."	No. Location is flexible. Church is spread out in every domain of society, making disciples and forming simple expressions of church that are connected with larger, more organized expressions of church that work to make the kingdom tangible. Church is an identity, so we can only "be the church."
If you thump it on the head, will it die?	Yes. Take out the lead pastor/board/boss and it dies, unless you quickly sew on a new head.	No. If you take out the leaders, new leaders emerge because reproducing disciples, leaders, teams, and churches is normal.
Is there a clear division of roles?	Yes. Divided into centralized departments and programs with delineated staff and volunteer roles for people to fill. There are slots to fill to help run the centralized programs. Invite your friends to church so they can do the same. Reach and accumulate.	No. Anyone can do anything based on the development of character (fruit of the Spirit) and calling (gifts of the Spirit) in each person. Leaders equip everyone to discover their calling and develop their character. People are deployed into mission where they live, work, learn, and play, where they make disciples, form kingdom initiatives, make disciples, see microchurches emerge, etc. Equip and release.
If you take out a unit, is the organization harmed?	Yes. Every department is necessary, especially the weekend services. Remove the weekend services and the church disperses.	No. The network can rebuild itself and is connected like cells in a starfish's body. Even without weekly weekend services, the collective of disciples and smaller expressions of church keep reproducing.
Are knowledge and power concentrated or distributed?	Centralized. Information and power are concentrated at the top with the lead pastor or lead team.	Decentralized. Information and power are dispersed throughout the network of reproducing disciples and churches.

Is the organization flexible or rigid?	Rigid. Has a lead pastor who fills the staff team, which runs the church. This structure will never change.	Flexible. The organization is amorphous and fluid, leading to agility, constantly growing, shrinking, mutating, spreading, dying, and rebirthing. New leadership teams are constantly emerging, which relate dynamically to other leadership teams in the decentralized network of the church, filling a city or a region.
Can you count it?	Yes. Weekend attendance and church membership in a particular location or brand of church are fixed and can be counted.	Not fully. Membership is fluid and open as disciples work together in networks and neighborhoods, even though they may connect with different congregations. No one can fully keep track of the discipling relationships and reproducing disciples, leaders, teams, and churches in the city or regional network.
How Is It funded?	Centrally funded. Offerings come to center and are distributed, with a priority on the center. Without funding, departments or programs quickly die.	Self-funded. A liberated financial model where disciples, leaders, teams, and micro-churches are responsible for sourcing and stewarding funds. The need for resources at the center is minimized so the apostolic mission at the margins can be prioritized.
How does communica-tion work?	From the top down, from the pastors through intermediaries. Important information is processed through HQ. The pastors are paid to be the experts endowed with special knowledge others are dependent on, who always have the answer. "All roads lead to Rome." Every church has its own pope.	From the bottom up, directly between the disciples, leaders, and churches in the network. The greatest learning happens at the edges, where discipleship and mission collide. Leaders facilitate collective intelligence by listening and reporting to the network. No roads lead to Rome because there is no Rome. Jesus is the head of the church.

* Ori Brafman, *The Starfish and the Spider: The Unstoppable Power of Leaderless Organizations* (New York: Penguin, 2006), 174–75). This original chart designed for business leaders has been reinterpreted for church leaders.

Without a doubt, the early church is a story told at the starfish end of the continuum. To truly begin this journey, we must reimagine church through the original starfish design Jesus gave it. We'll explore that in the next chapter.

CHAPTER 3

The Movement Starfish

Reimagining the Church as a Missional Movement

The starting place is theological, not structural or methodological. An institutional temple spirituality primarily oriented around church buildings, Sunday services, programs, formalized professional clergy, or standardized denominational frameworks, is not likely to produce a viral spiritual force of Christ followers and churches. Only a rigorous recovery of Christology— doctrine of Christ—will revitalize Christians.

—Roger Helland, *Magnificent Surrender*

Figure 3.1

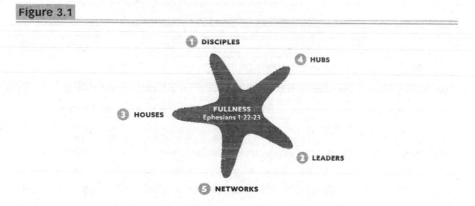

Starfish #1: The Movement Starfish

Purpose: The movement starfish helps us reimagine the church as a decentralized network of multiplying disciples, leaders, houses, hubs, and networks that fill a city or region with the fullness of Jesus.

Gospel Saturation

To reimagine church as a missional movement, we must explore saturation, imagination, and multiplication.

Consider what it would look and feel like to experience a missional movement in a city. Let's head back to Jerusalem. The church's enemies said of her, "You have filled Jerusalem" (Acts 5:28).

That's what a missional movement feels like. Fullness. Another word for that is *saturation*. A missional movement feels like a city saturated with God, like water fills an aquarium. Everyone and everywhere is saturated with the gospel!

In the context of this book, we are using the term *gospel saturation* to describe such an occurrence. What is gospel saturation? It is the church owning the lostness of an identified people in a defined place, ensuring that every man, woman, and child has repeated opportunities to see, hear, and experience the gospel in community and then to respond to the good news of Jesus Christ.[1]

Saturation = Shalom = Fullness

Perhaps the most compelling expression of gospel saturation is Paul's consummate vision for the church and the entire cosmos in Ephesians 1:22–23: "God placed all things under his feet and appointed him to be head over everything for the church, which is his body, the fullness of him who fills everything in every way." How big are you when everything is under your feet? How big is Jesus?

Consider the size of our planet for a moment. Most of us were quarantined in our homes for months during the COVID-19 pandemic. We could feel the walls closing in. Let your imagination run wild and envision again how vast the earth is.

Jim Lovell, of the Apollo 8 mission, reflecting on the size of the cosmos, discovered that from the vicinity of the moon, he could totally block his view of the earth by holding his thumb in front of it.[2] Another astronaut, Jim Irwin, described the earth as a fragile ornament hanging in the blackness of space. He said, "The Earth reminded us of a Christmas tree ornament hanging in the blackness of space. As we got farther and farther away, it [the Earth] diminished in size. Finally it shrank to the size of a marble."[3]

Pull back a little farther.

On February 14, 1990, as the Voyager 1 spacecraft left our planetary neighborhood for the fringes of the solar system, engineers turned it around for one last look at its home planet. Voyager 1 was about 4 billion miles away from the sun and approximately 32 degrees above the ecliptic plane when it captured a portrait of our world, now known affectionately as the *Pale Blue Dot*. Caught in the center of scattered light rays, earth appears as a tiny point of light, a crescent only 0.12 pixels in size.[4]

Pull back a little farther.

Not just the earth but the entire cosmos is like a speck of dust in Jesus' hand. Back in Genesis, Jesus took the chaos, what was formless and void, and ordered and filled it. Jesus turns chaos into cosmos. His wisdom and understanding have no limit. Each of us has an image of Jesu—the one comprised of our current knowledge, experiences, and cultural influence—that hangs in the gallery of our soul. We must understand how impoverished and warped the image is. It needs to be constantly reformed by the Word and by the Spirit.

Jesus is so much bigger and so much better than we imagine.

Alan Hirsch: Heresies—effectively what we can call theological reductionisms—occur when we reduce our understanding of God, Jesus, the gospel, people, or the church down to a lifeless and one-dimensional formula. This is essentially what the idolater does, making God smaller, making him into a god that can be controlled. But God won't have it! In *A Grief Observed*, C. S. Lewis noted that "images of the Holy easily become holy images—sacrosanct. My idea of God is not a divine idea. It has to be shattered time after time. He shatters it Himself. He is the great iconoclast. Could we not almost say that this shattering is one of the marks of His presence? The Incarnation is the supreme example; it leaves all previous ideas of the Messiah in ruins. And most are 'offended' by the iconoclasm; and blessed are those who are not. . . . All reality is iconoclastic."* Repent! Open your hearts and minds to the ever-greater God!

---

* C. S. Lewis, *A Grief Observed* (San Francisco: HarperSanFrancisco, 2001), 76.

Paul says that *Jesus fills everything every way* (Eph. 1:23). He is big enough to fill every need, big enough to be the solution to every problem, big enough to redeem every mistake, big enough to restore everything broken. Jesus fills everything every way with all that he is. At the end of the story, heaven and earth will collide and comingle completely, evil will be vanquished, and all that Jesus is will fill everything every way (Rev. 21–22).

As the church, we are called to be "his body, the fullness of him" (Eph. 1:23). *We are the fullness of him who fills everything every way?* Have you seen us? Have you seen the state of the church? This verse describes who we are meant to be as the church and what we are ultimately destined for.

The church is a living, breathing organism. The church is a people, not a program. The church is an identity, not an activity. We are the body of Christ. What are we designed for? To join Jesus by manifesting his fullness, making it tangible in every domain of society, that everything in every way will be filled with all that Jesus is.

They said of the early church, "You have filled Jerusalem" (Acts 5:28). Jesus said we are to begin there, continuing onward "in all Judea and Samaria, and to the ends of the earth" (Acts 1:8). Eventually, they will say of the church, "You have filled the earth!" Jesus says, "Fill it all with my fullness." This is the most expansive vision for church one could possibly imagine! As Alan proclaims in *The Permanent Revolution*,

> What are God's original purposes in and through his people? Is the gospel capable of renewing the world and transforming the hearts of all human beings? Did God really mean for the ecclesia to be the focal point for the wholesale renewal of society? . . . The ecclesia that Jesus intended was specifically designed with built-in, self-generative capacities and was made for nothing less than world-transforming, lasting, and, yes, revolutionary impact.[5]

Fill everything every way with the fullness of Jesus.

Let's be honest, there have been many times in our past when our vision for mobilization has gone something like this: "Lord, I need you to fill the chairs in the auditorium. I need you to fill all the volunteer slots in the nursery during the third service. And the offering bags too, Lord." The temptation for church leaders is to make the end zone of mobilization the institution of the church and its programs. If we say, "Our church is healthy," but the murder rate in our city is still high, fatherlessness is increasing, addiction is increasing, and we're not making any gains in universal flourishing in every corner of culture, is the church in the city healthy? If we continue to mean a building and a service when we say "church," we'll never fill everything in everywhere. We aren't even filling our buildings anymore.

Perhaps the best biblical word for the state of gospel saturation is the word *shalom*. Neal Plantinga, former president of Calvin Theological Seminary, in his book *Not the Way It's Supposed to Be*, described the idea as follows:

The webbing together of God, humans, and all creation in justice, fulfillment, and delight is what the Hebrew prophets call *shalom*. We call it peace, but it means far more than mere peace of mind or a cease-fire between enemies. In the Bible, shalom means *universal flourishing, wholeness, and delight*—a rich state of affairs in which natural needs are satisfied and natural gifts fruitfully employed, a state of affairs that inspires joyful wonder as its Creator and Savior opens doors and welcomes the creatures in whom he delights. Shalom, in other words, is the way things ought to be.[6]

That's the end game of the movement starfish: *to fill everything every way with the fullness of Jesus*. The movement starfish is designed to embody, in a practical and measurable way, the end we are seeking—a missional movement.

> **Alan Hirsch:** A missional church measures its effectiveness not just by what goes on inside the church building (the so-called butts and bucks metric) but also by its impact beyond the church. In other words, what impact is the church having on youth suicide, drug addiction, domestic violence, exploitation of the poor, and more? These things can, and should, be measured alongside the insider metrics we have been using for so long.

That's what began happening in Jerusalem shortly after the ascension of Jesus. The early church saturated the city with the good news, beauty, and justice of Jesus. That leaves us with this question: How in the world did that happen? The movement starfish is our best answer. Near the end of this chapter, we will explore ways to measure that fullness. But first, to understand the movement starfish, we need to make a radical commitment to *imagination first* and *multiplication forever*.

Imagination First

First, we must begin by engaging a missional form of imagination. Missional imagination is the blending of courage and creativity. It is more than getting swept up in a daydream; it is allowing the Divine to show you what could be. Missional imagination is sitting down with all your limitations and brokenness yet letting a seed of faith push up a dandelion through a crack in the concrete of your current paradigms. It creates something fresh within you as a response to the Lord's invitation to us: "See, I am doing a new thing! Now it springs up; do you not perceive it?" (Isa. 43:19).

The subtitle of this chapter is "Reimagining Church as a Missional Movement." That prompts the question, what exactly is that? This book is an invitation to reimagine the church as a decentralized network of multiplying disciples, missional leaders, microchurches, and networks thereof.

This work of reimagining is exceedingly difficult for us because the Constantinian Christendom template of church sits in our heads, having dominated our imagination for 1,700 years.

Take a minute to examine this table from *The Forgotten Ways* that distills three distinct eras of the church.[7] Our institutional way of thinking about church—through the lens of buildings, programs, rituals, denominational templates, and religious professionals—stems mainly from when Constantine legalized Christianity. Prior to this, the Jesus movement was grassroots, an underground people movement made up of multiplying networks of disciples and gospel communities marked by signs and wonders.

	APOSTOLIC AND POSTAPOSTOLIC MODE (AD 32 TO 313)	CHRISTENDOM MODE (313 TO CURRENT)	EMERGING MISSIONAL MODE (PAST 10 YEARS)
Locus of Gathering	Doesn't have dedicated sacral buildings; often underground and persecuted	Buildings become central to the notion and experience of church	Rejects the concern and need for dedicated "church" buildings
Leadership Ethos	Leadership operating with at least a fivefold ministry-leadership ethos as in Eph. 4 (apostle, prophet, evangelist, pastor, teacher)	Leadership by institutionally ordained clergy, thus creating a professional guild operating primarily in a pastor-teacher mode	Leadership embraces a pioneering-innovative mode, including a fivefold ministry-leadership ethos; noninstitutional by preferences
Organizational Structure(s)	Grassroots, decentralized, cellular, movement	Institutional-hierarchical and top-down notion of leadership and structure	Grassroots, decentralized, movements
Sacramental Mode (Means of Grace)	Communion celebrated as a sacramentalized community meal; baptism by all	Increasing institutionalization of grace through the sacraments experienced only "in church"	Redeems, resacramentalizes, and ritualizes new symbols and events, including the meal

Position in Society	Church is on the margins of society and underground	Church is perceived as central to society and surrounding culture	Church is once again on the fringes of society and culture
Missional Mode	Missionary, incarnational-sending church	Attractional	Missional; incarnational-sending; The church re-embraces a missional stance in relation to culture

But most of us have had no significant experience of church in this form.

How difficult is it for us to conceive of church without a special type of building? We've dubbed them "churches," and we "go" to them. Can we imagine all God's people as equally activated into ministry and mission? Most church leaders have received ordination from a centralized institution with accredited degrees. What about sacraments? Communion, for example, has been extracted from the context of a feast with an extended spiritual family in a home and turned into paper-thin, tasteless wafers and a thimble-size cup of grape juice distributed by an ecclesiastical professional. Baptism has been extracted from the immediate riverside celebration upon conversion to something that has to be controlled by the institution and fit into the programming of a service. What of the structures of the church? Consider Alan's observation:

> The organizational structures of Christendom are in a real sense worlds away from that of the early church—something like comparing the United Nations to Al Qaeda (one being a thoroughgoing institution with centralized structures, policies, protocols, and the other being a reticulated network operating around a simple structure with a focused cause). In the Christendom era the church perceived itself as central to society and hence operated in the attractional mode. In this situation people come to church to hear the gospel, to be taught in the faith, and to partake of the sacraments.[8]

Oh, how we need to open our minds and stretch, man, stretch! Even now, stop and pray, "Spirit, help me perceive the new thing. Free me from that which blinds me from seeing the church as you do." The movement starfish will provide a simple way to *imagine* the church as an unstoppable force of *multiplying* disciples, leaders, gospel communities, and networks, filling everything every way with the fullness of Jesus. Imagine first!

Multiplication Forever

Multiplication is the normal state in God's creation and God's kingdom.

The ultimate outcome of the creation narrative, and God's first command to humanity, was, "Be fruitful and multiply. Fill the earth" (Gen. 1:28 NLT). Later God entered the creation through his Son to re-create this world and restore shalom. That plan for restoration would once again be contingent on the ability to multiply. The same command he gave humanity in the garden he gives now to the church in the Great Commission: "Multiply and fill the earth!" In the creation narrative it was, "Make babies! Fill the earth!" In the new creation narrative, it is, "Make disciples! Fill the earth!"

Multiplication and fullness go together. Multiplication is the means to the end of fullness.

If something isn't multiplying in God's creation or kingdom, something is wrong, something is sick or malnourished, something is suppressed or oppressed, or something has been forgotten.

With many metaphors, Jesus embedded endless multiplication in the imaginations of his disciples. Here are a few examples:

- **Fruit (John 15):** Fruit-bearing is referred to more than fifty times in the New Testament. In John 15:2–8, Jesus reiterates that fruit will multiply in the lives of his disciples. He told them to expect not only "fruit" (v. 2) but "much fruit" (v. 5) and again (!) "much fruit" (v. 8). Ultimately, Jesus says it is "much fruit" and the multiplication of fruit that glorifies the Father.
- **Talents (Matt. 25):** The two-talent servant, through his faithfulness, multiplied the two into four. The five-talent servant multiplied his five to ten. Both of these multipliers were told, "Well done, good and faithful servant!" (vv. 23, 25). Faithfulness leads to fruitfulness, which leads to multiplication.
- **Seed (Mark 4):** With the seed, we are promised that multiplication is the expected outcome: "Other seed fell on good ground and yielded a crop that sprang up, increased and produced: some thirtyfold, some sixty, and a some a hundred." (v. 8 NKJV). When the seed hits that good soil, it multiplies and spreads. To drive home the point, Mark stacks a couple more multiplication stories on top of the parable of the sower, including the parable of the growing seed and the parable of the mustard seed, with the outcome of multiplication being the smallest seed producing the "largest of all" (v. 32).

- **Yeast, Dough, and Bread (Matt. 13:33):** Once the yeast is in the dough and the heat in the oven is cranked, multiplication happens. To add a surprising twist, the amount of dough this woman is working with is ridiculously large. But it's nothing the power of multiplication can't handle. Those little pockets of CO_2 will multiply and expand, lifting the entire loaf. Big problems can be solved only through multiplying small. We all know what happens when Jesus gets a few loaves in his hands—he multiplies them and makes it a meal for thousands.

Robert Coleman, author of *The Master Plan of Evangelism*, emphasizes, "The ultimate goal of Jesus for his disciples was that his life be reproduced in them and through them into the lives of others. . . . Reproduction was our Lord's desire. . . . But multiplication was the ultimate end."[9]

The book of Acts tells the story of the church of Jerusalem quickly multiplying to the edges of the Roman Empire. Multiplication is emphasized in the record of the early church (Acts 1:15; 2:41; 4:4; 6:7; 9:31; 12:24; 16:5; 19:20; and 28:30–31). Jesus' commission is for us to continue this multiplication forever until disciples multiply among every tribe, every tongue, and every nation (Matt. 28:18–20).

With that in mind, we must ask and imagine, "What are the various dimensions of multiplication that yield a missional movement that advances us closer to gospel saturation in a given context?

CHAPTER 4

The Movement Starfish

Five Points of Multiplication

Figure 4.1

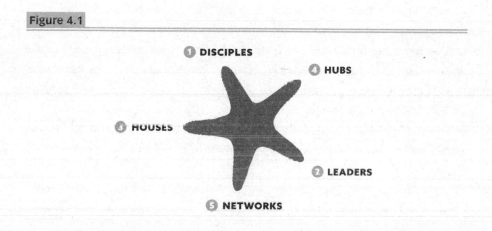

What are the various dimensions of multiplication that yield a missional movement that advances us closer to gospel saturation in a given context?

That's an important and dangerous question. If we can answer it, we will know where to focus our best multiplying initiative.

We contend that there are at least five points of multiplication in the New Testament, which make up the five points of the movement starfish: disciples, leaders, houses, hubs, and networks. All five points of multiplication are synergistically and organically connected in a decentralized network of networks. The favored structure of dynamic missional movements is always that of a fluid, decentralized, adaptive network where power and function are dispersed throughout, even at its outer edges.

Alan Hirsch: Talking about multiplication assumes that the most basic unit of church is, in fact, multiply*able*. In other words, scalability must be factored into the very DNA of the organization itself. Most Western expressions of church are inherently unreproducible in that they require leaders who have at least two degrees to be ordained, an audience of at least two hundred, and a $1 million budget to be considered successful and viable. But how does this make sense of the remarkable multiplication movements in history (e.g., Celtic, early Methodism, China), let alone the New Testament church?

Let's reimagine the church as a decentralized network of disciples, leaders, houses, hubs, and networks. At this point, we will seek to define what we mean by each of these terms. *Disciples* and *leaders* are more intuitive terms. The second and third sections of this book are devoted to defining them and creating a culture where each can multiply. So, although we will provide brief definitions for these in this chapter, we will come back and fill those in later. In this chapter, we will begin with *houses* and *hubs*, seeking to define and clarify these two essential points of multiplication. Both appear in Acts 5:42: "Day after day, in the temple courts and from house to house, they never stopped teaching and proclaiming the good news that Jesus is the Messiah."

The form and function of the early church in the temple courts approximates what we call a *hub*. The form and function of the early church embodied in the house to house expression approximates what we call a *house*.

Table 4.1

HUB	HOUSES
More *organized*	More *organic*
Gathered	Scattered
An apostolic team, using a shared space for equipping and empowering the houses in a city or region	Extended spiritual families planting the gospel in neighborhoods and networks
More *formal*	More *informal*
More *structured*	More *spontaneous*

Hubs and houses are the genius of Jesus. The early, Spirit-empowered church built their lives around a particular set of rhythms.

They devoted themselves to the apostles' teaching and to fellowship, to the breaking of bread and to prayer. Everyone was filled with awe at the many wonders and signs performed by the apostles. All the believers were together and had everything in common. They sold property and possessions to give to anyone who had need. (Acts 2:42–45)

Where did these rhythms play out? Through hubs and houses.

Every day they continued to meet together in the temple courts. They broke bread in their homes and ate together with glad and sincere hearts, praising God and enjoying the favor of all the people. And the Lord added to their number daily those who were being saved. (Acts 2:46–47)

If your faith community is like many, you may be thinking, "We already do this. We have small groups and weekend services." But we are talking about something substantially more robust and categorically different.

The church in Jerusalem had a rhythm of both centralized connection at the hub of the temple courts and decentralized connection within the houses. The early church tended to have two social spaces to meet and organize around. Admittedly, not much about the early church was dogmatic. It defied neat categories. But we will approximate what is described.

In the temple courts, the apostles taught, performed miracles, and evangelized. In the courts, the people of God learned, worshiped, prayed, and fellowshipped within the temple structures. Hundreds or thousands could gather in the temple courts.

In houses, the church lived as extended spiritual families in everyday gospel community, led by ordinary people owning the mission of Jesus in their relational network. Let's call these microchurches. A couple of dozen or more people could gather in the multigenerational homes of the day, which gives us a general size for the microchurch. The houses weren't primarily about the meeting but rather the conversion of a relational network into a new extended spiritual family on mission together.

The Greek word used in the New Testament for those networks is *oikos*. The gospel transformed oikos into microchurches. The oikos were the major social structure of Rome. Oikos went beyond immediate family to include extended family, household slaves, and their network of friends, neighbors, and business associates.

Rodney Stark, in *The Rise of Christianity*, documents the exponential growth of the church from one thousand in AD 40 to over thirty-three million by AD 350, crediting the microchurch strategy.[1]

Michael Green, author of *Evangelism in the Early Church*, proclaims the central nature of oikos: "Consisting of blood relations, slaves, clients, and friends, [oikos] was one of the bastions of the Greco-Roman society. Christians . . . made a deliberate point of gaining . . . households as lighthouses . . . from which the Gospel could illuminate the surrounding darkness."[2]

Dan White Jr., in his book *Subterranean: Why the Future of the Church Is Rootedness*, proclaims, "The oikos is the imperfect, messy, relational, organic but organized amoeba of the first-century church. Oikos was the hot mess of God's inbreaking kingdom that supported early Christians for mission in a city, for maturing in love, for the practice of the Eucharist, for the collision of racial diversity, for resistance to paganism, and for being shaped as disciples."[3]

The microchurches set entire oikos ablaze with the grace of God, like wildfire igniting an entire relational network with the gospel. By now you might be sensing how different this is from what most churches call small groups. Unlike traditional small groups, microchurches are a pure missionary endeavor, where the gospel is planted into a network or neighborhood and disciples emerge and form a new community. These groups are proximate and incarnational in that neighborhood or network, unlike traditional small groups in which professionals usually organize people from many networks and neighborhoods into groups. Because microchurches are embedded into a particular neighborhood or network of relationships, daily discipleship and gospel community become the norm. This is vastly different from most small groups, which are typically formed for assimilation and content delivery to churchgoers.

In Acts 12:12, we are told that one of these microchurches met in Mary's house. The church in Jerusalem was a starfish network of microchurches that also gathered at the hub of the temple. Those microchurches began to fill the neighborhoods of Jerusalem with disciples of Jesus. The gatherings at the hub were catalytic and empowering to the houses. Through the combination of multiplying disciples and microchurches (houses), equipped by apostolic leadership and teaching in the temple courts (hub), the early church filled the city of Jerusalem.

But don't miss this: the starfish network of microchurches was primary. How do we know that? "Saul approved of their killing [Stephen]. On that day a great persecution broke out against the church in Jerusalem, and all except the apostles were scattered throughout Judea and Samaria" (Acts 8:1).

In Acts 8:1, after the martyrdom of Stephen, the church was persecuted, and the public gatherings at the temple courts were shut down. Then the church ceased functioning, right? Wrong! The church continued to multiply disciples at an increasing rate across the Roman Empire. How did that primarily happen? Houses.

Learning the Art of the Small (Alan Hirsch)

1. One person can make an impact.
2. Concentrate your efforts on smaller and smaller areas. When your efforts are diffused over a wide area, they won't have much of an impact. So focus on smaller areas, and your efforts will be felt more fully. It could take time for change to happen, but keep the focus narrow.
3. Try to find an area that will cause a tipping point. You'll have the biggest impact if you can change something that will cause further changes—the rock that causes the avalanche. This isn't easy. It takes practice and experience and luck and persistence, but that area can be found.
4. Don't try to beat an ocean. You'll lose. Instead, focus on small changes that will spread.

Look for the word that is repeated in the next three passages. See if you can find the pattern.

One of those listening was a woman named Lydia, a dealer in purple cloth from the city of Thyatira, who was a worshiper of God. The Lord opened her heart to respond to Paul's message. When she and the members of her household were baptized, she invited us to her home. "If you consider me a believer in the Lord," she said, "come and stay at my house." And she persuaded us. (Acts 16:14–15 NIV 1984)

They spoke the word of the Lord to him and to all the others in his house. At that hour of the night the jailer took them and washed their wounds; then immediately he and all his family were baptized. (Acts 16:32–33 NIV 1984)

> Paul left the synagogue and went next door to the house of Titius Justus, a worshiper of God. Crispus, the synagogue ruler, and his entire household believed in the Lord; and many of the Corinthians who heard him believed and were baptized. (Acts 18:7–8 NIV 1984)

What word was repeated in all three passages? *House*, or *household*.

The book of Acts records clearly how the gospel spread from one household to another, with many of them being specifically named. We can unmistakably see the microchurch starfish networks by turning to the end of almost any of the epistles to specific cities. As the gospel spread, these starfish networks of microchurches formed.

Romans is a classic example. In chapter 16, Paul addresses different microchurches meeting in different households, including Priscilla and Aquila, the household of Aristobulus, the household of Narcissus, and so on. Leading New Testament scholar James Dunn says of Romans 16 that these groupings indicate that at least five microchurches were networked as the citywide church of Rome.[4] The same is true of the Laodicean church, which apparently gathered in various places, with Paul needing to give a greeting to a specific group meeting in the house of Nympha (Col. 4:15). Also consider the possibility of what could have been happening in Corinth, where the houses of Titius Justus (Acts 18:7), the household of Crispus (Acts 18:8), and the house of Stephanas (1 Cor. 16:15) are all mentioned. Yet Paul says "the whole church" came together (1 Cor. 14:23).

That microchurch framework makes sense of virtually all the instructions given in the epistles. The "one another" commands about community can be best fleshed out within a microchurch. When it comes to worship instructions—"When you come together, each of you has a hymn, or a word of instruction, a revelation, a tongue or an interpretation" (1 Cor. 14:26)—Paul envisioned a microchurch where everyone in the room could participate, not a large corporate worship service with hundreds or thousands of people where the only participation by the vast majority is through singing.

When the citywide church could pull together the households into a corporate gathering, they did. At the beginning of Acts, the church had a hub in the temple courts. At the end of Acts, Paul was using the hall of Tyrannus (Acts 19:9) as a hub. Antioch became a hub for the equipping and launching of missionaries before Ephesus did. This larger corporate expression had a huge impact on the city of Jerusalem and the church in Ephesus. It provided inspiration, momentum, celebration, teaching, and a shared identity as the church in a city. Some apostolic leaders provided oversight over all the microchurches—people like James and Peter in Jerusalem and Paul, Timothy, Priscilla, and Aquila in Ephesus (Acts 15; Acts 18; 1 Cor. 16:19; 2 Tim. 4:19).

Houses and hubs. Long live the starfish church.

But in our world, autonomous, independent churches dominate the landscape. Our driving question is usually, How can I grow my church? We're obsessed with the spider expression of the church. Yet in the New Testament, we see the microchurches in homes, in the cities, and in the regions working as one church, a starfish movement with multiple leaders and elder teams, interdependently networked as a body. Their driving question was, How can we multiply the number of people entering and experiencing the kingdom, and the influence of the kingdom, regardless of who gets the credit or increase?

Imagine our cities being filled with the life of heaven here on earth.

Imagine developing a missionary on every street and a microchurch in every neighborhood or network of relationships.

Several years ago Lance coined a term that became the name of a missional conference he and our friend Brad Brisco organized: *sentralized*. The word emphasized the centralization of hub and the decentralization of households of God's people *sent* into the various neighborhoods and marketplaces of our cities.

Imagine if every street had at least two people who said, "I will *bless* the people on this street! I will begin in prayer for each neighbor. I will listen deeply to the story of my neighbors and my neighborhood. I will eat with them. I will serve them. I will share the good news." As the gospel is planted in that context, Jesus draws people to himself, disciples are multiplied, and a house—a new expression of the church—emerges.

Imagine what it would be like if a house—an extended spiritual family— owned the mission of Jesus in every neighborhood and network of relationships in your city. That kind of movement would be present enough, deep enough, and personal enough to transform both the spiritual landscape and the culture of your city. Imagine the gathered church as a collection of those many microchurches, a hub for equipping, evangelizing, and sending. Imagine those hubs multiplying into networks, working toward gospel saturation in a city. That's a story that feels like the early church.

Now that we've fully explained what we mean by houses and hubs, let's go back to the five points of multiplication that make up the movement starfish.

Five Points of Multiplication

Figure 4.2

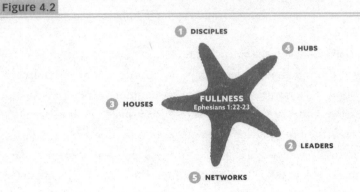

Remember, the movement starfish helps us reimage the church as decentralized network of multiplying disciples, leaders, houses, hubs, and networks that fill a city or region with the fullness of Jesus.

Multiplying Disciples

Disciple: *a person who hears and obeys Jesus.*

The movement starfish begins with developing disciples, people who hear and obey Jesus in all of life. Then those disciples make other disciples. The critical starting point of any faith movement is the flourishing and multiplying that happens when individuals become owners of the faith. The third section of this book, the lengthiest portion, is dedicated to the priority of disciple-making, which is the obsession of true missional leaders. We will explore both the ingredients of disciple-making environments and the elements of a transformative and multiplicative disciple-making ecosystem. Personal engagement in making new disciples, a clearly articulated vision for disciple-making, and a clear and reproducible process to ensure that disciple-making happens are the beginning of any starfish movement. On this, Alan proclaims, "When dealing with discipleship and the related capacity to generate authentic followers of Jesus, we are dealing with that single most crucial factor that will in the end determine the quality of the whole—if we fail at this point, then we must fail in all the others. In fact, if we fail here, it is unlikely that we will even get to doing any of the other elements of mDNA in any significant and lasting way."[5]

In addition, two of the starfish in the third section of the book focus exclusively on disciple-making.

Multiplying Leaders

Leader: *a disciple who has made disciples.*

As people begin to multiply disciples, they become leaders, often without knowing it. As each disciple becomes one who makes one, who can make another, then all followers are invited to be leaders. In a Jesus movement, everyone follows and everyone leads. Therefore, disciple-making is the beginning of and the most potent form of leadership development in the starfish movement. Disciple-making movements catalyze leaders like crazy. If you pay attention to an epistle like Romans, the list of leaders popping out of the network of microchurches is amazing. Paul lists more than twenty-five leaders by name in chapter 16. When people focus on disciple-making, leadership will always follow. Discipleship is the tree. Leadership is the fruit.

The opposite is not always true. Churches that become obsessed with leadership pipelines that focus on skills, techniques, and specific roles—whether volunteers or church planters—but aren't built on the foundation of disciple-making will find those pipelines spitting out the wrong sorts of leaders. Four of the starfish we will cover will equip you to create a culture for multiplying starfish leaders, which we explore in the second section of the book. As we multiply disciples and leaders, we get teams. The teams own the mission of Jesus in a neighborhood or network, then become the core for microchurches (houses).

Multiplying Houses (Microchurches)

House: *an extended spiritual family, led by ordinary people, who live in everyday gospel community and own the mission of Jesus in a network of relationships. Also known as a microchurch.*

Some call these missional communities or organic churches. As we multiply missional teams and microchurches, we start filling neighborhoods and networks. These usually range from ten to fifty people who can meet in homes or second and third spaces while living in daily gospel community.

The microchurches in Jerusalem, in those first honeymoon days of this emerging movement, had everything in common, sharing possessions, meals, laughter, joy, and conversation. These communities daily adopted new people as family. Stories of life with Jesus were shared with openness and honesty. Dinner was prepared by many hands, and the meals were accompanied by laughter and stories, for the people were sincerely glad to be together. Each would say, "These are my favorite people!" The conversation moved to rediscovery of the apostles' teachings, each retelling what they heard about Jesus and his ways, and the discussion was catalytic. They had been taught "to obey everything" (Matt. 28:20), so they discussed how each would live it out. Prayer flowed continually. It was difficult to figure out who was "in charge," as each person brought "a hymn, or a word of instruction, a revelation, a tongue or an interpretation" (1 Cor. 14:26) to share. Everyone knew Jesus was in charge of the meetings and their daily life together. He was guiding and shaping them.

Gene Edwards summarizes it this way:

> Behold! The church had learned from the twelve how to meet the way the twelve had "met" when they were with the Lord. They met with Him yet were not even conscious it was a meeting! That embryonic "body life" the twelve knew with Christ was now known by all! Those "meetings" (which weren't really meetings at all) which twelve men had while living with Christ, had now become the way the whole church met! The home meetings were to the church what sitting around with Christ had been to the twelve.[6]

Alan Hirsch: One of the key principles of incarnational forms of mission is to redeem and repurpose the organic structures of life in a given community or cultural context. The use of the household as the basic unit of ecclesia in the New Testament—and not just the so-called sacred places of the temple(s) or dedicated religious buildings—in effect meant "the church had left the building" and was discovered to exist in ordinary people's households and in the organic structures of the extended family. This is part of the genius of authentic Christianity—it redeems and reorients ordinary life and makes it sacred. The missional principle is this: The closer we can bring the gospel to the rhythms of ordinary life, the more likely it is both to be sustained and to spread.

Multiplying Hubs

Hub: *an apostolic team using a shared space to fuel and equip a network of disciples, leaders, and microchurches in a city or region.*

The Jerusalem Hub

In Jerusalem, an apostolic team made up of the twelve disciples used a shared space—Solomon's Colonnade, a large open area located on the east side of the outer temple courts—to equip and evangelize a network of disciples. The hub meetings were supercharged, filled with teaching, along with signs and wonders (Acts 2:42–43). People were filled with awe! A daily flow of encouragement and equipping poured forth from the apostles to the microchurches in the city.

Although we can't examine the explicit content and architecture of these hub gatherings, we can extrapolate their function from their exponential impact. The hub's equipping of microchurches was so successful in Jerusalem that when hub gatherings ceased, the house-to-house expression of the church continued to thrive and reproduce! That is the proof of effective equipping: what you equip someone with not only continues without you but also multiplies as the equipped become equippers.

The Ephesus Hub

In Ephesus, we see an apostolic team made up of Paul and the gang of eight he had collected in his missionary journeys:

- Titus from Antioch[7]
- Timothy from Lystra[8]
- Gaius from Derbe[9]
- Sopater from Berea[10]
- Aristarchus from Thessalonica[11]
- Secundus from Thessalonica[12]
- Tychicus from Ephesus[13]
- Trophimus from Ephesus[14]

This apostolic team used a shared space, the hall of Tyrannus (Acts 19:8–10), to fuel a network of microchurches that started in Ephesus and spread throughout Asia Minor. Frank Viola, in his book *The Untold Story of The New Testament*, summarizes the development of the Ephesian hub and house story with simplicity and clarity:

When Paul arrives in Ephesus, he meets twelve disciples of John the Baptist. Paul leads them all to Christ and baptizes them in the name of Jesus. He then lays his hands on them, and the Holy Spirit falls on each one. The twelve men begin to speak in tongues and prophesy. These twelve men, along with Priscilla, Aquila, and Epaenetus, form the nucleus of the Ephesian church....

For three months, Paul preaches Christ with great power in the Ephesian synagogue. The Jews reject and malign his message, so Paul moves his ministry center to the Hall of Tyrannus—a lecture hall that he rents. Every day from

11 a.m. to 4 p.m., Paul preaches Christ, trains the eight apprentices that are with him, and lays a foundation for the Ephesian church. (Tyrannus probably lectured in the morning, while Paul used the hall in the afternoon.[15] In the Greco-Roman world, the business day ended at 11 a.m. when most of the city ate a meal followed by a siesta.) . . . *

The community of Christians in Ephesus is meeting from house to house while Paul conducts the work from the Hall of Tyrannus. One of the homes where the church gathers is the house of Priscilla and Aquila.† Paul has received a wide-open door to preach the gospel in Ephesus; however, he encounters many adversaries.‡ On top of this, on a daily basis he experiences anxiety over the well-being of the eight churches he has planted.§

Paul will preach and teach in the Hall of Tyrannus for two years. During that time, he will unfold the "whole will and purpose of God."¶ . . .

At the end of two years, Paul will send his eight apprentice-companions throughout the region. These men will plant new churches all over Asia Minor. Some of these churches are listed in Revelation chapters 2 and 3. As a result of Paul's ministry in Ephesus and his sending out of these men to the neighboring cities, "the whole of Asia Minor" will hear the word of the Lord.** The Body of Jesus Christ—the community who expresses God's nature—is growing in Ephesus as well as throughout all of Asia Minor.[16]

As in Jerusalem, a hub may be a preexisting religious body, structure, or building that is repurposed and reorganized as a mission agency. As in Ephesus, hubs may be planted by renting spaces and starting from scratch. We'll do a deeper dive on hubs a little later in this chapter, as we believe this is a point of multiplication that requires more clarity. As hubs begin to multiply in a city, region, or nation, they can network for greater impact. The book *Underground Church* by Brian Sanders offers a deeper examination of this. As odd as it may sound, his chapter on governance was a game changer for me (Rob) and opened a way forward for a fresh structure, including hubs, that is vitally strategic in supporting a missional movement. Do yourself a favor and read that book.

---

* Acts 19:1–10; 20:4
† Acts 20:20; 1 Corinthians 16:19
‡ 1 Corinthians 16:9
§ 2 Corinthians 11:28
¶ Acts 20:27
** Acts 19:10

Multiplying Networks

Network: *two or more hubs/churches intentionally and collaboratively working together in a city or region around a shared kingdom mission.*

In the New Testament, we witness the power of networks. A microchurch is a network of disciples that make up a new spiritual family on mission. The church in a city—like Jerusalem, Rome, Corinth, or Ephesus—is a network of microchurches. The churches/hubs in a city network work together with other churches/hubs in other cities, forming a regional network.

One of my (Rob's) greatest joys is serving on the leadership team of NewThing, a catalyst for movements of reproducing churches relentlessly dedicated to helping people find their way back to God. NewThing helps leaders, churches, and church plant-ers establish healthy reproducing churches to achieve the Jesus mission (Acts 1:8). We are aligned around this mission and uphold that alignment through these core values: relationships, reproducing, residents, and reproduction. Jesus' words in John 17:20–23 describe what Patrick O'Connell, the director of NewThing, calls the Great Collaboration:

> My prayer is not for them alone. I pray also for those who will believe in me through their message, that all of them may be one, Father, just as you are in me and I am in you. May they also be in us so that the world may believe that you have sent me. I have given them the glory that you gave me, that they may be one as we are one—I in them and you in me—so that they may be brought to complete unity. Then the world will know that you sent me and have loved them even as you have loved me.

Shared doctrine and practices: helped each other in terms of orthodoxy and orthopraxy (Acts 8:14–25; Gal. 3).

Shared leadership: *relocated leaders* to strengthen other situations (Acts 11:19–23, 25–26; 12:25; 16:1–3); sent *individuals and teams* on strengthen-ing visits (Acts 11:27; 19:21–22; 1 Cor. 4:15–17; Phil. 2:19–29; 2 Tim. 1:18).

Shared resources: sent *money* to help each other and bless the wider society (Acts 11:28–30).

Shared work: helped advance the gospel together and made new disciples; new churches emerged (Rom. 15:24; 2 Cor. 10:15–16).

This call to collaborate in John 17 is as essential as the command to go in Matthew 28. Patrick says, "Jesus prays that his church would demonstrate missional unity. Jesus is praying that we find ways to work together. Not only will this honor his command, but he adds that our witness will become a new apologetic. Wow!"[17] We must collaborate in networks to see a missional movement emerge. On this, one of the greatest missional leaders of our time, Samuel Stephens of India Gospel League, which has seen more than seventy-five thousand churches emerge from missionary disciple-making among the lost, explains, "Networks are the backbone of movement."[18]

NewThing has seen more than 185 networks form from more than 3,046 churches committed to the four Rs. Together, those networks have equipped residents and provided resources for 855 churches to be planted.[19] We highly recommend you read the free Exponential ebook *Together*, by Patrick O'Connell and Dave Ferguson, for a deeper dive on the need for, various forms of, and practices of healthy multiplying networks.[20]

Most cities and regions require multiple networks working together on different areas of mission—like best practices in disciple-making, church planting, social justice, business as mission, prayer, and poverty—to reach the goal of gospel saturation. Those networks must remember that, at the end of the day, their most important functions are to be filled with the Spirit, make disciples who can make disciples, move in prayer, and plant the gospel, not just planting churches or addressing social justice issues.[21]

A Word of Clarity on the Function of Hubs as Revealed by the Coronavirus

Before we look at the goal of each of the five points of multiplication, let's drill a little deeper into the concept of a hub, as that will be the area where leaders may be most tempted to take what is currently being done in their church and relabel it a "hub" without making any significant changes.

As we write this, 75 percent of the American population is still under a shelter-in-place order. Our families are quarantined at home. The coronavirus has blindsided all of us. The whole world feels as if it's changed overnight. With hundreds of millions of people on lockdown, how do we mobilize God's people when folks can't leave their homes and social distancing keeps us out of reach from one another?

In the coming months, churches around the country will find that they are no longer able to offer weekend services or any other type of large gathering without putting people at risk. I (Rob) have spent most of my adult life as a pastor in very large churches, so I understand that this scenario has turned over the apple cart.

Currently, NewThing, along with a network of partners like Christ Together, the Send Institute, and Catapult, has launched a crisis coaching initiative. More than 1,500 church leaders joined in a matter of days. Immense fear, anxiety, and uncertainty bubbled in the hearts of leaders who genuinely wondered, "Will my church survive this?"

While I was serving as a pastor at a large church in northern Indiana, the leadership team had a few occasions when we had to cancel weekend services due to severe weather. We lived in what was known as the snow belt, where lake effect from Lake Michigan could dump six to eight feet of snow during a winter season. Our worst-case scenario was canceling services two weeks in a row. We operated with a minimum of a three-week cushion of operations costs in savings, so the threat was minimized.

Churches navigating the coronavirus pandemic have had to navigate not holding public services for months. That's a sobering situation that may feel as an existential threat because of how the centralized church is structured. This is where we can begin to discover new clarity on what it means to be a hub. When we say "hub," we must understand that it is not equivalent to the prevailing model of church.

This is where opening the hood on the Underground approach, initiated by the Tampa Underground, will be helpful. In KC Underground, we function with a two-entity structure: a mission agency and a network of microchurches. Our mission agency, our definition of a hub, equips normal folks to be loving missionaries and effective disciple-makers in new contexts. We have seven teams that make up the service platform to equip and launch missionaries who plant the gospel. As new disciples are made in a new context, a microchurch emerges. At that point, you have an extended spiritual family on your hands. When four to six microchurches in a geographic region or affinity group emerge, they network together in what we call collectives, with a shared mission and shared elders and resources.

Hubs support the missionaries, microchurches, and collectives. We currently have one hub in our city but envision a day when we will have twenty or more throughout the city. A hub has a physical location, an office that services as coworking space for the missionaries and microchurch leaders, as well as for the seven equipping teams. In a city of 2.2 million, we want every missionary and microchurch leader to have easy access to a hub, with its services and support proximate to them.

We are attempting to reimagine church as a decentralized network.

When the coronavirus hit, by God's grace we were able to pivot quickly. I knew I needed to write a letter to our microchurch leaders and the faithful missionaries in our movement to keep them abreast on our response to this crisis. As I wrote that letter, I realized that the form of church we equip for, a decentralized network of missionaries and microchurches, is perfectly positioned for this type of culture moment.

Less a warning about what we couldn't do anymore, the letter was more of a rallying cry for things we could do as a movement of microchurches. First, we quickly gave free access to a video conferencing platform to all our microchurches. All the microchurches leaned in, increasing both frequency of community touches and community depth.

Second, the hub increased activity and equipping because it isn't bound by a building or service in a particular location. For example, the hub offers a weekly equipping gathering for all the missionaries and microchurch leaders. This is not a weekend service but a combination of inspiration, storytelling, and practical equipping for leaders. It's conversational and interactive. We immediately moved that gathering online and saw an increase in attendance and participation. The liminal space of the crisis catalyzed creativity and new initiatives through our microchurch leaders as they shared their ideas. They don't need us to tell them what to do.

For example, a number of our missionaries launched new online Discovery Bible Studies, inviting new people from their neighborhoods and networks to join them to find community and comfort in the storm. New disciples of Jesus emerged quickly. We've seen four new microchurches start already. This is accelerating us in mission. Ninety-five percent of our giving is online, as we don't collect offerings in microchurches. As I write this, twelve weeks into the pandemic, we've not yet seen a dip in giving. In fact, in the third month of the pandemic, our giving went up. As we increased our local investment in feeding the hungry and caring for the poor, as well as investing more in disciple-making movements among unreached people groups in Africa who are suffering dramatically from this crisis, God's people rose to the challenge with generosity.

Alan Hirsch: I recently heard a Ghanaian pastor in England say that many of his colleagues in ministry were lamenting that because of COVID-19 all the churches were closing. He suggested that the churches weren't closing; instead, they were opening up in thousands of new places throughout the city. In saying this, this leader highlighted how deeply captive the imagination of the vast majority of church leaders is to clergy-operated weekend services and church buildings. Most leaders couldn't even recognize, let alone name, what they were seeing as legitimate (potential) expressions of ecclesia. But the question one must ask is this: How do these selfsame leaders, who claim to believe in the Scriptures, not consider the New Testament expression of church as a legitimate expression of church? Herein lies one of the serious flaws in our idea of church.

The church as a decentralized network is virtually immune to any pandemic or crisis. Historian Rodney Stark, in his book *The Rise of Christianity*, says pandemics that caused social chaos in the Roman Empire fueled both the viral growth of the early church and the depth of community in the households of faith, what we call microchurches. As others abandoned family and friends and hunkered down in fear, the households of faith led by ordinary people engaged the sick and the suffering. Their communal love and witness convinced the world that the good news of Jesus was real and for everyone.[22]

May this be our story in these coming days!

Whether church leaders wanted to or not, when the pandemic hit, they were forced to reimagine their church as a decentralized network of disciples and microexpressions of the church. We know theologically that the church is not a building; it's a body. The church is not a place or a program; it's a people. It's not an event; it's everyday people living out the mission of Jesus in every area of life and everywhere they go.

The COVID-19 crisis made us experience those ideas literally. Though the church has buildings, places, programs, and events, they aren't necessities. They don't define us. The church is not an activity but an identity. We have been forced to reimagine the church without those tools.

In the first few weeks of the crisis, many church leaders scrambled to move services online or to upgrade the online experience as the most important strategy because that is essential for the centralized form of church. We support having "the voice" of the church being broadcast to its people. Yet if done without reflection, as an end in and of itself, this still uses the same rubric of centralized delivery of religious goods and services as the main strategy. That play still leaves us vulnerable and far from the movemental form of church. The medium is the message, as the saying goes.

A Fitting Word from Alan, in *The Forgotten Ways*

It is worth noting again at this point that the church in the West is facing a massive adaptive challenge—positively in the form of compelling opportunity and negatively in the form of rapid, discontinuous change. These twin challenges constitute a considerable threat to Christianity, locked as it is into the prevailing Constantinian (Christendom) form of church, with all its associated institutional rigidity. Our situation is what Canadian missiologist Alan Roxburgh calls *liminality*. Liminality, in his view, is the transition from one fundamental form of the church to another, *necessitating* the apostolic role. Environments of discontinuous change require adaptive organizations and leadership. As the apostolic role is responsible and gifted for the extension of Christianity, so too the missionary situation requires a pioneering and innovative mode of leadership to help the church negotiate the new territory in which it finds itself.*

---

* Alan Hirsch. *The Forgotten Ways: Reactivating the Missional Church* (Grand Rapids: Brazos, 2016), 51.

In our crisis coaching, we emphasized a different response. First, we offered reminders of two theological truths the church rests on. Then we encouraged two priority pivots for action.

Reminder #1: Our God Is Unchanging

Jesus is the same yesterday, today, and forever. Heaven is not panicked; neither should we be. Jesus is seated on his throne. He's not pacing back and forth. Because of that, our foundation is joy and shalom. He will lead us through this together as we listen to his voice and obey. So begin with prayer, fasting, and repentance. May we go forward only as fast as we can on our knees, in totally God-dependency. Put the oxygen mask on yourself first, breathe in the gospel, and quiet yourself in his presence.

Reminder #2: Our Mission Is Unchanging

Make disciples who make disciples. This crisis environment is a richer environment for disciple-making because people are living with a real awareness of eternal realities. We are always hanging on a thread between life and death, but most of the time we can ignore it. Not anymore. Most of time we live with the illusion of control. Not anymore. Most of the time we can distract ourselves and keep ourselves busy. No longer. When you are in lockdown, the desperate need for authentic community is palpable.

I saw a picture on Instagram of a pastor who was going to buy supplies. Of course, half the shelves were empty. But you know what else he noticed? He posted a picture of the book section of Walmart where the Bibles are. All of them were gone. Not one left. That reveals the unparalleled hunger for spiritual truth during this pandemic. Thus far, this is the most potent opportunity for disciple-making in our lifetime! How will we leverage this opportunity?

Priority #1: Pivot Harder to Small Groups (Starfish) than You Pivot to Streaming Services (Spider)

As helpful as streaming services are, what people need most in a crisis isn't more content (there's a glut of great content already) but deep, Jesus-centered community to sustain them. The second wave of churches' response to COVID was to move whatever microelements it had (small groups, life groups, Bible studies) to video-conferencing platforms like Zoom. That's terrific.

Reimagine church as a decentralized network of microexpressions of church.

> **Alan Hirsch:** If you want to learn how to play chess, you should start by removing your own queen. Once you've mastered the game without the most powerful piece, then put the queen back in and see how good you are! Applying this metaphor to our understanding of church brings numerous insights; for instance, the Sunday service in a building can be considered a queen. We've been relying on it too much. Now that this queen has been taken off the board, it's time to rediscover what all the other chess pieces of ecclesia can do.

The harvest is ready to be brought into the barns. The fish are jumping into the boat. But the barns and the boats are not church buildings. They are not online streaming services. The barns and the boats are those microexpressions of the church, the small groups, where people can truly be part of the family of God in an embodied way, (and for now) even in a virtual space.

Priority #2: Pivot Current Staff to Equipping the Leaders Who Lead Those Microexpressions

As mentioned earlier, in the Underground, we offer a weekly equipping gathering for the leaders of the microchurches. We seamlessly moved that gathering online, where they work in huddles in breakout rooms. That's a virtual re-creation of what we had been doing when we met in one location. In addition, every microchurch leader in our movement has a coach. Our coaches are increasing their connections with those leaders. All seven of our equipping teams, because they are built on a coaching model, can operate at 100 percent capacity, totally unhindered by this crisis.

Wise church leaders are realizing, "The staff I had to support all the centralized programs and services of the church now have to be redeployed to become coaches to equip those who are leading the microexpressions. That's job one." When crisis hits, we find out what is essential. If this crisis is forcing the prevailing model to reorganize, prioritizing smaller groups, then perhaps that is always the most essential expression of church.

That leads to the real purpose of a hub: equipping ordinary people to be loving missionaries, effective disciple-makers, and spiritual parents of microchurches. If you consider what was really happening with the apostolic influence in the temple courts and hall of Tyrannus, do you think it consisted of people gathering to consume a Christian TED Talk, sing a few songs, and then repeat the next week? Or did Paul use that hall to equip missionary disciple-makers who spread out all over that region of the Roman Empire to plant the gospel and see new microchurches and networks emerge?

Hubs can be independent of congregations, like they are in the KC Underground. Our collectives (networks of microchurches) operate like congregations with shared worship gatherings (one to two per month) and shared leadership. The hubs support the collectives by equipping the missionaries and microchurches within them. We are more at the starfish end of the continuum, a starder reaching toward starfish.

Or hubs can exist within a larger organized expression of church. Those within the prevailing model can transition by creating a new mission agency inside the church and make that an essential part of their framework. That would be more at the spider end of the continuum, a spiderfish.

Both types of hubs are needed to get the job done. Either way, we can equip to see multiplication happening at all five points: disciples, leaders, houses, hubs, and networks. With the definitions of the five points of multiplication in mind, let's look to see what we can measure so the use of the word *movement* will be meaningful.

CHAPTER 5

The Movement Starfish

What Makes a Movement, and How Do We Measure It?

What makes a movement a movement?

Movement is one of the latest buzzwords in the church leadership world. These days everything seems to be a movement. When everything is a movement, nothing is. Words matter. Definitions matter.

We are seeking to ground the movement starfish definition in the more than forty years of analysis of the greatest movements in the history of church that have occurred in our lifetime. These disciple-making movements (DMM) and church planting movements (CPM) have been documented and researched in such seminal works as *The Forgotten Ways* by Alan Hirsch, *Church 3.0* by Neil Cole, *Church Planting Movements* by David Garrison, and *Miraculous Movements* by Jerry Trousdale, along with the work of David Watson, through CityTeam and New Generations, who has been instrumental in starting over one hundred DMMs globally through his training of local leaders. It would seem foolish to ignore the definition of *movement* that has emerged from the CPM and DMM world, where we can learn from the church in its finest expression around the world.

In his book, Garrison defines a church planting movement as "a rapid and multiplicative increase of indigenous churches planting churches within a given people group or population segment."[1]

Here are four key points to note about a movement:

1. It's rapid and viral. Momentum grows and appears out of control.
2. It's multiplicative, not growth by addition. Four generations on more than one strand.

3. It's indigenous. The church planting doesn't occur because outsiders come in (although they may be catalytic in the early stages) but because local, indigenous people are making new disciples that form new churches.
4. It diminishes lostness within a given people group. Previously unreached, unsaved people are reborn.

In the last twenty-plus years, the number of movements has increased dramatically, spreading to every continent. It truly is the greatest hour in the history of the church from that front. We live in an era of "missional movement" in terms of the global church. Currently, there are over 4,500 reports of active DMM/CPM engagement. Of those, 1,369 meet all four criteria! There are currently more than 76.9 million disciples in those 1,369 movements. From that total, 4.8 million churches have emerged, with an average size of 16.[2] Microchurch is the "normal" church around the world. When you place that against the backdrop of "normal" in the New Testament, perhaps it's time to consider the average church in the US as abnormal.

These indigenous movements start with extraordinary prayer and fasting and focus on obedience-based discipleship, discovery forms of Bible engagement, and passionate and fearless sharing of the gospel. Authority is decentralized, so finding the "top leader" feels impossible, and the form of church is small, simple, and easy to produce.

David Watson further defines *movement* as having at least one hundred churches, at least three generations deep.[3]

How do DMMs and CPMs relate? Roy Moran, another Kansas City native, who is a mentor and a recognized expert on both DMMs and CPMs, provides an answer: "The term disciple making movements . . . is what started the process. While Garrison was describing the result—planting churches—the New Generations tribe preferred to describe the process—disciple making. Multiplying churches was the result."[4]

Disciple-making movements (DMMs): *rapid, immediately viral, multiplicative, indigenous movements, creating new disciples from lostness four generations deep on multiple strands. The direction of mobilization is from the harvest toward the church. The focus is regeneration of the lost into disciple-makers.*

Generally, a DMM follows a two-to five-year timeline with an outcome of one hundred or more churches with thousands of new disciples.

The leading analysts, such as 24:14,[5] which spark and measure DMMs around the world, report no such movements among Caucasians in North America. We have zero DMMs.

Many people have co-opted the labels CPMs and DMMs, redefining them in any way that serves them. Our desire is to build on the foundation of these hard-fought, well-founded definitions. We also seek to add to it.

We would like to propose for the consideration of the DMM world and the rest of the disciple-making and church-planting world a new term: movements of disciple-making (MDMs). Our hope is to celebrate what has been developed as a technical and measurable definition by the DMM world, but to add another term for another type of movement that is, in our opinion, just as critical in a larger missional movement. What we offer is embryonic, yet it builds on long-established biblical frameworks and demonstrable orthopraxy in the history of the church. By God's grace, we hope it moves the conversation forward in an inclusive and inquisitive way without compromising the integrity of what has already been established, while offering another emerging framework to further establish the foundation of the different types of mobilization needed.

Movements of disciple-making (MDMs): *slower, eventually viral, multiplicative, indigenous movements, creating new disciples from believers four generations deep on multiple strands. The direction of mobilization is from the church toward the harvest. The focus is catalyzation of believers into disciple-makers.*

Let's compare.

Table 5.1

	DISCIPLE-MAKING MOVEMENTS	MOVEMENTS OF DISCIPLE-MAKING
Type of Growth	Viral and multiplicative	Viral and multiplicative
Generational Impact	Four generations on more than 1 strand	Four generations on more than 1 strand
Source of Leadership	Indigenous	Indigenous
Timeframe	Rapid explosion (occurs in 2 years or less)	Slow build (takes 2 years to start)
Outcome	Regeneration of the lost	Revival of the believer
Direction of Mobilization	From the harvest to the church	From the church to the harvest
Cultural Focus	Premodern/postmodern	Christendom/Christian subculture
Acts 1:8 Reference Point	From "Samaria"	From "Jerusalem"
Biblical Example	Woman at the Well	The Twelve
Archetype	Pauline	Petrine

Both forms of mobilization were present in the story of the early church. Consider the stories of Paul and Peter as prototypes for these two forms of mobilization. Alan Hirsch and Tim Catchim have done profoundly important work on these different types of apostleship in the seminal book *The Permanent Revolution*. The following excerpts provide clarity on the synergistic differences.

The Petrine Catalyst: The Mobilizer of MDMs

Alan and Tim note in *The Permanent Revolution*,

> Although they retain an entrepreneurial orientation, the Petrine catalysts, true to their gifts, will not likely pursue specific opportunities far beyond the established organization. Instead, they are likely to develop an approach designed to address the community's inherent capacities for mission. To generate an urgent reaction in God's people, mobilizers have to generate motivation internally by connecting believers to the church's core theological truths. . . .
>
> If Petrine explorers mine the community to reveal both its dysfunctions and its potentials, Petrine catalysts accelerate the process of mobilization for mission by helping a community become inherently more creative and entrepreneurial. Effectively they are optimizers; they help mainly established communities become more focused on purpose and geared toward their missional calling. The mobilizers are helpful in remissionalizing established organizations and operationalizing movements. In other words, the Petrine catalyst cultivates an internally generated pressure for movement and after achieving that works to maintain motivation and momentum. . . .
>
> Mobilizers call the church to remember that God is a redeemer and that the church is the uniquely called people who exist to extend that mission (Acts 2:39; 1 Peter 2:5, 9).[6]
>
> Petrine apostles tend to have a somewhat more internal ecclesiocentric focus, are less missionary in the truly cross-cultural sense of the Word, and are called primarily to serve the already existing people of God. So while they might go into new geographical territories, their initial destination is not to unreached groups of that area (the markets and the philosopher's forums) but to existing churches in a select region. We clearly see this pattern in Peter's ministry throughout the book of Acts.
>
> Furthermore, we seldom see Peter directly engaging marketplaces,

philosophical discussion forums, and the like as Paul seems to do (Acts 2 is the exception; but even there he is speaking to Israel). Rather, in Acts 9:32–42, while traveling the country, a sure application of the translocal implications of his ministry, Peter visits the two predominantly Jewish cities of Joppa and Lydda, where he spends the majority of his time. As a result of his impact on them, many people were converted to Christ (v. 42). His primary work was in and through the ecclesia itself. . . .

Petrine apostles remove barriers to authentic ecclesia, in effect mobilizing the church to fulfill its mission and calling in the world.[7]

The Pauline Catalyst: The Networker of DMMs

If Petrine catalysts mobilize existing communities for mission, Pauline catalysts accelerate movement by establishing the pathways by which the gospel travels from person to person, from group to group, and from one culture to another. This is why we have opted to call the Pauline catalyst the networker. Pauline networkers make the connections and subsequently move on to broaden the network; they don't seem to stay long in a single place. Their influence and leadership are therefore very much translocal. Their home, as well as the locus of their ministry, is the movement at large (not the local church)—the church as a translocal social force—and they thrive at this level of ecclesia.

Alan writes in *The Permanent Revolution*,

> As [Paul] crisscrossed the empire, planting the gospel, establishing communities, knitting them together, developing and sending leaders, and resourcing and catalyzing the movement, he was cross-fertilizing the Israel story with that of the various Gentile nations. The result was the creative generation of new forms of ecclesia unbound from the distinctly Jewish template and culture and allowing them to follow the indigenizing cultural logic of the incarnation.[8]

On the need for both forms of mobilization, Paul and Peter eventually come to the same conclusion. Paul starts with a DMM strategy. But when he finally arrives in Ephesus, he slows down for three years, training "his twelve," which was technically ten (the gang of eight apostolic leaders he had picked up on his missionary journey, plus Priscilla and Aquila). He starts a hub in the hall of Tyrannus, trains them along with the microchurches in the town for three years (sound familiar?), and sends

Table 5.2*

CHARACTERISTICS	PAULINE (DMMS)	PETRINE (MDMS)
People skill set	Culturally savvy	Politically savvy
Primary metaphor	Pioneer	Mobilizer
Specialization	Founding	Refounding
People Orientation	Outsiders	Insiders
Response to status quo	High dissonance	Medium to low dissonance
Missional focus	To the nations	To the people of God among the nations
Leadership type	Entrepreneurial	Intrapreneurial
Assignment Duration	Shorter term	Medium to long term
Level of risk	High	Low to medium
Relation to Institution	Dissenter (change agent)	Agitator (change manager)

* Table adapted from Hirsch and Cathim, *The Permanent Revolution*.

them out. They plant the gospel and see new disciples and microchurches emerge across Asia Minor. Paul eventually engages both a DMM and MDM strategy.

The same can be said of Peter. After Peter spends six to seven years building on an MDM strategy in Jerusalem, Stephen is martyred (approximately AD 33–36), the hub meetings are shut down, and the church disperses throughout Judea, Samaria, Galilee, and some as far as Damascus, Syria. After a few more years in Jerusalem, Peter takes a tour of churches outside Jerusalem. What a novel idea, since Jesus gave him that command eight years prior! Eventually this tour lands him in Caesarea, where he experiences the gospel spreading like wildfire among the gentiles. The folks back in Jerusalem are uncomfortable with this crazy DMM and aren't even sure if it's legitimate. Peter comes to its defense.

Eventually, both Peter and Paul convert to both forms of mobilization. It was just a matter of time, as their Master had clearly modeled both. But he first went to the lost sheep of Israel:

These twelve Jesus sent out with the following instructions: "Do not go among the Gentiles or enter any town of the Samaritans. Go rather to the lost sheep of Israel. As you go, preach this message: 'The kingdom of heaven is near.' Heal the sick, raise the dead, cleanse those who have leprosy, drive out demons. Freely you have received; freely give." (Matt. 10:5–8 NIV 1984)

Jesus doesn't ditch the calling for God's people to be the light of the world. Jesus starts there. Where does he go first? He goes to the synagogue, not Samaria. He goes to the religious structures, not Rome. He starts by reviving the people of God. He offered again to them the calling to fulfill the mission given to them two thousand years before. But he doesn't stay there. On to the gentiles:

> Leaving that place, Jesus withdrew to the region of Tyre and Sidon. A Canaanite woman from that vicinity came to him, crying out, "Lord, Son of David, have mercy on me! My daughter is suffering terribly from demon-possession."
>
> Jesus did not answer a word. So his disciples came to him and urged him, "Send her away, for she keeps crying out after us."
>
> He answered, "I was sent only to the lost sheep of Israel."
>
> The woman came and knelt before him. "Lord, help me!" she said.
>
> He replied, "It is not right to take the children's bread and toss it to their dogs."
>
> "Yes, Lord," she said, "but even the dogs eat the crumbs that fall from their masters' table."
>
> Then Jesus answered, "Woman, you have great faith! Your request is granted." And her daughter was healed from that very hour. (Matt. 15:21–28 NIV 1984)

This is a difficult passage. On the surface, it appears that Jesus is at best a snob and at worst a racist. Some interesting ideas about the interpretation of this passage help us move beyond the confusion. One is that he is enacting a game of wordplay. *Dogs* may sound like an offensive term, but Jesus just called his own people "lost sheep." When you consider the stupidity of sheep, being called a dog isn't much worse.

But let's let Jesus' actions speak for themselves. Notice that Jesus changes his mind regarding the woman's requested miracle. This wasn't the first woman who was able to talk Jesus into a miracle he initially appeared opposed to. The first example was his mother, Mary, at the wedding in Cana. As you may know, she requested chardonnay and got it. Now this woman receives the gift of her daughter's healing.

Israel had a long history with Canaan. In Deuteronomy 7, the original encounter between Israel and Canaan, the Israelites are preparing to drive out the Canaanites, who were mercilessly conquered. Now instead of a Jew conquering a Canaanite with no mercy, we have a Canaanite woman conquering a Jewish man, who surrenders an act of mercy.[9]

Grant LeMarguand sees this as a turning point in Jesus' ministry. Just as Mary's request became a trigger to "go public" with Jesus' miracles, this woman's request triggers a "go multicultural" focus for Jesus' ministry.[10] In the chapters that follow, he begins to heal multitudes, which Matthew specifies as gentiles who are now praising "the God of Israel" (15:31).

Now Jesus feeds four thousand gentiles, whereas Jesus previously fed five thousand Jews. How many baskets were left over after the feeding of the five thousand? Twelve. How many tribes where in Israel? Twelve. But when he feeds the four thousand, how many baskets are left over? Seven. Why that number? We find a clue in Deuteronomy 7:

> When the LORD your God brings you into the land you are entering to possess
> and drives out before you many nations—the Hittites, Girgashites, Amorites,
> Canaanites, Perizzites, Hivites and Jebusites, seven nations larger and stronger
> than you. (Deut. 7:1)

Seven nations are listed in the conquest target list. Jesus takes the old "destroy the Canaanites" story and turns it on its head. He takes the "no mercy" policy and instead shows mercy to a Canaanite woman. Seven nations are to be destroyed; Jesus leaves seven baskets to feed them. Instead of heading out with swords and spears, we are to head out with bread and fish to serve and heal.

Jesus mobilized in both directions.

This same symbiotic relationship has been repeated throughout the history of the church in the cyclical relationship between revivals and spiritual awakenings, which were the major theme of revivalist scholar J. Edwin Orr's many books. Revival begins in the church. The corresponding effect of the revived church spills out into society, or the harvest field, triggering a spiritual awakening. Large numbers of new converts are added to the church in a short period of time. As a result of such harvest, a reformation of culture takes place to some degree.

Both forms of mobilization are required in a missional movement in contexts where a form of Christendom or cultural Christianity has taken hold, like Western Europe and North America. Already in this book, you've heard stories from places like India and China, where DMMs are breaking out. There are more than 1,300 DMM movements in the world right now![11] In addition, MDMs are beginning to emerge here in the West, as a great reformation around disciple-making is underway. In chapter 8, you will meet Brian Phipps, a Petrine catalyst for an MDM in Kansas City of more than 4,000 new disciples, all grassroots, six to seven generations deep on multiple strands, that has led to unbelievable kingdom impact, catalyzing believers into missionary disciple-makers.

Our hope is that both movements of disciple-making and disciple-making movements will be seen as essential in any starfish movement. With that foundation, let's consider how to measure a movement.

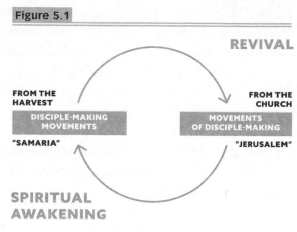

Figure 5.1

REVIVAL

FROM THE HARVEST

DISCIPLE-MAKING MOVEMENTS

"SAMARIA"

FROM THE CHURCH

MOVEMENTS OF DISCIPLE-MAKING

"JERUSALEM"

SPIRITUAL AWAKENING

The Measurement of the Movement Starfish: Four Generations of Reproduction on Multiple Strands at All Five Points

The goal in each of these aspects of the movement starfish—disciples, leaders, houses, hubs, and networks—is reproduction to the fourth generation and beyond on more than one strand. "The things you have heard me say in the presence of many witnesses entrust to reliable people who will also be qualified to teach others" (2 Tim. 2:2).

This is an example of four generations: Paul (generation 1) to Timothy (generation 2) to reliable people (generation 3) to others (generation 4). Since we are all called to be disciples who make disciples, that means every disciple is called to initiate more than one strand of four-generation multiplication.

In figure 5.2, you can see what four generations on a multiple-strand disciple-making movement look like. When we see four generations of reproduction on multiple strands in each of

Figure 5.2

A MOVEMENT
4 Generations of Reproduction
on More than One Strand

these areas—disciples, leaders, houses, hubs, and networks—you have a genuine movement on your hands. The good things are officially running wild. Jesus' plan from the beginning was for the church to reproduce at every level. If we keep reproducing consistently at every level, eventually we get to multiplication. Multiplication will produce an unstoppable, transforming missional movement.

Alan Hirsch: Factoring in reproducibility at every level is one definite factor of healthy scalability. But to lead a multiplication movement and keep it cohesive requires that leadership look to identify and develop common principles and practices that together create a ubiquitous culture throughout the movement. Again, we should look to the ingenious design of all organic life—reproducible DNA in *every* cell in a body. Movement leaders are advised to work hard to identify and develop replicable DNA and also preserve the utter centrality of Jesus in the equation. When a body loses control of its own reproducibility, doctors call that cancer.

In Kansas City Underground, we are working on environments and tools for multiplication at each of the points of the movement starfish. We will explore those with the disciple-making ingredient starfish and the disciple-making ecosystem starfish in the second half of the book.

Mindset, Momentum, Movement

Cory Ozbun, my (Rob's) friend and partner in the KC Underground who is a catalytic, DMM-style leader in our city, describes the journey toward the movement starfish this way: *First, mindset. Next, momentum. Then, movement.*

Counting vs. Measuring

Most church leaders have been obsessed with counting. What is needed is measuring.

Counting gives attention to numbers.

> When counting, the question to be answered is "How many?" Conversations about "How many?" are most frequently conversations about resources. Conversations about resources, in a time of limited resources, are commonly conversations about scarcity—"Do we have enough?" or "How can we get more?"
> *Measuring gives attention to change.*
> When measuring, the question is not "How many?" but rather "How far?" Conversations about "How far?" are frequently about change that can be measured over time, as in "How far have we come, over the past year, toward our goal?"

It starts with the right mindset: the commitment to gospel saturation through the multiplication of disciples. When you multiply disciples, then, as disciples make disciples, eventually leaders and microchurches multiply, with hubs and networks following in suit. If things are moving that way but you've not yet reached four generations on multiple strands, you have momentum. Momentum is good! For example, we saw a 500 percent increase in microchurches last year in the KC Underground, most of which was from multiplication, along with a few adoptions. By God's grace, that's momentum. But we're not a movement yet, not until we hit four generations on multiple strands with a holistic vision of all five points of multiplication. We will count it from both directions, harvest to the church and church to the harvest.

We believe the movement starfish is meant not just for national church planting movements or large networks like NewThing, Acts 29, ARC, and the like. This kind of movement always starts with a handful of disciples. In other words, you and your friends could be the catalyst for a starfish movement. A small or medium size congregation could be unleashed into a starfish movement with the right kind of leadership. Using a dated metaphor from our teen years, this is an "all skate." Everyone gets to play. Large faith organizations could be reimagined this way. Adaptive changes can create new forms.

This brings us to the hybrids again: spiderfish and starders. The spiderfish is a more centralized institution that decentralizes parts of their organization. They lean more heavily into centralization of staffing, teaching, and resources but are willing to decentralize certain aspects like local or global missions or microchurches.

This book is designed for leaders who find themselves drawn toward the middle of this matrix, with a strong gravitational pull toward the starfish corner, our north star. If you find yourself in a spider quadrant but you'd love to get to spiderfish territory, keep reading. If you currently find yourself leading a franchise multisite model in the spiderfish quadrant, but the Spirit is leading you to starder territory, we hope to be helpful guides. If you're a church planter and you already know God has placed a vision in your heart for the starfish quadrant, then it is our hope that this book, by God's grace, will shorten your learning curve and speed up your timeline. The remainder of the book will provide ways of thinking and practical tools, each encapsulated in a different starfish, to move faith communities toward the starfish quadrant. As with all sustained change, before we can talk about structural reformation in the church you lead, we need to speak to personal reformation in the soul and life of the leader.

Let's discover what it means to be a light-load leader. But first, an introduction to the next section and a deeper sharing of our stories.

Figure 5.3

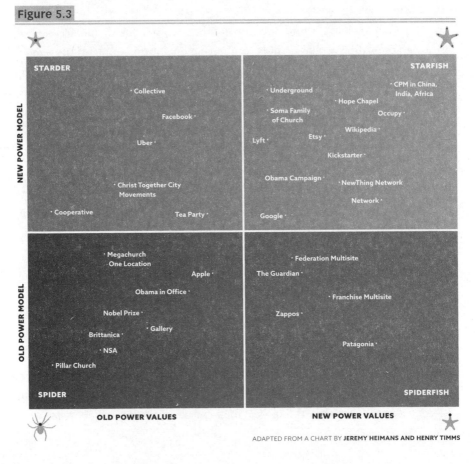

ADAPTED FROM A CHART BY **JEREMY HEIMANS AND HENRY TIMMS**

A Culture for Multiplying Leaders

Section 2 Introduction

Now that we have reimagined the church as a missional movement, we must recognize that not just any form of leadership will catalyze and sustain this decentralized, networked form of the church. In this next section, we will look at the ethos, language, and practices required to create a leadership culture that will multiply starfish leaders. We will explore the following starfish:

Starfish #2: The Light-Load Leader Starfish

Purpose: The light-load leader starfish helps leaders equip others in a fivefold fashion (Eph. 4:11–13) with five postures, distributing the weight of leadership throughout the entire body rather than on the shoulders of a few.

Starfish #3: The Structure Starfish

Purpose: The structure starfish helps leaders structure around organic systems by repeating five patterns in every cell of the body.

Starfish #4: The Self-Management Starfish

Purpose: The self-management starfish helps leaders create a culture of empowerment and self-management through activating five potentials in every leader and team.

At the end, after the third section, "A Culture for Multiplying Disciples," we will close out the book with the final starfish, which is the culmination of a culture that multiplies disciples and leaders.

Starfish #7: The Collective Intelligence Starfish

Purpose: The collective intelligence starfish helps leaders unlock the shared intelligence of every member of our living system for the purpose of better decision-making and constant improvement through implementing five simple processes.

After just a quick review of these four starfish, you may feel this particular form of leadership is quite foreign. For most of us in church leadership, starfish leadership has not been required of us, desired, or understood (if attempted).

For example, a well-meaning leader on our team, whom I respect tremendously, recently shared concerns about the number of teachers we have rotating in our equipping gathering for the missionaries and microchurch leaders. His feedback was clear: "We need you up front more." I've been a teaching pastor in large churches for years, which means I've put my reps in, and it shows. If we were rating teaching on quality alone, we should put up the person with the most reps. But in a starfish leadership culture, the higher value is on development and multiplication, not excellence alone. Why do we have so many trainers? Our plan is to equip enough equippers to have twenty or more hubs in our city. And yet even with that vision in place, for those of us who have been in centralized forms of church our whole lives, this new way can seem weird or ineffective.

Most of you, dear readers, have likely been charged to lead a centralized form of the church. And you had to learn the form of leadership required to grow, manage, and sustain a centralized church. Before we explore the new forms, let us slow down and do an honest gut check about the old forms.

Let us consider that something about the centralized form of church (or any other institution) lends itself to a strict hierarchy, where power is consolidated in a few hands. Has this not been your experience? Has not history proved that time and again? Does it not concern you? Can we not see that no human soul can withstand such pressure over time without degradation? Do we think we would be the exception to that rule?

If the next section of the book is to have the desired impact, we must begin with repentance.

Repentance is sometimes associated with feelings of shame. But true repentance has nothing to do with shame or condemnation. Repentance is turning to receive the embrace of Jesus, placing your head on his chest while sighing, "You are right. You are what I need." Repentance is turning from unbelief in Jesus to belief in Jesus in every area of life. It is the way to Life itself.

The Hebrew word for repentance is *teshuvah*, which comes from the biblical Hebrew verb *shuv*, which means "to return" to home or to an original state of wholeness.[1] In a prayer of repentance, we recognize that we are all the prodigal son, sitting in a pig pen in one way or another. When we repent, we wake up and head home to find the Father already running toward us with a robe and ring to cover us.

> **Alan Hirsch:** While the Old Testament term for repentance is *teshuvah*, the primary New Testament term for it is *metanoia*, which literally means "above/beyond mind."* This is best translated as a paradigm shift or simply "having your mind blown"! While the Hebrew terminology emphasizes shift in direction, the Greek term emphasizes a necessary radical shift in our thinking. Both are necessary for complete repentance to take place.

* Alan Hirsch and Mark Nelson, *Reframation: Seeing God, People, and Mission through Reenchanted Frames* (Edinburgh: 100Movements, 2019), 124–6.

For repentance to be meaningful, we have to look at the error fully and name it. We have to stop our speeches of explanation and accept the unearned embrace. We would like to share our stories of repentance with you so you know you are with a couple of ragamuffins, not experts or pissed-off prophets. In these stories, we will also share how we have been bitten by spider leadership.

As you read, we invite you to be a ragamuffin too. Resist the desire to rationalize, and consider joining us in the embrace of repentance if the Spirit leads you.

For those who have been crushed by toxic forms of leadership, these stories may be difficult to read. If they trigger too much trauma, please feel free to skip over them. When you've done what we do, as pastors, for as long as we've done it, please know we validate that your scars are real and spiritual abuse is as real as physical abuse. We are so sorry for your pain. We hope you will sense our solidarity with you and our compassion for you. We tenderly invite you to forgive those who have wounded you, rather than "drinking the poison and expecting the other person to die."

What a Tangled Web (Lance's Story)

The first time I (Lance) *knew* a spider leader had bitten me was shortly after joining the staff of a medium-size West Texas church, straight out of Bible college. My initial stint on a church staff had been as a youth pastor at a small but healthy fellowship during my Bible school years. Sam, the pastor of that church led from a joyful and loving humility. He was patient, forgiving, sharing, secure in who he was and treated no one as lesser than himself. Resolute when necessary but always fair and open to viewpoints not his own, Sam had a leadership style that seemed to match up with the character and fruit I imagined from the shepherd leaders I had studied in the Bible.

But things would be different at my first postgraduate assignment on the dusty West Texas plains. Within three months, I had been screamed at over the phone, physically shoved against an office wall, reprimanded through gritted teeth multiple times, and had my complete wardrobe replaced—all by the senior "shepherd." This was the first time I ever heard a pastor declare, "Church is a business, and it has to be run like a business." It wouldn't be the last time.

Over the next ten years or so, I would take on spider leadership tendencies myself. Like thousands of other young pastors and church planters, I sought the best leadership conferences and read every leadership book I could find, especially those recommended by pastors of well-known and growing churches. I sought wisdom and advice from my heroes, pastors who had grown big churches. As I was about to embark on starting a new church near St. Louis, when I asked one such pastor for the most important ingredient in planting a successful church, his answer was two words: "the guy." By this he meant a single standout hero type. In other words, my inner Peter Parker would need to get his spider game on.

So for the next few years, I continued to focus on learning leadership from the most notable authors and speakers, and the theme continued to galvanize: being a great leader must be a main goal, and leadership is about being a person who has the charisma, talent, expertise, and authority to get others to follow him or herself.

The overarching idea was that building a great church or faith community involves creating a well-oiled leadership machine, with structures and systems promoting the vision of the visionary and the mission he or she lays out and charts the course toward. As the years wore on, I developed a growing unease and disenchantment with much of what I was seeing, reading, hearing—and quite frankly was doing myself—in relation to church leadership, along with the weight and pressure to "make it work" and "make it grow."

Many of the ways and means of leadership seemed to ignore the habits and character of Jesus and what I read in the New Testament epistles regarding the treatment of others. On top of it all was a particular loneliness of being *the guy*. Something seemed off. I wondered how one person could be expected to have the stamina and energy to carry so much leadership weight and pressure. And who in their right mind—or ego—believed one human could have the talent, giftings, and wisdom capacity to always know what should be done?

After ten years of leading the church I founded in St. Louis, I resigned—out of senior pastor exhaustion—to lead the church planting efforts and serve on the pastoral staff of a large church in Texas. The mistake I made was that I ran deeper into the very system and leadership myth I had wanted to escape. I went from being the spider to being the one caught in the spider web. This would be the highest command-and-control environment I had ever been part of.

Not long before I arrived, a new executive pastor had been installed, with the task of overseeing and managing the entire pastoral staff. He was a brilliant and nice guy who was never even remotely harsh toward me or anyone else, to my knowledge. But it seemed odd that someone who had precisely zero experience as a pastor or church leader, much less any formal theological training, was giving daily marching orders to the entire spiritual leadership community of the church. Several of us on the staff had pastored flourishing churches. Nevertheless, this second-chair leader (as some call them) had an impressive résumé from the corporate world and therefore was deemed perfectly suited to lead this church in its operational basis. This practice has become common among contemporary churches.

The executive pastor stood between the senior pastor and the rest of the staff and was in control of day-to-day functions in a clear line of authority. Policy decisions, schedules, strategic initiatives, all of it, were the prerogative of the EP. Those under the EP were in place to implement the marching orders of the senior and executive pastors without question. This leadership paradigm assumes the need for clear lines of demarcation or boxes that separate the thinkers from the doers. It is classic top-down leadership. Thinking happens at the top, and doing happens at the bottom. Information, disseminated on a need-to-know basis, created a cloud of unease over the pastoral staff. Otherwise secure, gregarious, boisterous men and women became subdued and even childlike when the senior pastor entered the room. The atmosphere contained a discernable aspect of secrecy and distrust. And it was the SP and EP who decided what and who would know whatever, whenever.

Coming from a corporate command-and-control culture, the executive pastor considered it his job to manage everyone's schedules. One morning after hearing that a couple of staff pastors and I were spending the first twenty minutes of our mornings together in a time of worship with a guitar, he called me to his office to tell me we would need to "do that on your own time."

Taken aback, I asked him if he thought I was doing well with my area of responsibilities: "Mike, do you think I'm getting my job done? Do you think the other guys are getting their jobs done?"

He enthusiastically said, "Oh, yeah, you guys are doing great."

"Then what is the rub? What does it matter to you how we start our days?" I asked.

He answered, "Because this is the office. The office is for business, and it's my job to maintain that."

Leadership cultures fueled by *management* systems such as this contain a belief that people perform best under controls and guidelines. It is as if there are only a few adults in the mix and the rest are incompetent or lacking the crucial self-motivation or self-discipline to carry out the areas they are tasked to. Church business has come to this.

By the mid-1990s, two decades of what was called the church growth movement shifted focus as more and more leaders in the field of faith became fixated on the subject of leadership. The trend has continued to the present. The mantra "everything rises or falls on leadership" is almost universally unquestioned by "learned" pastors and faith leaders. There is at least a shade of truth in that saying. But what is seldom questioned is the *type* of leadership our future depends on.

Today the primary idea in these circles is that to develop a healthy and flourishing faith organization, there must be a single leader who stands out as the best strategist, theologian, visionary, communicator, and CEO. Over recent years, as the leadership emphasis took front and center, and before anyone seemed to notice, the faith community looked outside itself and the wisdom of the sacred texts for its primary leadership answers from the old models of the corporate sector.

It wasn't long until tens of thousands of faith leaders had attended church-sponsored summits with speakers from Bill Clinton to Melinda Gates and kept bookshelves housing volumes written by or about such luminaries as Attila the Hun and "Neutron Jack" Welch. Here was the rationale: If church is a business, then why not learn from those who are best at business? This is not to say there is not much to be learned from business leaders. In fact, in this book we draw on concepts from the business world. The issue in such learning is that the advice and practices we accept from anyone must pass through the filter of Jesus—his ways, ethics, commandments, and heart.

Alan Hirsch: While movements require leadership (they will not happen without it), both Lance's and Rob's testimonies highlight that it is the *kind* of leadership that matters. If our primary understandings of leadership are derived from the image of the CEO (or the "lords of the earth" in Jesus' day), then we have introduced a profoundly un-Christlike form of leadership at the heart of Jesus' church or movement. This will almost always undermine the advance of the gospel in any context. Jesus modeled a fundamentally different form of leadership—one based on the Suffering Servant who is also Lord of all (Phil. 2:5–8; Luke 22:27; Matt. 23:11).

The F-Word (Rob's Story)

I was one of those eager students, learning all I could from leaders from every sector of society. I believe all truth is God's truth. Therefore, leadership truth can be discovered and applied from every sector. But my mindful critique of these sources wasn't thorough enough. Without realizing it, I imported extrabiblical frameworks and principles—more explanation on that is coming shortly. Over time, I felt the corrosive effect. It came to a head at a surprising moment.

Some twenty years into my vocational ministry journey in a large church, I was on a five-day retreat. This was part of a longer sabbatical given to me after those twenty years of service. Prior to the sabbatical, my wife and I had begun engaging spiritual direction with a wise couple, and the plan was to spend extended time with them at their retreat center. But first I carved out a week to spend in solitude and silence at a monastery.

The first two nights I tossed and turned the whole night. Nightmares plagued me. I was exhausted by day three. That afternoon, I had finished praying the mid-afternoon office with the monks. As I made my way back to my cabin, my thoughts drifted toward a church leader whom I loved dearly: my boss. He was without a doubt one of the most meaningful mentors of my life. I stand on his shoulders. He has believed in me and blessed me in ways beyond number.

Yet as his face came to mind, a torrent of anger burst out of me, along with a string of expletives that I won't repeat here. To say I was shocked would be an understatement. I felt dizzied, and I mumbled, "Where did that come from?"

Up to that point, I hadn't been living with any vivid awareness of the venom in my soul. I thought I experienced the typical frustrations common in any church. My soul was telling me otherwise. The explosion of rage felt primal and involuntary, like vomiting a bad meal that has given you food poisoning. This poison was from spider bites—many of them.

In the aftermath, as the wave of rage passed, I was at first ashamed that I had said the f-word, cursing someone I loved. But the revelation of that feeling was the beginning of the healing. I prayed, "Lord, help me to understand what is going on in the mystery of my heart."

Over the next few hours and days of solitude, as I prayed and journaled, the scales fell off my eyes. Yes, this individual's habitual behaviors had wounded me, but the problem was more systemic than that. A tangled web of "leadership" values and tactics had enmeshed me and many others, perpetuating spider bites. Our church wasn't unique in this. These were values and tactics championed in the church growth movement and studied in church leadership conferences, which had now become normative in thousands of churches.

Suddenly, this twenty-year, singular hero story about a progressive, prevailing church plant that became one of the most influential megachurches in America flipped into a multilevel horror story. Later, I would be able to see the complexity and nuance of the story—both its beauty and brokenness, the hero and horror—in a fuller way. No story or life is just one thing. In that moment, however, the dark side of the story, which I had largely repressed, looked away from, and excused, swallowed me.

In the darkness, we usually look for someone else to blame to absolve ourselves from the problem. But in that moment, I knew I was complicit.

During those days of solitude, in prayer and journaling, I revisited the deep places of idolatry in my soul that had allowed me to lose my way. I revisited the wounds and wept. Jesus met my four-letter f word with an even stronger f word: forgiveness. By God's grace, I was able to receive and also pass on what had been given to me in limitless measure.

What I had seen as powerful and progressive in church leadership in my twenties now felt crushing and suffocating at the dawn of my forties.

Upstairs, I looked like I had it going on. Down in the basement, I had a heavy, dirty soul. The hurt inflicted by that pastor, the impact of a toxic culture, and the shame I felt over the ways I exerted my influence for my benefit—all of it had been buried deep in the basement of my soul and hidden behind a false wall. Of course, in some aspects of the church's life, God was so clearly at work redeeming and restoring people in amazing ways. Simultaneously, I knew other facets of our life together had drifted far from Jesus' intent for the church.

I remember one particularly disturbing meeting, shortly before the sabbatical, that embodied the drift. In this important private meeting, with just me and the other "top" two guys, one of them said, "I see this church as a business with three co-owners. That's whose sitting at this table—the co-owners of this church."

I nodded my head and was afraid to speak up, but my stomach hurt. After I left the meeting, it was as if something unraveled in me. "How did we get here?" The leadership model championed in the modern church, which we had embraced, had become a confused web of unanchored Bible verses, cut-and-paste business practices, unedited marketplace values, and unchecked motives, where "leaders" were unconsciously working out of their own woundedness through narcissism and power tactics.

That model was crushing my soul, yet I was perpetuating it and hurting others.

The tactics and values seen as necessary for the maintenance of leadership excellence in the church had too often become shaming and bullying tactics. Patterns lauded as surefire ways to build a culture of honor and gratitude had instead created a culture of celebrity for a few in each church and a caste system for the rest. When the church is dysfunctional, it is the most appalling of all institutions. The stakes are so high precisely because the church's potential for beauty is so great and our love for it is so deep.

My feelings toward that leadership culture had all been building up in me. But up until that moment, it had been too painful and humiliating to look straight at.

The combination of the three days of silence and prayer mixed with the physical exhaustion—not to mention the preceding detonations set off by the spiritual directors my wife and I had been meeting with—caused that wall to crumble. The years of hurt I had buried, the undercover sense of shame over my contribution to a contaminated leadership culture, and all the unforgiveness I had harbored came pouring out.

By the end of the retreat, I felt a hundred pounds lighter. I slept like a baby those last few nights of the retreat. But the most difficult season of my life lay ahead. The soul work had only begun.

During the next season, I found myself at a crossroads, as the pastor and the culture of that church continued harder and faster in the same direction. Prior to this sabbatical, the pathway was clear. Most people assumed I was the heir apparent. Now I felt lost. Dante describes the experience this way: "In the middle of life, I found myself in a dark wood."[2]

I was experiencing the dark night of the soul. I remember the darkest point.

On a pitch-black night in the dead of winter, I walked alone on the gravel berm of a country road. A few hundred yards away, a pair of headlights were barreling toward me, on my side of the road. A thought played in my head, stuck on repeat, skipping like a scratched record: *End it.*

As the car closed in, I thought, "It would be so much easier to just step in front of that car. I'm just two feet away from the pain being over." That's where my two-decade journey with church leadership had landed me. By God's grace, I saw how foolish that thought was. It was also terrifying. I went home immediately, told my wife, and began to weep.

A collision of crises in the church and our family, a toxic church leadership culture, and unresolved wounds from my past combined into a season of depression that was so dark, there were days when I was nonfunctional. I questioned all my deepest held beliefs. More than once I thought, "They'll have to pull my pastor card if I end up an atheist."

The darkness went on for months. I kept muscling my way through. Externally, I was the envy of my peers. A church of thousands. A national reputation. A book published with just the right publisher in just the right book series. Gigs at the cool conferences. Coaching and training other church leaders. But internally, I was crushed to the point of despair.

As I continued to do deeper soul work with a spiritual director and moved regularly into inner healing prayer with another mentor, I felt like the blind man who had the two-stage restoration of sight. First things were blurry, but with Jesus' continued touch, clarity increased. Of course, this miracle in Mark 8:22–25 was proceeded with a question meant to provoke Jesus' "blind" disciples in Mark 8:21: "Do you still not understand?" A bit at a time, I understood and experienced more deeply: Jesus and the gospel could meet my deepest needs!

In Closing

Our stories aren't uncommon. As we mentioned earlier, in just the last few years, we have witnessed a pattern where every few months we receive news of yet another "at-the-top leader" either resigning or being forced to step down in light of confession or accusations of some form of bullying, abuse, or manipulation of staff members or the opposite sex. For example, famed Seattle pastor Mark Driscoll resigned after the board of elders at his church declared he had "been guilty of arrogance, responding to conflict with a quick temper and harsh speech, and leading the staff and elders in a domineering manner."[3] Or consider the tragic descent of Bill Hybels as numerous women courageously stepped forward to uncover a pattern of oppression and manipulation that was rampant for years.[4] Both of these individuals were lauded as "best in class" in church leadership by the public, up until the very moment the veil was pulled back. By all means, we long for their full restoration. Their stories serve as a warning to *all of us* in church leadership who at some level or another have been complicit with oppressive and self-benefiting forms of leadership at some point in our lives.

But it is also about more than just individual character flaws. A system behind these failures must be addressed. It would be naive to write these off as merely personal failures and not question the form of leadership and the institutional systems that form of leadership creates. Each of these situations would find difficulty gaining traction in a starfish leadership culture. Was *more* leadership needed, or was a far different type of leadership required?

Rigid systems are a great fit amid the drive for predictability, but there's a human cost because they tend to foster cultures of fear and depersonalization instead of expectation, creativity, and uniqueness. Worse yet, they are greenhouses for domineering, bullying, and sexual abuse. To say the least, they quench the Holy Spirit. London Business School professor of organizational behavior Dan Cable writes,

> This so-called executive disease is common because power changes how leaders view other people—research shows that power causes people to see others as a means to their ends rather than as intelligent humans with ideas and emotions. In organizational life, power can result in arrogance and self-importance, and executives too often use their power to bully and frighten employees into compliance.[5]

Rank-based concepts create a hierarchy. At the top are leaders, a select and privileged few. Below them are followers, the vast majority.[6] This type of thinking quashes the collective intelligence of an organization. It shuts down creativity, heart, and drive under the mindset that only a small group of "gifted" ones contain the competence for decision-making. Sadly, leadership like this slams the door on the unlimited potential of most of our team members. Even more tragic is that the gifts God wants to give our organizations via the silenced majority are summarily rejected by the upper echelon. When this happens, we aren't playing with the full deck God has dealt us.

By sharing our stories, we hope we don't come off like angsty teenagers, because honestly, we love the church leaders involved in these practices. These are our people. We are for them. We are them.

If you've been bitten by a spider, it's easy to objectify and hate the pastor or church leader who hurt you. Please know we validate your loss and pain. We commend you to find your healing in Christ, which will eventually involve your forgiving those who wounded you. Hurt people hurt people—that includes those who hurt us.

Here's something else observed. The megachurch pastor or church leader we want to resent, dislike, or slam may make us angry precisely because they remind us of our own dark side. Jesus says, "Love your enemies." If we follow this command, eventually we'll realize that a lot of our enemy-hating is at least partially about us projecting our own darkness onto someone else. In our lives and leadership, repentance—turning back to Jesus—is the only way forward.

Before you turn the page, would you first turn to the embrace of Jesus? Did the Spirit convict you of anything as your read these stories? Did a certain memory push its way to the surface?

Sit now at the feet of Jesus. That's where starfish leadership begins.

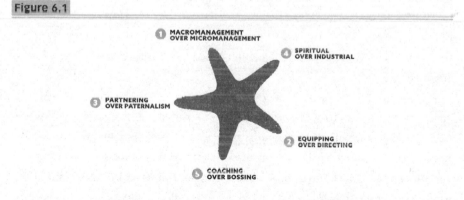

CHAPTER 6

The Light-Load Leader Starfish

Equipping Others and Distributing the Weight

Behind the facade and the bravado, the lives of powerful corporate leaders are ones of quiet suffering too.
—Frederic Laloux, *Reinventing Organizations*

Come to me, all who labor and are heavy laden, and I will give you rest. Take my yoke upon you, and learn from me, for I am gentle and lowly in heart, and you will find rest for your souls. For my yoke is easy, and my burden is light.
—Matthew 11:28–30 ESV

Figure 6.1

Starfish #2: The Light-Load Leader Starfish

Purpose: The light-load leader starfish helps us equip others in a fivefold fashion (Eph. 4:11–13) with five postures, distributing the weight of leadership throughout the entire body rather than on the shoulders of a few.

Meeting at a local coffee shop, Steven, the founding pastor of a church that had grown to around 1,100 members, and I (Lance) sat down to discuss the young pastor's discontent after over a decade of leading the church he started. "I can't pinpoint what it is I'm feeling," Steven said. "Don't get me wrong. I love our church, and I'm not looking to move on. But I am just so weary of the weight and pace of carrying this thing. Something seems off."

Over the next couple of hours, I asked Steven to give an overview of how day-to-day workflow and responsibilities were carried out—the way the church was governed and the methods with which accountability and authority were practiced among the staff. Next I had Steven draw the church's organizational structure with the names and titles of those involved. The result was a classic pyramid leadership chart. At one point I spun the sketch 180 degrees. "All that weight is on the point, Steven. You're the point because so much *points* toward you. That's a lot of weight on your shoulders," I said, before steering the conversation to a prophetic promise of the coming Messiah: "For to us a child is born, to us a son is given; and the government shall be upon *his* shoulder, and his name shall be called Wonderful Counselor, Mighty God, Everlasting Father, Prince of Peace" (Isa. 9:6 ESV, emphasis ours).

Steven pushed back from the table and sighed deeply, saying, "Wow, that sounds so refreshing and hopeful."

Just imagine the momentous value this familiar verse can bring if we stop limiting it to glittery Christmas cards and cantatas and allow it to shape and inform our leadership approach. It is a promise! The weight of governing rests on the triune Godhead of the Holy Spirit (counselor), Father, and Son (Prince of Peace). The burden of leadership rests there. When we acknowledge it as such, our leadership role opens up to God's counsel, might, and peace. The *government* shall be upon *his* shoulder.

There are two ways you can operate: (1) you live like Atlas and exhaust your soul, or (2) you learn to share the pressure on Jesus' shoulders via shared responsibility and accountability with your trusted team members. The various gifts the Lord has poured out on each team member serves as his shoulders.

Remember the old myth of Atlas? He carried the weight of the world on his shoulders. While Atlas is often depicted holding a globe, the original story says he held up the sky. He did so as punishment, so he wasn't at liberty to simply drop the weight (and it would have caused devastation if he had).

Granted, regardless of the operating system, leaders must expect a degree of pressure. Even Paul expressed as much (2 Cor. 11:28). Too often pastors feel as if the weight of the (church) world is on their shoulders. It is not uncommon to hear pastors doing a bit of humble-bragging about all the pressure they are under. But much of the torturous stress leaders strive under is either self-inflicted via a sense of playing the Clint Eastwoodesque hero, or it comes from imposed expectations from a board or congregation that "expects" such performance as fulfillment of the job description of *pastor*. As you read this, to what degree to you feel that weight on *your* shoulders?

Figure 6.2

Many readers will remember Darrin Patrick, founder of the Journey, a megachurch in St. Louis that developed into a multisite church. Darrin was my (Lance's) friend for two decades, and I was one of three pastors that served as his council for the first couple of years as he initiated the Journey church plant. Darrin's story is one of triumph, despair, brokenness, and restoration. From conversations I had with my friend, I am certain the weight of leading in the wrong way systemically played a large part in Darrin's story, which ended with him taking his own life. Thankfully, and redemptively, Darrin engaged the work of deep personal repentance. Furthermore, he helped a multitude of young leaders by urgently and lovingly warning them not to repeat his mistakes. We celebrate his legacy and grieve deeply for this immeasurable loss.

In these situations, however, it is easy to miss that it wasn't just an individual who was responsible. Behind the scenes, in thousands of churches, a system and set of practices built on the wrong assumptions are crushing church leaders with the weight of the world on their shoulders. The expectation is for the pastor to be the expert, the smartest person in the room, and the "answer person" for every question. The load for the health and vitality of the church rest in an absurd degree on one person's shoulders.

But what is the witness of the Scripture?

Speaking the truth in love, we will grow to become in every respect the mature body of him who is the head, that is, Christ. From him the whole body, joined and held together by every supporting ligament, grows and builds itself up in love, as each part does its work. (Eph. 4:15–16)

We celebrate Jesus' headship theologically and philosophically, yet our systems demonstrate our true belief that a pastor or tiny group of leaders are, in reality, the "real head." Instead of leadership being lifted and integrated into Jesus' headship, in the current model a single leader's shoulders bear the weight.

This system is an offense to the lordship of Jesus.

Notice Alan's observations on lordship and headship of Christ:

Jesus's executive lordship goes deeper than merely being put in a favored position. Paul suggests that the actual function of lordship, normally associated with the Father, is now passed on to Jesus.

> He [God] raised him from the dead and seated him at his right hand in the heavenly realms, far above all rule and authority, power and dominion, and every title that can be given, not only in the present age but also in the one to come. *And God placed all things under his feet and appointed him to be head over everything* for the church, which is his body, the fullness of him who fills everything in every way (Eph. 1:20–23; emphasis mine).

In 1 Corinthians 15:25–28 Paul says, "For he [Jesus] must reign until he has put all his enemies under his feet. . . . When he has done this, then the Son himself will be made subject to him who put everything under him, so that God may be all in all."

This redefinition of biblical monotheism around the role of Jesus I will call Christocentric monotheism because it realigns our loyalties to God around the person and work of Jesus Christ. Jesus thus becomes the pivotal point in our relation to God, and it is to him that we must give our allegiance and loyalty. Jesus is Lord![1]

Jesus alone can bear the weight of headship. Yet many, if not most, churches see the lead pastor or a handful of leaders as the "head in residence" in lieu of Jesus. This happens subtly and subversively, not so much intentionally, because church leaders have inherited a centuries-old social contract that must be actively deconstructed in order for Jesus' rightful headship to become apparent to all.

Whereas this model of false headship is characterized by a crushing weight and level of difficulty that is hard beyond bearing, the headship of Jesus offers us a refreshing and radical alternative.

Come to me, all you who are weary and burdened, and I will give you rest. Take my yoke upon you and learn from me, for I am gentle and humble in heart, and you will find rest for your souls. For my yoke is easy and my burden is light. (Matt. 11:28–30)

How good does that sound? That's what we need: the way of the light-load leader. When Jesus says, "Take my yoke," he's saying, "Let me train you so your soul is as light as a feather, fluid as water, deep as the ocean, and strong as a mighty oak."

Alan Hirsch: If the basic task of the disciple is to become more and more like Jesus (to be increasingly Christlike), and the way Jesus is embodied in the life of the church is in and through discipleship, then we can say that nondiscipleship lies at the root of many problems in the life of the contemporary church. We can also further extrapolate that if there is no real discipleship in the church, then we should not be surprised if there are un-Christlike leaders directing the show. Nondiscipleship at every level undermines everything Jesus wants to do through his people.

Way too many leaders believe the weight of the church should be on their shoulders alone. For example, hear what Seattle pastor Eugene Cho shared with the congregation he led for eighteen years during his announcement of resignation: "I haven't been able to honor my responsibilities as the lead pastor. As such, some of the burden has trickled down to the other pastors, which simply isn't fair to them, our staff, and to the church. . . . The church needs a lead pastor who can be fully invested and drive the vision and mission of the church."[2] Again, we aren't called to be Atlas.

How might we ensure that the leadership (government) of our organizations rest on Jesus' shoulder? This book is titled *The Starfish and The Spirit* because we are seeking to convey what the Spirit of God wants in his church. Therefore, we are speaking here as to the *ethos* and *essence* of governance via the Spirit of the Lord.

Returning to the idea of living systems verses institutional structures, Alan describes that ethos and essence this way:

The task of missional leadership here is to bring the various elements in the system into meaningful interrelationship. This will require the leader to focus on developing a relationally networked, as opposed to an institutional, structure for the church. We must become an effective expression of the "body of Christ" (1 Cor. 12:12–27 is not just a metaphor, after all—it's a description of the church in its interrelationship with each part to its Head). It is critical to share information and ideas and to cross-pollinate in terms of gifts and callings around common tasks (Eph. 4:1–16). We must bring all necessary parts of the body into the missional equation if we want to truly function as a body. In nonecclesial settings, this would mean getting the various departments and specialists to relate meaningfully and share information functionally around common tasks, thereby bringing diversity into a functioning unity. It seems that in living systems, the real answer is always found in the grander perspective—when diverse gifts and knowledge rub up against each other, new forms of knowledge and possibilities will arise.[3]

In this chapter and the ensuing chapters, we will seek to make the missional leadership task of developing a relationally networked, cross-pollinating, gift-leveraging, information-sharing, Spirit-empowered living system of leadership both practical and accessible. In many ways, we hope what you hold in your hands will function as just that, a handbook.

What is the starfish way of the light-load leader? How do we grow up into Christ's headship and help activate the leadership strength of the entire body to carry the load together? Let's explore the five postures and practices of the light-load leader.

Posture #1: Macromanagement over Micromanagement

First, picture a system of *macro*management whereby the responsibility of self-managing is distributed to every individual rather than a micromanagement system of superiors in pockets of the organization.

Missional movements, with organic leadership DNA as its guidance system, is integral to releasing the people of God to go forth in the name of the Lord. In *The Forgotten Ways*, Alan conveyed the nonhierarchical ethos of genuine apostolic environments:

Part of the resistance to the reception of apostolic ministry in our churches has been that at times people who claim to be apostles have assumed that it involved a dictatorial approach to the leadership of the church. All too often, this has resulted in a disempowering of God's people, who, instead of maturing and growing in the faith, remain basically childlike and powerless, dependent on the autocratic and overwhelming paternal power of the "apostle." This is both a distortion and a misrepresentation of authentic apostolic ministry. Apostolic ministry is authenticated by suffering and empowerment, not by claims of positional leadership, with its institutional levers.[4]

Four Signs of Micromanagement

- **Delegation doesn't happen.** Micromanagers don't believe others can do the job, so they do it themselves.
- **Over-reporting is required.** Everyone must make periodic reports. Micromanagers make it seem like reporting is the job.
- **No power to make decisions.** Team members feel like the smallest task may require a sign-off.
- **The hoarding of skills and knowledge.** Micromanagers see knowledge and skill as *their* currency, so sharing it means they feel they will lose value.*

---

* Diane Baily, "Am I Being Micromanaged?—8 Signs You Work for a Micromanager," Honestly, March 11, 2019, https://www.honestly.com/blog/how-to-deal-micromanager-part1/.

In his letter to the church at Philippi, the apostle Paul speaks of his companions as fellow workers (Phil. 4:3). The word is also translated as "yokefellow," a term that expresses collegiality, camaraderie, and partnership. *Yokefellow* harkens to the tool used to join two oxen in unison. A yoke is a simple mechanism made from a pole with two side-by-side U-shaped devices that fit over the necks of the oxen. The word in Greek means "to pull together in harness."

To call someone your yokefellow is to say, "We are in this thing together, shoulder to shoulder. We may have differing strengths, but we are both just a couple of oxen whose reins are in the hands of the same Master." Jesus says, "Take my yoke upon you, and learn from me, for I am gentle and lowly in heart, and you will find rest for your souls" (Matt. 11:29). We see that Paul uses the language that helps us take Jesus' yoke and work within the soul-fulfilling rest our Lord promised.

The Pathway toward Macromanagement and Equipping

Delegation is an art. Jesus walked with his disciples incrementally. Delegation is a leadership development process, not a product. The goal is to replace yourself and to develop others to their maximum influence while maintaining clarity and increasing authority along the way.

- **Level 1: Do exactly what I have asked you to do.** Don't deviate from my instructions. I have already researched the options and determined what I want you to do.
- **Level 2: Research the topic and report back.** We will discuss it, and then I will make the decision and tell you what I want you to do.
- **Level 3: Research the topic, outline the options, and make a recommendation.** Give me the pros and cons of each option, but tell me what you think we should do. If I agree with your decision, I will authorize you to move forward.
- **Level 4: Make a decision and then tell me what you did.** I trust you to do the research, make the best decision you can, and then keep me in the loop. I don't want to be surprised.
- **Level 5: Make whatever decision you think is best.** No need to report back. I trust you completely. I know you will follow through. You have my full support.*

* Gavin Adams, "The Art of Delegation," https://www.gavinadams.com/wp-content/uploads/2015/07/art-of-delegation-gavin-adams.pdf.

When we view church and faith-based organizations as typical businesses, we end up viewing those who should be our yokefellows and peers as employees and subordinates. As we will show later, this is not to say everyone has the same role or ability. Different giftings and talents equip us all for different roles. What causes us to go off the rails—through the sin of lording over others—is the tendency to rank the rarer gifts and talents of a few servants above the more common gifts and talents held by others. We will touch on how this plays out in starfish leadership later in the book.

Alan Hirsch: When an organization has (1) clarity and covenantal *commitment at the level of purpose* and (2) an *agreed-upon set of principles* (practices) by

> which all operate, then leadership can dispense with coercive command-and-control type management. This is because people will know how to behave in accordance with the purpose and principle, and they will do it in thousands of unimaginable and creative ways. The organization develops into a decentralized movement by becoming a vital, living set of beliefs.

We don't claim that starfish leadership is stress-free, but we are confident it sets us free from many of the stresses and burdens currently associated with leadership as we've known it. By its very design, *modern* leadership particularly has factors that make it hard in ways it doesn't have to be. If you have ever watched a spider build a web, it looks like a difficult, complex, and lonely endeavor, something that is often said about leadership. Though bullies and jerks certainly exist, and we have had our own share of experiences with them, this book isn't about focusing on the villains and tyrants. Like Steven, the vast majority of leaders in faith-based organizations we have encountered, even when they are leading in spider practices, are good and sincere people who are just doing the best they can with what they know.

Posture #2: Equipping over Directing

Take a few minutes to think through the things that stress you out as a leader or one who is or has been under leadership. What is the root source of most of the stress? Where does the pressure come from? For most leaders, stress comes from the pressure to produce results. We call it "the bottom line" or "the main thing." First off, we must make sure we know what our *main thing* is. We must make sure we have kept to the main thing. In doing so, it is vital for us to use only the tools and methods that correspond with what we are seeking to produce. Blowtorches and sledgehammers aren't seen in gardens.

What is the main thing of missional leadership that can spark and sustain a missional movement? Equipping.

Christ himself gave the apostles, the prophets, the evangelists, the pastors and teachers, to equip his people for works of service, so that the body of Christ may be built up until we all reach unity in the faith and in the knowledge of the Son of God and become mature, attaining to the whole measure of the fullness of Christ. (Eph. 4:11–13)

Unfortunately, we often choose coercive directing over catalytic equipping. When we create cultures based on the following, we undercut our primary directive from Jesus to engage fivefold equipping as the main thing:

- Titles and rank (under the guise of "authority")
- Charisma and personality (under the guise of "alpha leader")
- Stamina (under the guise of "work ethic")
- Technique (under the guise of "ingenuity")

A spider leader who directs others from these categories alone creates a weighty burden that is unsustainable over time. It shuts down the spirit in the majority of our coworkers and leaves little room for the Spirit of God to guide and speak to us and to do the heavy lifting necessary to bring about the wins we are looking for. The endgame too often is crash-and-burn stories whereby leaders flame out through narcissistically driven habits. The organization ultimately can't take it anymore and confronts the leader directly, or credible accusations eventually surface to force the leader into stepping down or being removed. Other scenarios play out with a leader who burns out or succumbs to addictions of one sort or another.

> **Alan Hirsch:** It doesn't take long to see that Jesus embodied and fulfilled all the APEST functions perfectly in his flawless human life. APEST aren't just what Jesus does; they are his very purposes and identities that he bequeaths to the body of Christ in his ascension to the throne room of the universe. Barth says APEST are "the modes of Christ's presence."* APEST are therefore the way Jesus is present and operative in the life of the Body. If the body of Christ exists to extend the logic and impact of Jesus' fivefold ministry, then it simply has to have all five operatives in its ministry. Mess around with APEST typology and the ministry becomes dysfunctional as a result.

* Markus Barth, *Ephesians: Translation and Commentary on Chapters 4–6*, vol. 2, The Anchor Bible (New York: Doubleday, 1974), 434.

However, Ephesians 4 provides the solution: a fivefold system of equipping. The five styles listed in Ephesians 4—apostle, prophet, evangelist, shepherd, and teacher (sometimes called APEST)—aren't leadership roles that reflect the calling of just a few individuals; they are lifelong influencing styles given to every follower of Jesus. Only Jesus fully lived out all five purposes to their full potential. And each of us can grow in all five purposes. But each of us has one style that is primary among the five. Here are brief working definitions of each of the APEST gifts:[5]

- The **apostle** sends and extends. These people are tasked with the overall extension of Christianity as a whole, primarily through missions and church planting. The apostle (from the Latin term meaning "sent one") is one who is on a mission of being sent, and those who have the apostolic style influence others by emphasizing the work of sending and multiplying.
- The **prophet** questions and critiques. These people feel called to maintain faithfulness to God among the people of God. Prophets are guardians of the covenant relationship, calling out sin and challenging God's people to greater fidelity to God, his Word, and his ways.
- The **evangelist** invites and gathers. These people influence and recruit others to the cause and love to share the gospel and proclaim the truth about Jesus. They are naturally infectious and able to enlist people into the movement through their communication and actions.
- The **shepherd** protects and provides. These people are called to nurture spiritual development, maintain communal health, and engender loving community among the people of God.
- The **teacher** explains and organizes. These people mediate wisdom and understanding. This philosophical style of influencing others brings comprehensive understanding of the revelation bequeathed to the church.

Activating a starfish movement, by the power of the Spirit, will happen only through sustained and scalable fivefold equipping. Once again, Alan, in *The Permanent Revolution*, highlights,

What is ultimately at stake is the church's capacity to embody and extend the mission and purposes of Jesus in the world. When Paul says that APEST is given to "equip" the saints, he uses the Greek word *kataptismo*, which, among its various nuanced meanings, is applied to the act of setting a broken bone. APEST helps us mature so that the "body" can "walk" and ultimately "stand" against the principalities and powers that dehumanize and then crush humanity (Ephesians 6:10–16). Our capacity as a movement to engage the spiritual powers that be is at stake when APEST is not fully operative.[6]

In the next section, we'll explore how to active all God's people by helping each discover his or her own APEST profile. Once that discovery is made, ongoing fivefold equipping is *job one* of the light-load leader.

In the book *Find Your Place*, Rob and his coauthor, Brian Phipps, describe it this way:

> In your body there are nine different systems. You have a circulatory system, a respiratory system, a central nervous system, a skeletal system, a digestive system and so on. When these nine systems are all in balance, we say that the body is healthy. And when a body is healthy, life and growth happen naturally. Just ask the parents of any healthy kid . . . you can't keep them in shoes for very long. They keep growing too fast! Any time one of the systems in your body gets out of balance, that's called disease, and at that point, you head to the doctor. The task of health care professionals is to diagnose where you are out of balance and advise you on how to bring your body back into balance so all the systems work together again.
>
> In the Bible, "Dr. Paul" writes in Ephesians 4 and describes the body of Jesus, the church. He explains that we have several "systems" in the body. We have an Apostle system, a Prophet system, an Evangelist system, a Shepherding system, and a Teaching system. All of these "systems" work together to keep the body in balance, leading to health and growth in the Body of Christ.[7]

The health of any church, and the possibility of starfish movement, is contingent on all five of these influencing styles operating synergistically.

Many church leaders assume they are supposed to be directing, that they are supposed to be the "big man or woman" pulling all the levers and calling the shots. But here's the dirty little secret: directing as the head honcho is ultimately less productive. Equipping will unleash untold productivity! Furthermore, directing can be dangerous to the soul, as it props up and puffs up a false sense of self.

If you've seen *The Wizard of Oz*, you will remember that near the end of the film Dorothy's little dog, Toto, pulls the green curtain back on the "powerful" wizard. We find out he is just a little man with a big microphone who operates pulleys and levers.

In the end, the wizard has no *true* authority. He only has the brutish powers of manipulation and volume. All along he has reduced himself to playing a cheapened role that falls way short of who he was made to be. As the scene unfolds, the wizard is at first startled to be exposed but is quickly relieved to come out from behind the curtain. And then something incredible takes place: he becomes who he was meant to be all along.

Leaving behind command and control, the wizard transforms into an equipper and encourager, a phenomenal leader! A new, authentic confidence and strength emerge. The former wizard helps the scarecrow see his own untapped potential and get the brain he has longed for. He transforms the cowardly lion into a full-fledged member of the Legion of Courage and helps the tin man understand the importance of love and what makes a heart what it is meant to be. Leaving behind the role of commander and controller, the little man steps into the joy of being a catalyst and starts changing lives for the better.

Alan Hirsch diagnoses the challenge of conventional leadership as The Oz:

> The problem with CEO-type leadership is that it tends to disempower others, and when, for various reasons, that leader should leave the group, the organization tends to be weak and underdeveloped. This is the very thing that apostolic influence is at pains not to do—rather, apostolic ministry calls forth and develops the gifts and callings of all of God's people. It does not create reliance but develops the capacities of the whole people of God based on the dynamics of the gospel.[8]

Let's get practical. What are the differences between equipping and directing?

Equipping others involves first discovering what the person needs to fulfill his or her calling. For example, a baseball coach may have a pitcher who is very good but struggles with keeping base runners from getting huge leads away from first base and easily stealing second base. A coach that equips works with the pitcher through situational practice, better coordination, and *reading* the runner in order to keep the runner from getting too much of a lead. Next, the coach will focus on helping the pitcher develop a quicker and more accurate pick-off move to first base. With *directing*, the coach has a system in place that has the pitcher look only at a bench coach for a signal of when to throw over to first base to keep the runner close. When properly equipped with a refined skill, the pitcher doesn't need direction in the moment. He has become a much better player because of the hard work his coach put in with him. At some point, as the pitcher further develops his skill, he will become equipped not only to be effective himself but to help others refine the skill as well.

Table 6.1

EQUIPPING	DIRECTING
Long-term	Short-term
Interactive	Reactive
Exponential potential	Limited potential
Mentors	Manages
Trains	Tells

THE SEVEN PRACTICAL STEPS OF EQUIPPING

1. Discover—assess for the needed skill or resource
2. Practice—the skill
3. Debrief—the experience
4. Tweak—fine-tune the skill
5. Play—with the skill
6. Release—freely use the skill
7. Reproduce—equip someone else by walking with them through the seven steps.

As this process of equipping unfolds in all five APEST dynamics, the combination of these five influencing styles creates an unstoppable force for unity in the church, the building up of the Body, and the unleashing of movement potential.

Alan Hirsch: A quick way to get a "blink" on the (dys)functionality of your system is to try to view it in terms of all five APEST functions: Which one is the highest and which one the lowest? Rate all of them accordingly. I guarantee the answer to this gives you vital clues about what the problem is and how you might go about fixing it. For instance, if the teaching (T) function is your highest capacity by far (as it is in most evangelical churches) and the apostolic (A) is your lowest, then it's no good doing more teaching to try resolve all your problems. You simply won't become more missional by doing more teaching! You need to bolster those functions and systems that are weak to have overall strength and functionality. (See www.5Qcentral.com for personal and organizational assessments.)

Posture #3: Partnering over Paternalism

Much of what keeps us as leaders from experiencing the easy yoke and light burden Jesus offered can be traced to basic but misguided assumptions that organizations are machines and that most people lack the necessary self-discipline and acumen to carry out their tasks. These assumptions create wizard roles whereby otherwise gifted and good-hearted equippers and mentors are reduced to lever-pulling controllers with volume-enhanced voices.

This mode of organizational management was designed within and for the industrial age. It came from the need for prediction and precision through engineering and architecture, delivering products forged from cold, hard steel. Assembly-line workers were measured with clocks and quotas. They were constantly hovered over by the lingering eye of the shift boss in an open-windowed upper office on the factory floor. The conflict is that our faith communities aren't factories. They are more so gardens. They aren't full of robots. They are families. Margaret Wheatley writes, "The tension of our times is that we want our organizations to behave as living systems, but we only know how to treat them as machines. It is time to change the way we think about organizations. Organizations are living systems. All living systems have the capacity to self-organize, to sustain themselves and move toward greater complexity and order as needed."[9]

We have discovered a vast number of organizations, both for profit and nonprofit, that have grown phenomenally successful endeavors by structuring themselves in nonhierarchical ways—such as Morning Star, founded in 1970, which dominates the tomato processing and transport space in the United States. If you have indulged in pizza, spaghetti, or just about any other meal with a tomato paste ingredient, you have almost certainly tasted their product. This company operates sans human bosses and hierarchy. It is organized through shared principles and self-management and held together by its "principles, mission, processes and a culture of learning and coaching."[10]

Or consider Resources for Human Development, an almost fifty-year-old Philadelphia-based nonprofit with over 4,500 staff members focusing on providing services to those facing homelessness, addiction recovery, and mental disabilities. They provide over $200 million to tens of thousands of people across fourteen states. RHD is built on a system of self-management and a safe and open environment where information is shared freely, early, and often. If non-faith-based organizations can operate in such ways, it is more than reasonable to imagine that churches and other faith organizations can function likewise.

Many faith organizations, particularly those in North America, have unwittingly imported the human resources manuals of corporate America straight into their day-to-day workforce policy. We have let systems that make no claim whatsoever of being informed by the Word and Spirit of God set the rules for us. Earthly thinking never creates heavenly results. Most of the earthly leadership thinking of our day creates paternalistic cultures. Again, that does not mean we can't learn from all sectors of society. As Aquinas argued, all truth is God's truth! Paul quoted the philosophers and poets of his day, as we do in this book. But we must be wise not to simply cut and paste marketplace leadership structures and strategies without theological reflection. Pragmatism is the hubris of the West, and too often it is the fundamental driver for church leaders: "Does it work?" Not everything that "works" is holy. All methodology in the church should flow from our theology.

Paternalistic relationships limit the freedom and responsibilities of others, seeing others merely as subordinates. This is vastly different from the biblical model of spiritual parenting. Paul was a spiritual parent to many. His goal wasn't an ongoing relationship of gridlock paternalism, but a growing partnership whereby others became equals in authority, credibility, and practice. Paul was looking for others to become coequal coworkers.

We are co-workers in God's service. (1 Cor. 3:9)

Greet Priscilla and Aquila, my co-workers in Christ Jesus. . . . Greet Urbanus, our co-worker in Christ. (Rom. 16:3, 9)

Consider the phases of Paul's relationship with Timothy. In Paul's first letter to Timothy, he addresses him as "my true son in the faith" (1 Tim. 1:2). We first meet Timothy in Acts 16. As Paul is launching out on his second missionary journey, he makes a pit stop in Lystra to invite Timothy to join him. Along the way, Paul bonds with him, equips him, and raises him up. Phase one is parenthood, but the end goal is a partnership where Timothy is able to parent others toward partnership, as Paul had done with Timothy. Paul expressly invites Timothy to this in 2 Timothy 2:2: "The things you have heard me say in the presence of many witnesses entrust to reliable people who will also be qualified to teach others."

Paul had been setting the pace for Timothy through his example and availability. In his second letter to Timothy, for example, he states, "You . . . know what I teach, and how I live, and what my purpose in life is. You know my faith, my patience, my love, and my endurance" (2 Tim. 3:10 NLT). Basically, "Timothy, you've seen me do this. You can do this too!"

Finally, in a somewhat hidden passage in the book of Romans, Paul drops a title on Timothy that had to make him put his shoulders back and stick his chest out: "Timothy, my fellow worker, greets you" (Rom. 16:21 ESV).

Timothy has gone from being a son and student to a colleague and co-laborer. No doubt that fatherly role and affection continued through their entire relationship, but Paul considered Timothy an equal partner.

You see this celebration of partnership come up again and again in Paul's letters.

In all my prayers for all of you, I always pray with joy because of your partnership in the gospel from the first day until now. (Phil. 1:4–5)

I always thank my God as I remember you in my prayers, because I hear about your love for all his holy people and your faith in the Lord Jesus. I pray that your partnership with us in the faith may be effective in deepening your understanding of every good thing we share for the sake of Christ. (Philem. 1:4–6 NIV)

In this very chapter, Paul, while describing his approach to confrontation with Philemon, basically says, "I could throw down on you. In Christ, I could order you to do this, but I'm not going to. Rather, I will appeal to you as a partner." "Although in Christ I could be bold and order you to do what you ought to do, yet I prefer to appeal to you on the basis of love" (Philem. 1:8–9).

Unfortunately, this phased approach with the end goal of equality is a rarity in the church.

Take this typical example from a member on staff at a large southern church. Dan was an exceptionally competent and productive leader of an entire sector of the church. He asked for a day off to take his college freshman son to move into his new dorm. Dan was told he would have to use one of his vacation days to take the day off. It was all referred to as *policy*.

But no one stopped to ask, "Why do we have such policies? Where did we get this policy?" First, the time Dan spent serving the church was far beyond a forty-hour work week. Anyone who has served on a church staff knows that work does not stay at the office once you leave for home. Yet this capable adult was required to ask permission from the executive pastor for a day off.

Second, like a child going to a parent, Dan was required to ask permission from someone—someone that would never have to ask permission of *anyone* to do the same thing.

The two top pastors were the only ones allowed to set their own schedule and clear their own vacations. The unspoken dynamic in such scenarios is that only two adults in the entire organization have the competency, credibility, and trustworthiness to make self-managed decisions. Let that sink in.

Compare that with Jesus' affirmation and invitation in John 15:15: "I no longer call you servants, because a servant does not know his master's business. Instead, I have called you friends, for everything that I learned from my Father I have made known to you."

If the Son of God is willing to condescend to make fishermen and tax collectors his peers and partners, how can we do otherwise?

Perks and privileges for a select few at the top is a telltale sign that servant leadership is not functioning. Servants never have perks and privileges that those they are serving don't have. Paternalism is a classic trait of modern leadership. It treats adults as children and is demeaning, demoralizing, and unnecessary in a healthy spirit-led organization.

10 SIGNS OF PATERNALISM AND PARTNERSHIP SOLUTIONS

1. *Paternalism*: A select few have the power to make decisions.
   Partnership: Using an agreed-upon *advice process*, decision-making is made by those whose roles place them closest to the issue at hand.
2. *Paternalism*: Senior leaders and executives determine quotas and goals for the organization.
   Partnership: Individuals and teams set the goals for the projects for which they have to work on the tasks.
3. *Paternalism*: Senior leaders and executives come and go at their own leisure while other team members have no such prerogative.
   Partnership: Everyone in every role is respected as a capable adult who is trustworthy to get their job done—and is held accountable to other team members for the final results.
4. *Paternalism*: The HR department determines work schedule, holidays, days off, vacation time, and more.
   Partnership: Working with one another, team members set their schedule— with respect and reverence for all team members.

5. *Paternalism*: Benefits are greater for executive positions.

   Partnership: Regardless of role, equal job performance and tenure are rewarded equivalently.

6. *Paternalism*: There are frequent closed-door meetings where the higher the rank, the narrower the information portal.

   Partnership: Information is shared freely among all roles.

7. *Paternalism*: Sabbaticals are for senior pastors only.

   Partnership: Sabbaticals are a healthy and biblical ordinance. If sabbaticals are offered for any role, they should be offered at the same scale for all roles.

8. *Paternalism*: The church or organizational website lists staff in order of rank.

   Partnership: Presents the team in alphabetical order, demonstrating that all are equally valued.

9. *Paternalism*: A limited group, by rank, receives higher education benefits.

   Partnership: If such benefits are available, they should be for anyone who desires to expand their skill and knowledge set.

10. *Paternalism*: Senior pastors have reserved parking.

    Partnership: Nope!

Posture #4: Spiritual over Industrial

Our guiding metaphors are of utmost importance. Our metaphors determine our mental maps, which will always shape our behaviors. Consider the earth. If our unconscious guiding metaphor for the earth is that of "supply store" for the industrial complex, then our attitude will be that of a consumer, a master, and an exploiter, and our actions will follow suit. We will see the earth as something to be used and controlled for our benefit, without concern for setting limits.

However, if I adopt biblical metaphors for the earth, I will respond to the world like Saint Francis did, with an attitude of stewardship, reverence, fraternity, and beauty. Saint Francis, faithful to Scripture, invites us to see nature as a magnificent book in which God speaks to us and grants us a glimpse of his infinite beauty and goodness. "Through the greatness and the beauty of creatures one comes to know by analogy their maker" (Wisd. Sol. 13:5); indeed, "God's invisible qualities—his eternal power and divine nature—have been clearly seen" (Rom. 1:20). He saw creation as a living system or great dance between the Creator and the creatures, of which humans are only one. Centuries before the ecology movements of our day,

Francis had already demonstrated with his life how inseparable the bond is between concern for nature, justice for the poor, commitment to society, and interior peace.[11]

His view of the earth was spiritual, not industrial.

Now, let's translate that from ecology to ecclesiology.

Dan White Jr. proposes that the unconscious guiding metaphor for ecclesiology in the West is that of the "industrial complex."[12] There is an unquestioned, undergirding concept of the church that is highly informed by these modern ideas of success in industry. To be successful in the church as industrial complex, the church must:

- grow bigger
- collect more resources
- consolidate power
- create stronger hierarchical structures
- experience exciting rapid growth
- connect with consumers so they can purchase the goods and services[13]

Our concepts of being the church are heavily weighted by our modern notions of success in the industrial marketplace: more resources, more programs, more power, more paid staff, more property, and more people in attendance. Therefore, leaders begin to desire to be CEOs and "captains of industry."

The use of force and person-to-person unilateral authority is the most commonly used modus operandi of industrial-age leadership. Exercising rank, using intimidation, or leveraging sheer personality power comes not from the Spirit of God but from the lower primal parts of creature behavioral dominance. Remember, management was originally developed to depersonalize work so that employees could be easily stationed, evaluated, and replaced when deemed obsolete. It was and is a form of dehumanization.

Alan Hirsch: You can be sure Jesus did not multiply metaphors (birds, seed, corn, farming, and more) to make the Bible understandable for children; rather, he offered us ways to reimagine ourselves, our tasks, and our purpose in the world. These metaphors are concentrated visions or paradigms of what we can and must be to be faithful to God. And important for movemental thinking, since metaphors awaken the imagination, they are our best tool for thinking creatively. New metaphors invite vision and innovation.

Anyone who has been unceremoniously fired or harshly talked down to can attest to feeling depersonalized. This is why the Industrial Revolution instituted hierarchy in the first place, where leaders were given heavy-handed power over others. Relationships and human feeling and emotions were considered as needless distractions. Who ever heard an ironworker asking a furnace how life was going or a mechanic asking an engine if it had any thoughts on how to produce more horsepower? People began to be treated as if they were cogs, parts, and machines. They were expected to do their appointed job, nothing more, nothing less. Leave it to the architects and engineers to figure out improvements and better ways.

There is a far better way. As we've already mentioned numerous times, the guiding metaphors for a biblical ecclesiology are primarily that of a living system; a family and a field, a body and a bride. On this, Alan states,

> Here we are on fertile biblical ground, because organic images of the church and the kingdom abound in the scriptures—images like body, field, yeast, seeds, trees, living temples, vines, animals, etc. These images are not just verbal metaphors that help us describe the theological nature of God's people but actually go to issues of essence. Therefore, they will need to be rediscovered, re-embraced, and relived in order to position us as Jesus's people for the challenges and complexities facing us in the twenty-first century. We must find a new way to experience ourselves, beyond the static, mechanistic, and institutional paradigm that predominates in our ecclesial life.[14]

We have grown accustomed to operating from the power of human will and unrefined human strength within an industrial framework, rather than the fuel of God's Spirit inside a multiplying spiritual family on mission. For many leaders who have never seen such living systems structures, this starfish talk may sound not only impossible but also outrageous.

However, with the structure Starfish, the self-management starfish, and the collective intelligence starfish, we will seek to make the way of living systems practical in everyday church leadership. Starfish structure is possible and incredibly life-giving, as these living systems' practices and structures flow from and with the biblical metaphors for ecclesia.

The brilliance in the processes and systems by which such living systems function can be summarized in two words: *family* and *freedom*. At the heart of this genius is a strident belief in the God-given capacity within people to freely choose to create and contribute, along with the value placed on human relationships—familial bonds—that incorporate ground rules that support healthy and prolific teamwork, while increasing freedom. Morning Star's Doug Kirkpatrick shares the story of a colleague, "To the degree that our people are free to perform to the best of their ability, they are also free to innovate change that improves performance even more. There will be no barriers to communication in the workplace—anyone will be able to discuss anything with anyone else regardless of area or process."[15]

Kirkpatrick's words serve to point us to scriptural passages of freedom.

Where the Spirit of the Lord is, there is freedom. (2 Cor. 3:17)

It is for freedom that Christ has set us free. Stand firm, then, and do not let yourselves be burdened again by a yoke of slavery. (Gal. 5:1)

Family and freedom are as important as anything for those who hope to perpetuate movemental endeavors. Leaders who trust their teams like family show the greatest trust in God because God is *in* the people that make up those teams. Developing cultures of freedom is the proof of trust and belief in the Spirit of God to do his work through his people. Any team member should be able to talk to anyone about anything relating to the organization and its endeavors. Freedom in our workplaces is the most natural and efficient way to operate. God has even designed our neurology so freedom within the safety of family environment is sought and rewarded.

In his book *Alive at Work*, Daniel Cable discusses the neuroscience behind what motivates or disengages people. He says, "Many organizations are deactivating the part of employees' brains called the *seeking system*. Our seeking systems create the natural impulse to explore our worlds, learn about our environments, and extract meaning from our circumstances. When we follow the urges of our seeking system, it releases dopamine—a neurotransmitter linked to motivation and pleasure—that makes us want to explore more."[16]

Many churches today have cultures that simply don't foster experimentation and creativity that reaches beyond predetermined job descriptions and preset decision-making boundaries. This grossly limits people's untapped skills and insight—a vast resource of problem-solving and potential for creative advancement. Amazingly, every day we all use technology that continues to develop at astonishing rates and was created by companies such as Google or Apple, which have flexible work cultures that encourage freedom and creativity and feel like a family. World-changing innovation most often arises in such cultures. These organizations are facsimiles of the living system design of the church, and yet they work because God's wisdom is universal.

Let us now, as God's people, reclaim our birthright as a living Spirit-empowered system, not a human-designed industrial complex.

Posture #5: Coaching over Bossing

Moving from hierarchical to humble leadership changes the role of a leader from boss and manager to coach and mentor. The leader's goal is to help one's teammates discover and develop their fullest potential. By choosing to relinquish the wizard role, we cease wearing ourselves down from the feverish pace of command and control. Instead, we work to unleash the brainpower, heart passion, and courageous fortitude of our team members.

Apart from such a posture shift, honest and transparent communication will likely never thrive. People will tell a boss only what they think the boss wants to hear. It decreases the likelihood of genuine relationships and familial community flourishing.

Coaches are still leaders, but they use a different style of leadership than bosses. Daniel Goleman, in his *Harvard Business Review* article "Leadership That Gets Results," proposed from his research that there are six essential leadership styles. Of these styles, coaching was shown to have a "markedly positive" impact on performance, culture, and the bottom line. Simultaneously, his research found it to be the least used style. Why? Goleman wrote, "Many leaders told us they don't have the time in this high-pressure economy for the slow and tedious work of teaching people and helping them grow."[17]

Bosses focus on the performance evaluation of the individual as the priority. Coaches focus on personal development of the person as the priority. Bossing leads to overdependence because others are waiting codependently for direction. Coaching leads to interdependence because others are increasingly empowered over time to grow in authority and decision making. Bossing leads to disconnection because it reinforces an entrenched caste system. Coaching leads to community because shared humanity and the potential for each person to reach their maximum influence are the goal. Bosses tell others what to do. Coaches ask questions to draw the best out of others.

Too often, bossing and leading become synonymous.

For example, one of the catchphrases poised in a keynote address at the Willow Creek Association Leadership Summit in the early 2000s was this: "Who's got the gun?" This celebrated pastor, in his annual session that summarized leadership lessons he had acquired during the previous year, chuckled as he reflected on the fact that sometimes you just have to remember, "You've got the gun." The crowd roared in laughter. He even drew a gun on the whiteboard. "Remember, you've got the gun." The phrase was clearly meant to communicate, "You have the power! You are large and in charge. You're the leader. You're the boss—so execute. Pull that trigger."

> **Alan Hirsch:** It's amazing how we have largely taken the idea of friendship and comradeship out of the equation of leadership. Jesus did not exclude a real relationship with him in the call to follow him. "I no longer call you servants, because a servant does not know his master's business. Instead, I have called you friends, for everything that I learned from my Father I have made known to you" (John 15:15). Discipling—which involves coaching and mentoring—is never simply a transactional program; it includes an offer of some level of life together.

Depending on the translation, at most the word *leader* is used only six times in the New Testament, while the word *servant* can be found over two hundred times. Let that sink in. How many leadership conferences have you been to? How many servantship conferences have you been to?

Jesus says, "I am among you as one who serves" (Luke 22:27). If you are a senior leader, can you say the same thing to your staff? Or would you have to say, "I am among you as the one who leads"?

To be genuine *followers* of Jesus—those who shadow his ways and means—our great obsession must be servantship rather than leadership. It means we will seek to be the best servant we can be. And this doesn't happen in abstract. We can't claim to be God's servant and not play it out among those he has placed around us. In other words, we serve God by serving others.

The apostle Paul clearly understood and highlighted the call of servantship. *Servant* is noticeably his favorite designation for himself. He opens his epistle to the Romans by declaring himself to be not a leader but a "servant" (1:1)—and not just any typical servant.

In *Unleader*, I (Lance) wrote,

The word Paul chose as his favorite label for himself was the Greek word *doulos*, which means "bondslave." A *doulos* is a slave who has given up his freedom and will. New Testament scholar Kenneth Wuest writes, "The word . . . *doulos*, [was] the most abject, servile term used by the Greeks to denote a slave. The word designated one who was born as a slave, one who was bound to his master in chords [*sic*] so strong that only death could break them, one who served his master to the disregard of his own interests, one whose will was swallowed up in the will of his master." I can just imagine Paul's bio if he were to speak at one of the large leadership conferences today. It would most likely read something like this: "Paul, formerly known as Saul of Tarsus, is an at-large janitor for Jesus. He is the property of Christ and has no purpose other than to be a slave, without personal rights of his own."[18]

Transforming our perspective of one another to that of yokefellows produces a peer-based culture rather than a traditional leadership culture. We no longer categorize people as leaders and subordinates. There is no elevating or superstarring of leadership because there is no thought of or leveraging of rank. Leadership emerges as a natural byproduct that materializes organically and exceptionally. Wheatley says, "In nature, change never happens as a result of top-down, preconceived strategic plans or from the mandate of any single individual or boss. Change begins as local actions spring up simultaneously around the system."[19]

Seven Coaching Questions That Will Forever Change the Way You Lead

Our coaches in the KC Underground use the following seven questions to develop our leaders. These are from *The Coaching Habit: Say Less, Ask More, & Change the Way You Lead Forever* by Michael Bungay Stanier.

- **The kick-start question:** What's on your mind?
- **The A.W.E. question:** And what else?
- **The focus question:** What's the real challenge here for you?
- **The foundation question:** What do you want?
- **The lazy question:** How can I help?
- **The strategic question:** If you're saying yes to this, what are you saying no to?
- **The learning question:** What was most useful for you?

Consider the relationship between Barnabas and Paul. Barnabas was a leader of great stature in the Jerusalem church (Acts 4:36). He was willing to leverage this status to elevate Saul's (Paul's) standing because of the suspicions of the understandably cautious church. Barnabas later invites Saul to join him in ministry, which he does until the end of this first missionary journey. When they set out from Antioch, they are referred to as "Barnabas and Saul" (Acts 13:2). Barnabas is the first partner and Saul is second. For example, in Acts 14:12 the crowds see Barnabas as Zeus, leaving Saul as Hermes, Zeus's sidekick. But during that journey together, Barnabas's encouragement lifted Saul and made space for him to emerge as Paul. From that point on, the Scriptures now list them as "Paul and Barnabas." In the language of Dave Ferguson, Barnabas was a hero maker. Coaches don't want to be the hero, but bosses often do. Coaches find their joy in making heroes of others. By the time they return to Antioch, Paul and Barnabas are peers.

When we allow our organizations to be ruled on the Spirit's shoulders, governance happens regularly, distributed throughout the organization. No longer does it rest on one single leader but becomes a key process shared by many. It changes the way we function in leadership by changing the way we view our roles. Distributed leadership means that "functions that traditionally reside with a CEO or executive team (move) into *processes* that are enacted throughout the organization, with everyone's participation."[20]

Clear processes are essential for a starfish leadership system to work. Moving forward in the book, we will deal with principles and practices that answer questions such as

- Who can make decisions, and what are the limits on those decisions?
- How is accountability held in place?
- What actions can individuals make without keeping the organization bogged down in meetings?
- What agreements should we come to in order to honor the spirit of being yokefellows?

Transitioning toward starfish and spirit leadership brings us to a place of trusting the Spirit of God to build his people and lead his organizations via the people that *are* the organization. The gifts and fruit of the Spirit are unleashed to flow freely throughout the group, unfettered and unlimited by a small elevated few. May these five practices lighten the load and empower all God's people as you seek a starfish movement.

CHAPTER 7

The Structure Starfish

Thinking outside Pyramids and Creating Circles

The modern organization cannot be an organization of boss and subordinate.

—Peter Drucker, "The New Society of Organizations"

Movements, by definition, cannot be led, and they cannot be planned really. They defy control and singular identity. A movement is an egoless enterprise.

—Brian Sanders, *Underground Church*

Figure 7.1

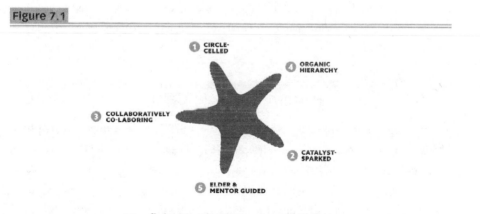

① CIRCLE-CELLED

④ ORGANIC HIERARCHY

③ COLLABORATIVELY CO-LABORING

② CATALYST-SPARKED

⑤ ELDER & MENTOR GUIDED

Starfish #3: The Structure Starfish

Purpose: The structure starfish helps us structure around organic systems by repeating five patterns in every cell of the body.

Have you ever tried to roll a triangle? Cavemen figured out a long time ago that circles make better wheels than pyramids do. This analogy is a clue for movement thinking. If we want our organizations to proliferate as dynamic movements, then we must seek to discover movemental types of leadership systems. The first challenge for most of us will be to think beyond the triangles of the most commonly used organization charts.

Whether you are a senior leader or staff member with leadership oversight in particular areas of your organization, when seeking to uncork the latent talent available, you must be willing to consider an entirely different function from a traditional CEO or executive. Reimagining leadership in the structure of the starfish, we certainly face challenges, but we can also crack the safe of greater inspiration as we consider the transformational possibilities.

Here we are now exploring organic systems. Phenomenal Jesus movements don't have the barriers of centralized institutions that hinder growth through control. They have the feel of a movement, structure of a network, and spread like viruses. In this chapter, we will offer five organic patterns that provide a simple structure that can be reproduced in every cell of an organization or missional movement, without constricting the flow of a movement.

The challenges are in abandoning the old ways of thinking while resisting our own knee-jerk reactions to new ways of doing things. Peter Block says, "The concept of leadership does not leave much room for the concept of partnership. We need a way to hold on to the initiative and accountability and vision of the leadership idea, and to abandon the inevitable baggage of dominance and self-centeredness."[1] In the following material, you will find five patterns of healthy starfish structures.

Pattern #1: Circle-Celled

Every living thing is made up of cells, and the starfish is of course no exception. Think of the cells of a starfish as circles. Within the starfish leadership structure, the circle is, in the words of Baldwin and Linnea, "essentially a gathering of equals, people who set aside external, hierarchical positions that categorize and separate them and sit down in a ring of chairs with a clearly defined intention or purpose symbolically represented in the middle."[2]

The Godhead is a circle! The old-world image of God is that of a singular monarch, seated on a throne: a pyramid. The Latin word for God is *Deus*, not a far cry from Zeus, a primitive image of God that still occupies the imaginations of millions.

Your image of God influences your entire life. You become like the God you worship. That's one of the reasons we have so much Zeuslike leadership.

Yet how radically did Jesus deconstruct this pyramid? God came as a vulnerable baby born among an oppressed people in a land occupied by Zeus worshipers. He lived as a simple man of trade, then kick-started his ministry by creating a leadership circle of fishermen and tax collectors. Gradually, he revealed the circle at the center: Father, Son, and Spirit. Of course, it took the church centuries to develop the doctrine of the Trinity until finally the Cappadocian Fathers used a word from Greek theater to describe it: *perichōresis*, which is a dynamic word to help us see God is a relationship or dance of equality and interdependence. We are invited into that the circle. How could we not model all our leadership on this theological foundation?[3]

We need circles of equality and interdependence that are open, inviting others in. That is the way of Jesus. In *The Permanent Revolution*, Alan describes it this way: "On closer examination, movements are composed of many circles, or a fractal-like network of networks. Each circle is an independently functioning decentralized network consisting of autonomous and interdependent units. And these tend to lack the hierarchy or structure normally associated with centralized command-and-control organizations."[4]

The circle changes the leader's role to that of a facilitator and coach who generates some, but by no means all, of the ideas while allowing those in his or her circle not only to follow through on concepts but also to add to and adapt them. The result is not a leaderless church or organization. Far from it. The upshot is more and better leadership.

> **Alan Hirsch:** Leadership is more about the success of your comrades in the ministry and mission than it is about you and your personal success. Being a leader does not mean having a fancy title or performing a job; rather, it involves developing a character committed to giving purpose, motivation, and direction to the people you lead.

For a starfish culture to thrive, leaders must reimagine their roles and practices. Several years ago, I (Lance) was part of a pastoral team that experimented with a form of shared leadership. Up to this point, the church was led in the typical senior-and-associate-pastors structure. I was one of the two associate pastors. The senior pastor was a true shepherd and teacher. He was selfless and sharing. The three of us had diverse gift mixes and therefore complimented one another tremendously, filling each other's shortcomings in both viewpoint and talent.

Our pulpit voices brought a healthy variety of insight and perspective to the discipling of the members, and the church exploded in growth. It was brimming in creativity, development, and an overall life-changing message. But it all came to a sudden end when the senior pastor finally could no longer handle sharing credit for the wonderful things that were happening in our midst. He felt a sense of diminishing value and initiated a devastating blowup that split the church. Over two decades later, he has repeatedly confessed his lack of maturity at the time, along with a deep regret for causing the end to what was a great work of the Spirit up to that point. Thankfully we have had a healthy, restored relationship for many years now.

Though this pastor had his share of blame in the botched leadership experiment, it was not altogether his fault. Looking back on the situation, we had failed to develop ground rules and necessary structures and systems vital to operating a shared leadership ethos. This omission served to create opportunities for poor communication and a lack of healthy sharing of information.

Previously, each of us had experience only in pyramid leadership structure, which runs on a diminished degree of relational intelligence. It lacks the holistic components that make a living body function. There was no systemic mutual understanding or practical habits to support our desire for shared leadership. Each of us led teams and programs, but without ground rules and processes in place, each of us was, in essence, doing our own thing. The cumulative effect bred inadvertent competition, insecurity, and a feeling of disorientation. We plainly lacked the necessary systems of navigation for the uncharted waters before us. Even a few simple practices would have helped tremendously. Understanding the power of circles would have been the perfect starting place. Alan's advice from *The Forgotten Ways* would have been helpful in those days:

> The problem is that most people see the church as an institution and not an organic movement (a living system).... The structures just revert back to default once the pressure of change is alleviated. The fact remains that for this very reason the vast majority of Christian institutions throughout history never renew and change. The institutional systems story informs so much of what we do. Machiavelli was right: "Nothing is more difficult to carry out, nor more doubtful of success, nor more dangerous to handle, than achieving a new order of things."[5]

Taking nothing for granted, Peter Block is a stickler for "circling up." He believes even the way we arrange meeting spaces weighs heavily on how groups of people relate to one another. One of the most helpful ways to convene collegiality and do away with prestige and control is to rearrange the room. Block's motto is "Change the room, change the culture."

> The task is to rearrange the room to meet our intention to build relatedness, accountability, and commitment. The room needs to express the quality of aliveness and belonging that we wish for the community. The circle is the geometric symbol for community, and therefore for arranging the room. No tables if possible. If tables are a given, then choose round ones (the shape of communion), which are better than rectangles (the shape of negotiation), or classroom-style tables (the shape of instruction). The ideal seating for a small group is a circle of chairs with no table. Put the chairs as close together as possible, which forces people to lean into one another.[6]

Assessing the Circle

Catalytic leaders understand the gifts, passions, and stories of their circle members. This awareness increases the possibility of a meaningful interdependent dance, where we move together, leveraging each person's strengths and buttressing each other's weaknesses. Without assessment, the dance diminishes as we step on each other's toes. Consider the following assessment tools. These are the assessment tools we use in the KC Underground.

- GPS: Gifts, Passions, Story (giftspassionstory.com)
- DiSC profile (discprofile.com)
- CliftonStrengths (gallup.com/cliftonstrengths)
- 5 Voices (5voices.com)
- Enneagram (enneagraminstitute.com)
- APEST (5qcentral.com)

The wisdom of tangibly circling up fleshes out and actualizes the symbols we say characterize us. For instance, Janette has served for over seven years as a pastor of a sizeable congregation on the East Coast. Throughout the past year or so, she has worked with her staff to shift to a peer-led, circle leadership culture. Janette has worked diligently to shape the culture of the team by encouraging others to share their thoughts, ideas, and creativity daily, and she is careful to use inclusive language throughout her interactions. In planning meetings, Janette and the team arrange the room in a circle, and she views a shift in her role from being decider and enabler to discerner and equipper.

Janette seeks to draw out of each team member the voice the Spirit has given him or her to speak to the overall leadership community, without limits. She has used multiple types of gifts assessments as she sought to bring teamwide understanding of one another across the organization. Janette senses a key part of her role for the organization is to help every team member have the opportunity to present their best insights, desires, and talent to the overall mission. Her thoughts constantly lean toward ways to crack open the latent insights the Spirit has imparted to each person. Frequently, prior to a meeting, Janette asks another team member to serve as catalyst for the gathering. She is content to meld into the circle with no greater status than any other participant. This pastor cedes the leadership to the Spirit's movement through all within the circle. It has become increasingly common during strategic meetings for a key idea or perspective to come forth through a team member that a couple of years prior would not have felt free or encouraged to share their viewpoint based on their role, rank, or fear of status loss. Leaders, who are first off servants, follow the model of Jesus—

> Think of yourselves the way Christ Jesus thought of himself. He had equal status with God but didn't think so much of himself that he had to cling to the advantages of that status no matter what. Not at all. When the time came, he set aside the privileges of deity and took on the status of a slave, became *human*! Having become human, he stayed human. It was an incredibly humbling process. He didn't claim special privileges. Instead, he lived a selfless, obedient life and then died a selfless, obedient death—and the worst kind of death at that—a crucifixion. (Phil. 2:5–8 MSG)

Pattern #2: Catalyst-Sparked

Shifting to shared leadership compels leaders who have been accustomed to being *in charge* to let go of insecurities that nurture their self-worth based on the importance they have to the group or organization. Their identity must go deeper than what they mean to the group as a leader. Faith leaders must incarnate the motto of John the Baptist—"He must become greater; I must become less" (John 3:30)—to trust God to rule supreme and move through whomever he chooses in the moment.

> **Alan Hirsch:** The great philosopher Martin Buber once noted that false leaders and prophets are in fact not godless people. Rather, they adore the god "Success." They themselves are in constant need of success and achieve it by promising it to the people. But they do *honestly* want success for the people. This craving for success governs their hearts and determines whatever arises from their idolatrous hearts. That is what Jeremiah called the "deceit of their own heart" (Jer. 23:26 KJV)! False prophets don't just deceive others; they themselves *are* deceived, and they thrive in the atmosphere of deceit.

The ego trap of leader identity breeds demands for respect and flawed definitions of success. It is an ever-present pitfall that must be backfilled with a soul-settling resolve that finds contentment and value simply as a treasured child of God, apart from status and titles. Leaders content in this mode find joy in seeing the gifts and talents of others bloom and flourish. This paradigm sets our teams free to work out of our true calling as servants for all God's children. Frederic Laloux, in his book *Reinventing Organizations*, shares,

> The pursuit of love, recognition, and success shapes our lives slowly but surely to the point that we end up, in the words of poet May Sarton, "Wearing other people's faces." Our journey toward inner rightness prompts some soul searching of who we are and what our purpose in life might be. The ultimate goal in life is not to be successful or loved, but to become the truest expression of ourselves, to live into authentic selfhood, to honor our birthright gifts and callings, and be of service to humanity and our world.[7]

The starfish goal is not to give everyone the exact same volume of power. The quest is to make everyone as powerful as possible. This means we let go of the overwrought identity of *leader* and embrace the roll of a *catalyst*. The catalyst shapes culture and DNA but is happy to cede control in the moment to the members of the team. In letting go of the headship role, the catalyst transfers deep, shared ownership and responsibility to the circle under the leadership of the Spirit of God. The results are freedom for creativity, greater buy-in, lasting stability, mutual respect, and deeper community.

Developing a culture of mutuality requires practical steps of addressing status language that undermines the ethos of collegiality. Jesus gave unambiguous instructions about his feelings and commands regarding leadership in his tribe. Yet what he demands in the following passage is patently ignored in almost every church and religious entity. "You are not to be called rabbi, for you have one teacher, and you are all brothers. And call no man your father on earth, for you have one Father, who is in heaven. Neither be called instructors, for you have one instructor, the Christ. The greatest among you shall be your servant. Whoever exalts himself will be humbled, and whoever humbles himself will be exalted" (Matt. 23:8–12 ESV).

Jesus says we are siblings. Churches are not businesses or corporations. They are family. His point? Stop elevating yourselves over one another. If you want to go up, do so by going down. Humble yourself and let God do the exalting. He flattened the hierarchical ideals. Jesus didn't say if you want to become great, become a leader. He said, "Whoever wants to become great among you must be your servant" (Matt. 20:26). He was emphatic. He forbade rank-based titles, permitting no place for them. Why so? we may wonder.

First, titles are meant to identify, but too often they are dividers. They highlight status, for better or worse. Titles too often position one person or group over another and create boundaries, fences, and doors that need permission or privilege for entry. Titles change the entire dynamic of a relationship, creating a new set of rules and limits of expression, openness, and authenticity. As soon as a title is applied to one person, the title "less than" or "greater than" is pinned to the other. Titles create psychological and sociological dynamics of hierarchy.[8] Holding on to rank-based titles undermines collegiality.

Leadership and Power

Making the titular shift from senior leader to coworker is not a negative change in status unless the leader feels the need to leverage his or her title or seniority. The starfish effect is not a demotion of any one leader. It is a promotion for everyone! It unleashes the servantship spirit throughout the organization. This is a shift in the perception of leadership power. It changes our view of how it best works and how the Spirit of God works it in us and throughout our groups and organizations. A commitment on this point means leaders that need to change can become better people. They can become humble, spirit-led humans as opposed to dominating personalities. It provides no quarter for bullies or tyrants.

Developing churches into starfish mode takes patience on everyone's part. Recall the saying "culture eats strategy for breakfast." A starfish strategy is not enough. Success or failure depends on the hard work of creating a new starfish culture. The challenge is to develop modes of leadership that maintain accountability and vision while dispatching with dominance and ego-driven self-centered command and control.

For organizations seeking to shift to starfish leadership, the temptation is to throw in the towel when emotions run raw, concluding that the industrial way was easier. We are the first to admit that hierarchical leadership is indeed easier in the beginning. But easier is seldom better.

Early in the quest to reinvent his fledgling construction company, Sid—an experienced owner of past businesses worth millions—took up my (Lance's) challenge to build something different, to start doing business as *unusual*. The first time I discussed the concepts from this book with him, Sid responded as if I had told him I believed in the tooth fairy. Unbeknownst to me, he read one of the books I suggested and a few weeks later came to me and said, "Okay, I believe this is right. Now, how do we do it?"

Over the next several months, Sid developed a company that has become profitable and filled with highly content coworkers, many of whom are using elements of wisdom and creativity that they were never permitted to exercise in previous work environments. Looking back at the experiment and its current yield, Sid says the biggest fear he had in a starfish leadership shift was "trusting others when the stuff hit the fan. In my past company I would just micromanage, and I knew everything would float. But as soon as I took that pressure off people, it all caved in. The early days of implementing a flattened leadership structure were met with some real bumps in the road, and I was really tempted to throw in the towel and just revert back to command and control. I'm so glad I didn't." Sid's biggest surprise of the experiment has been "discovering the indomitable spirit within people when they are trusted and permitted to bring their entire selves to the workplace. I now have an entire team of creative people who show up every day believing we are going to do something great together."

In *The Starfish and The Spider*, Ori Brafman stresses the differences in CEO-type leadership: "A CEO is The Boss. He's in charge, and he occupies the top of the hierarchy. A catalyst interacts with people as a peer. He comes across as your friend. . . .

CEOs must be rational; their job is to create shareholder value. Catalysts depend on emotional intelligence; their job is to create personal relationships."[9]

To attain what Ori speaks to it is crucial that the organizational culture abound in both spirit and practice of shared leading. In letting go of the leadership role, the catalyst transfers ownership and responsibility to the circle.[10] At the same time, when we attempt to develop starfish cultures, it is extremely important that we not abandon agreed-upon rules and well thought out systems. Jettisoning policies and guidelines altogether is both unwise and impractical. It sets the stage for abuse and emotional-driven collapses. Servantship and a starfish culture will not simply evolve in a vacuum of hierarchy.

Starfish thinking "does not mean that we are all interchangeable, or that we are all the same—with equal talents, experience, needs, ambitions, and so forth—or that we even make equal contributions. But what it does assert is that all members of the organization have equal *standing*."[11] This paradigm is rooted in the belief that the answers to our problems or opportunities are not relegated to top-tier leadership but can be found at any place within the circle. The answers emerge because of the culture that both supports and encourages mutual respect and ideation throughout the organization.

Ori wrote about the role of leader as catalyst: "In chemistry, a catalyst is any element or compound that initiates a reaction without fusing into that reaction. In open organizations, a catalyst is the person who initiates a circle and then fades away into the background."[12]

Catalysts trust that those in their circle have the knowledge, skill, and ability to bring the best answers to existing problems and opportunities.

Pattern #3: Collaboratively Co-Laboring

Let's do a bit of word study. First consider the word *collaboration*. It means to work with others on a shared goal. There is much to discover when we ruminate on the power in this term. The first thing we should notice is that its root is *co-labor*. Notice that no hierarchy is present. The prefix *co-*means "mutual" and "in common"; therefore, equality is assumed and by definition emphasized. The Greek word for "collaboration," *synergasia*, is used thirteen times in the New Testament, translated in multiple forms: fellow laborer, helper, fellow worker, fellow helper, workfellow, companion, and more. This is where we get the English word *synergy*. Co-laboring produces synergy! Synergy is the experience or effect that takes place when the combined interactions of people create more wisdom, ideation, and fruit than the sum of the individuals in solo mode.

> **Alan Hirsch:** It is precisely in the area of collaboration that *communitas*—a signature characteristic of movements that change the world—begin to emerge. *Communitas* arises when a group experiences liminality in the form of a crisis, a challenge, an ordeal, a compelling opportunity, or a task that simply cannot be done alone and therefore requires a deep commitment from all the members (e.g., a sports team in a grand final). In undergoing the liminal conditions together, the group discovers itself anew in an invigorated form of human togetherness. Just try some daring things together and you will find a greater sense of comradery on the other side.

Remember Brafman's quote from before: "In letting go of the leadership role, the catalyst transfers ownership and responsibility to the circle."[13] This makes way for the catalyzing of synergy. Co-laboring is about being a peer-based organization. The etymology of the word *peer* is fascinating. To peer means "to squint at,"[14] "to look intently in order to bring into focus."[15] The word also means "to consider as an equal."[16] Bosses are not peers because they often don't allow others to really see them, to really know them. This mindset goes hand in hand with considering certain members of the team unequal.

Time and again, both Rob and I (Lance) have heard senior pastors advise young pastors to keep a distance between themselves and their staff. The ideology is that if you become friends with your staff, you will lose authority over them. The myth surrounding such leaders is that they don't possess real authority in the first place. They brandish power via fear and intimidation. Such advice clearly thumbs its nose at Jesus and his model of relationship with his twelve disciples: "No longer do I call you servants, for the servant does not know what his master is doing; but I have called you friends, for all that I have heard from my Father I have made known to you" (John 15:15 ESV).

The principle of circle over pyramid yields limitless metaphors. One we have found useful is

Figure 7.2

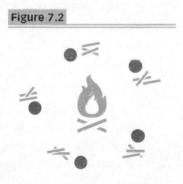

that of a firepit with a group circled around it. A good fire is necessary for warmth, illumination, and food. Collaboration means every member of the team is around the fire in view of one another. The fire represents the organization (church, company, guild, or something else), including its vision, values, initiatives, history, and present opportunities and risks. The flames will keep going only if fuel is continually added as needed. Each member brings wood for the fire. The wood is each member's story, experience, skills, ideas, wisdom, and opinion. Anyone is free to place wood on the fire—kindling, chunks, and chips, whatever they have. When routine updates and decisions are needed, "Let's gather around the fire" is a great metaphor for any team.

Pattern #4: Organic Hierarchy

We don't advocate for the total dispelling of hierarchy. What we encourage is a naturally organizing, fresh hierarchy that is not a cold, steel-framed ladder. It is a living system that replaces systems that subordinate most of the organization to a select few with "a hierarchy of processes, projects, and assignments."[17]

In the absence of a hierarchy of "bosses over subordinates, space becomes available for other natural and spontaneous hierarchies to spring up."[18] The new hierarchy constantly renews itself and manifests spontaneously and without fanfare, built on "recognition, influence, and skill (sometimes referred to as 'actualization hierarchies' in place of traditional 'dominator hierarchies')."[19]

Wheatley writes,

> Entering into a world of shared significance is only achieved by engaging in conversations with colleagues. Not debates or oratories, but conversation that welcomes in the unique perspective of everyone there. If we remain curious about what someone else sees and refrain from convincing them of our interpretation, we develop a richer view of what might be going on. And we also create collegial relations that enable us to work together with greater speed and effectiveness. When any of us feel invited to share our perspective, we repay that respect and trust with commitment and friendship.[20]

Collaboration through organic hierarchy does not lessen responsibility and accountability. To the contrary, it expands both by placing them on everyone within the organization. No longer is a worker responsible and accountable to one higher-up supervisor or manager. He is now responsible and accountable to his fellow workers.

Reviewing the Circle

Here's our way of doing peer-based review in the KC Underground. Each member of our circle, those who lead equipping teams and function as elders, are officially peer reviewed by the people to their "right and left," every four months. Those who are to your "right and left" shift as you cycle through the entire circle over time. Once a year, you receive the feedback of the entire circle in an annual review. Of course, between the official reviews is a continual cycle of peer-based feedback facilitated by weekly meetings and life together.

We look at areas like:

- **Celebration:** What are this person's unique contributions? What is their sweet spot?
- **Constipation:** Where are they stuck? What are this person's blind spots?
- **Disposition:** What level of emotional, relational, and spiritual maturity do they display?
- **Execution:** How productive are they? How well do they keep their promises? How well are they living into their sweet spot?

In the fall of 2018, my (Lance's) farming neighborhood near Panama City, Florida, was among those hit head-on by Hurricane Michael, a category 5 storm that was the third-most intense hurricane to ever strike the United States. The devastation was incomprehensible. Every major highway and country road in the county became little more than forest trails as over 2.5 million pine and other trees came crashing down. The most-needed commodities in the days after the storm were water, chain saws, generators, and fuel. These supplies could be found only well outside the counties hit by the storm. Two days after the storm, I was awakened by a voice whispering through my bedroom screen window: "Hey, Lance. We're driving to Dothan, Alabama, for supplies. You wanna' go?" Markus, my neighbor, had procured an enclosed twenty-foot cargo trailer and was rounding up neighbors to make the trip. That evening, we returned with pallets of water, dozens of filled gas containers, generators, and chain saws. The neighbors self-organized, acquired supplies, and cleared our road.

If competent people can self-manage and organize their day-to-day life, why do these same people lose that high level of expertise and ability when they show up for work?

Speaking on organizational intelligence, biologist Francisco Varela says, "It isn't the ability to solve problems that makes an organization smart. It is the ability of its members to enter into a world whose significance they share. Everyone in the group has to feel that what is occurring is significant—even as they have different perspectives."[21]

Pattern #5: Elder and Mentor Guided

Without counsel plans fail,
but with many advisers they succeed. (Prov. 15:22 ESV)

Jesus was the greatest leader ever, and he modeled servanthood at its best. We should be asking why our best books on leadership aren't filled with the way he formed his team and led them! Humility is the fuel that drives leaders who identify themselves not as bosses but servants. They have found great joy and strength in helping those around them discover and experiment with their own potential. This attitude makes for the best type of leader because it causes people to want to be around such catalysts. A practice that Jesus exemplified and that starfish structures use is mentoring. Clinton and Stanley highlight the departure from mentoring in contemporary times.

Mentoring is as old as civilization itself. Through this natural relational process, experience and values pass from one generation to another. Mentoring took place among Old Testament prophets (Eli and Samuel, Elijah and Elisha) and leaders (Moses and Joshua), and New Testament leaders (Barnabas and Paul, Paul and Timothy). Throughout human history, mentoring was the primary means of passing on knowledge and skills in every field—from Greek philosophers to sailors—and in every culture. But in the modern age, the learning shifted. It now relies primarily on computers, classrooms, books and videos. Thus, today the relational connection between the knowledge-and-experience giver and the receiver has weakened or is nonexistent.[22]

Eldering and Mentoring

Dispatching traditional management and rank-based titles as we develop a peer-based organization requires managers to reinvent their roles into those of coaches and mentors. This aspect is vital for implementing self-management. Judeo-Christian cultures all recognize the value of receiving the wise counsel of elders. In peer-based circle leadership, organizations' rank-based executive leadership gives way to relational-based elder leadership. The pressure of rank disappears as the advisory function emerges, releasing wisdom, knowledge, and experience-based understanding.

The primary reason why our ideas on church leadership have strayed so far from Jesus' example can be traced to our tendency to project Western notions of government and business onto our faith communities. When we read words like *pastor*, *overseer*, and *elder*, we immediately think in terms of governmental offices like president or business offices like CEO. At that point, we regard elders, pastors, and overseers as sociological constructs (offices). We erroneously view them as vacant slots that possess a reality independent of the people who populate them.

Alan Hirsch: It's interesting that, given our penchant for titles like "reverend," "pastor," "doctor," and the like, the New Testament knows nothing of using functions as titles. For instance, Paul never uses the term *apostle* as a title on a business card. It is always used as a function. So it is not "Apostle Paul" but "Paul, an apostle." It is not "Elder John" but "John, an elder." When leaders in the church use titles, they set up an inappropriate power differential among the people of God. The only one who gets the titles in the New Testament is the Lord Jesus Christ. All others (Peter, Paul, Mary, John) are known by their names. If your name is not good enough, a title will never help. Rather, it will only bolster insecurity and pride.

On this, Frank Viola notes,

Such biases have transformed simple words into heavily loaded ecclesiastical titles. As a result, they have eroded the original landscape of the church. Thus, a fresh reading of the N.T. in its original language is necessary for properly understanding certain texts. For instance, a look at the original Greek yields the following insights:

1. "Overseers/Bishops" are simply guardians (*episkopoi*), not high-church officials
2. "Pastors" are caretakers (*poimen*), not professional pulpiteers
3. "Ministers" are table-waiters (*diakonos*), not clergymen
4. "Elders" are wise old men (*presbuteros*), not ecclesiastical officers[23]

The New Testament uses three terms to refer to the same church leaders:

- *Poimenas*, translated as "shepherds" or "pastors"
- *Presbyteroi*, translated as "elders"
- *Episkopos*, translated as "overseers" or, rarely, "bishops"

Elders are . . .

- **Guardians** (*episkopoi*) protecting and defending the flock, not high-church officers who leverage their position for their personal advancement (1 Peter 5:1–4; James 5:13–15).
- **Caretakers** (*poimenas*) who serve with the spirit of one who is "among" the flock, not "over" the flock (Acts 20:35).
- **Wise guides** (*presbyteroi*) who know God's Word and how to apply it with discernment, orthodoxy, and specificity, not professional preachers (1 Tim. 5:17; 3:2; Titus 1:9; Acts 20:27, 32; Heb. 13:7, 17, 24).
- **Influencers** in that by virtue of their wisdom and spiritual maturity, they are accorded respect. Their godly character, spiritual stature, and sacrificial service to the people of God give them increased influence. They have an ability to help those who are immature, off track, or confused to reorient their lives under Jesus' lordship and the authority of the Scripture because of their persuasive power to convince and to win over rather than to coerce, force, or browbeat others into submission.
- **Appointed people** who aren't "elected" but recognized. The term in the New Testament is that of the "laying on of hands" by an established, elder-level leader (Acts 14:23; 1 Tim. 5:22; Titus 1:5). This appointment recognized the "elder life" they had already been living. The Spirit was active, helping current

elders identify the emerging elders and overseers (Acts 20:28). But this divine guidance does not short-circuit a frank assessment of a person's character (1 Tim. 3:2–7; Titus 1:5–9). Elders are to have healthy families, emotional and spiritual maturity, an ability to communicate and teach truth, and a sound reputation, not just with insiders within the faith community but also among those outside the faith community. The community recognizes together that these elders have become older siblings, whose leadership is worthy to be honored and respected.

The goal of eldership is that of facilitation, guidance, equipping, mentoring, nurturing, and ultimately, service.

Peer Coaching and Mentoring

For those in teams, the most important thing to remember is this: you are in a peer relationship with those around you. This means each member commits to be willing to both give and receive feedback, critique, encouragement, and opinion in the spirit of generous discourse among team members. The commitment is to actively view one another as peer mentors and for each person to broaden their view of their own responsibilities. Everyone vows to keep eyes, ears, and minds open to issues, opportunities, threats, and solutions.

When people work together with freedom as an overarching premise, they are motivated not by a single charismatic leader but by the shared vision and goals that come from the mission itself. In a setting such as this, team members are peers, working together as such and holding one another accountable for the overall performance and results of the group as a whole.

Conclusion

In *Servant Leadership*, Robert Greenleaf writes, "To be a lone chief atop a pyramid is abnormal and corrupting. None of us are perfect by ourselves, and all of us need the help and correcting influence of close colleagues. When someone is moved atop a pyramid, that person no longer has colleagues, only subordinates. Even the frankest and bravest of subordinates do not talk with their boss in the same way that they talk with their colleagues who are equals, and normal communication patterns become warped."[24]

Moving past pyramid-style organizational structures and circling up in our

Table 7.1

SPIDER STRUCTURE	STARFISH STRUCTURE
Boss/manager	Facilitator/coach/mentor/equipper
CEOs	Catalysts
Employees	Coworkers/peers
Leaders	Servants
Rank-based titles	Role-based titles
Executives	Equals
Hierarchy of positions	Hierarchy of processes
Limited accountability	Multiplied accountability

leadership systems does not create a dull or weak uniformity. Peer-led groups, churches, and organizations don't seek to equalize individual power and talent. They work to equalize opportunities across the field of their organization. Realizing that wisdom, knowledge, and understanding are exponentially available in the whole group rather than the select few, the circle-celled group leverages its best ideas and abilities in the moment of need or opportunity.

Through the structure starfish, may we see circles multiply, each carrying the DNA through the entire body, connected and structured organically as a living system.

How will these circles be managed? How can freedom be unleashed and order facilitated at the same time? On to the self-management starfish!

CHAPTER 8

The Self-Management Starfish

Unleashing Freedom and Facilitating Order

You don't manage your peers. You collaborate with them.
—Jeffrey Nielsen, *The Myth of Leadership*

The Spirit God gave us does not make us timid, but gives us power, love and self-discipline.
—2 Timothy 1:7

Figure 8.1

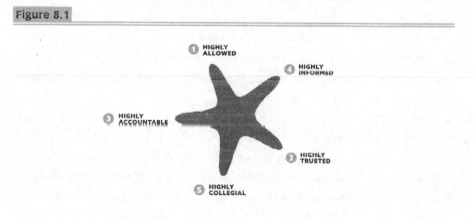

Starfish #4: The Self-Management Starfish

Purpose: The self-management starfish helps us create a culture of empowerment and self-management through activating five potentials in every leader and team.

One afternoon, the senior pastor knocked on my (Lance's) office door and stopped in for a brief chat. He was in a cheerful mood with nothing in particular on his mind. "Just wanted to drop by and see how you're doing," he said with a smile. We chatted for a few minutes before he went on his way. After he left, I went back to what I had been doing before he came in. But I became aware of something about my demeanor while in his presence. What is this strange feeling that's come over me? I wondered. After a couple of minutes of pondering, I had it. I felt like a little boy while I was in the presence of the senior pastor. It was a strange phenomenon, but that was precisely it. Here I was, a forty-one-year-old man who had managed to get married, purchase a home, raise three children, plant and pastor several churches, grill steaks without burning the house down, and drive myself to work. Yet I felt like an adolescent in the moment.

Something was being projected in the relationship between the senior pastor and me. We were not on equal footing. I was constantly looking up at him, and he was looking down on me. Relational dynamics change when we operate from rank-based systems. Colleagues are lost at the expense of subordinates.

This realization confused me at first because the pastor I am speaking of is a wonderful man. I love him dearly and am beyond thankful for so much that he has taught me. He is not a jerk. It would be much easier for people trapped in spider leadership cultures to pinpoint their situation if all senior leaders were jerks. We could just say, "My boss is a jerk and leads like a jerk."

It took a while to put my finger on what I was feeling. But after a few months of working at this church, I was finally able to wrap my head around it. The leadership environment was not only mechanistic, it was paternalistic. For anyone other than the select *executive* leadership team, self-management was out of bounds. Staff members outside that exclusive group knew in their hearts that they were more than capable of doing their jobs. But being subjected to a command-and-control culture projected a parent-child atmosphere on them, and it had produced a devastating effect among the most tenured of staff. It had eroded their confidence, and it showed. They had been reduced, and their souls were suffering.

I had wondered why there was a somewhat broken spirit in several of those who had served the church for some years. These were sharp, godly men and women full of talent and superb gift mixes and experiences. One evening I told my wife, "I can see something in their eyes. It's a longing. It's like an unfulfilled desire that diminishes their smiles. They're like a corral full of powerful mustangs that were once free to run and jump with boundless joy and energy but have become broken stable ponies relegated to loping walks and controlled trots in service of the dude ranch trail boss for the paying customers."

A handful of us joined the staff around the same time, and there was a discernable difference in our energy and spirit—early on. We were all upbeat. But we were changing too. The management thumb was like an improperly placed tourniquet, throttling our blood flow. We slowly became numb. As I experienced the overmanaged culture, it became clear that this atmosphere would likely break one's spirit. Margaret Wheatley speaks to why this is the case:

> We have people in the organization ready and willing to do good work, wanting to contribute their ideas, ready to take responsibility, and leaders holding them back, insisting that they wait for decisions or instructions. The result is dispirited employees and leaders wondering why no one takes responsibility or gets engaged anymore. We have known for more than half a century that self-managed teams are far more productive than any other form of organizing. There is a clear correlation between participation and productivity; in fact, productivity gains in truly self-managed work environments are *at minimum 35 percent higher* than in traditionally managed organizations.[1]

Alan Hirsch: I have always been amazed at the marvelous complexity of the human body. It is a sheer miracle of organization! Thirty-two trillion cells are in the average human body, and there is no CEO cell (or hierarchy) telling the rest of the cells what to do and when to do it. The whole thing is profoundly self-organizing. The genius of the organization is found in the DNA, which is fully embedded in every cell in the body. Each cell carries in itself the full code of the whole. There is an important metaphor for the body of Christ here. Movements are DNA-based organizations, and they are geared to self-organize and motivate toward further expansion.

What a difference self-management and empowerment make! Alan and Tim Catchim wrote,

> In light of this, apostolic leadership recognizes that every member or group in a movement already has everything it needs to get the job done. They just need

permission and empowerment to live into that truth. Rather than attributing more and more power to an increasingly centralized (centripetal) organization, movement dynamics require that power and function flow away from the center to the outermost limits, giving the whole movement a profoundly centrifugal feel.[2]

The purpose of the self-management starfish is to help leaders create a culture of empowerment that releases the untapped potential of every disciple, leader, and team through self-management and constant feedback from elders and peers in the movement. Each of the following five potentials, as they are invited and activated, will unleash exponentially greater creativity and productivity.

Potential #1: Highly Allowed

Everything we point to in this chapter gives obedience and process to Jesus' leadership philosophy. He put it out as a direct commandment to the small group of disciples he poured himself into as the future shapers of his church:

> Jesus called them to him and said, "You know that the rulers of the Gentiles lord it over them, and their great ones exercise authority over them. It shall not be so among you. But whoever would be great among you must be your servant, and whoever would be first among you must be your slave, even as the Son of Man came not to be served but to serve, and to give his life as a ransom for many." (Matt. 20:25–28 ESV)

Getting honest with the Lord and ourselves demands that we ask hard questions of ourselves and give honest answers as to whether we *lord* over anyone on our staff or in the organization:

- Do I dictate how they use their time?
- Do I interrupt their space or speech in ways they are fearful of doing in like kind to me, i.e., are they free to do the same with me?
- Can questions, critique, and challenges be shared without fear of demotion, firing, or sharp rebuke?
- Does everyone have free access to everyone else?
- Do I sometimes pull rank or project intimidation?

Lead Pastor?

The Bible never refers to a human being as a "head" or "lead" or "senior" pastor of a church. This title belongs exclusively to Jesus Christ. He is the only head of the church.

Quite simply, there is no analogue for the modern idea of "lead pastor" anywhere in the New Testament. Some might say, "The first three chapters in Revelation speak of an angel for each church. Isn't that symbolic of a lead pastor?" Scholars are unsure of what the angels symbolize. Beyond the obvious interpretation of them being actual angels, any other applications are speculative at best.

In the New Testament, every clear instance is that of a circle of elders (Acts 20:17, 28); leadership was always plural. No one in the KC Underground bears the title of pastor. We do have many who are elders, spiritual mothers and fathers. They typically use their first names, not titles or positions, to introduce themselves.

The answers to these few questions are hints as to whether we are embracing and obeying Jesus' ethos of leadership, which is based on serving and is in direct conflict to much of modernity's ways and means of leadership, which is being served by others.

In recent years the universally accepted rank-based title of senior pastor has become so ingrained in evangelical churches that it has yielded a spin-off some call the "second chair." Usually titled "executive pastor," this position joins the senior pastor to form a dynamic duo atop the local church leadership hierarchy. In the opening words of their book *Leading from the Second Chair*, Bonem and Patterson set the stage for the top-down ideology that is so prevalent across the evangelical church landscape today:

We have been frequent consumers of books, tapes, and conferences as a means of improving our leadership. Yet we have often felt frustration or discouragement after using these resources because they were not aimed at us. Their focus was the senior leader of the organization, the person who has the freedom and relative autonomy that comes with this top position. In the second chair, the amount of change you can initiate is limited because you are not the vision caster, the lead leader. You do not have to be the number two person in an organizational hierarchy to be a second chair leader. In fact, our definition can include anyone who is not the lead leader. Every organization has a perceived pecking order.[3]

There is no nuance of top-down language here. Phrases such as "senior leader," "top position," "lead leader," "organizational hierarchy," and "pecking order" make it staunchly clear that one person is on top and everyone else descends from there.[4] And there is no embarrassment or shame in the terms used. This is patent disregard for the ethos Jesus said he wanted for his church and his followers.

If you are a senior leader, think back to a time when you were not in a top-tier position. How did you feel being bossed and controlled? How did it affect your creativity and spirit? Few people want to be controlled.

In their book, *Accountability: Freedom and Responsibility without Control*, Lebow and Spitzer say, "As individuals become more self-confident in their ability to be great, they simply can no longer live in a management-employee context that continues to attempt to subtly manipulate or control them in a paternalistic way. And so, they eventually leave the organization looking for more freedom."[5] By its very nature, control perpetuates a search for escape by the one being controlled. Eventually the best talent in control-minded groups departs in search of freedom of expression. Not surprisingly, in the church described at the beginning of this chapter, almost the entire staff turned over in about a year or so.

Losing Control

The Lord Almighty created our world in such a way that many of its systems and processes organize and manage themselves. Some of our worst ecological problems come from the actions of humanity. The infamous dustbowl that ravaged the American and Canadian prairies of the 1930s came about because of irresponsible farming methods that damaged millions of acres of land. As rotation farming was learned, the land repaired itself, and another such disaster has yet to happen.

Chaos and eventual collapse will surely arrive if we simply jettison traditional management systems. Moving beyond the pyramid requires reinventing practices and processes in our organizations. A lot of questions need answers: Who makes decisions on what gets done? How are people held answerable for their actions and performance? What happens when team members aren't in agreement?

The first step toward creating leadership cultures of adult-to-adult relationships is to install systems of self-management. Choosing freedom strips "all of our control-based assumptions and challenges our capacity to trust our people ... that every staff member at every level is fully accountable for his or her ideas, actions, behaviors, and performance, without anyone looking over his or her shoulder."[6] This means we determine to stop controlling people. When we do so, we must commit to these foundational steps toward creating a self-management culture:

1. **We trust our people.**
   You will never see the best out of anyone when they must seek your approval. Policies and procedures that demonstrate a lack of confidence in our people not only stifle risk-taking creativity, they also bog down progress.

2. **Our people have the freedom to leave their fingerprints on their work.**
   Let individuals bring their style and creativity to bear upon their tasks. Just as there is no single correct batting stance for hitting a baseball (just take a look at videos of some of the all-time baseball greats) or one way to swing a golf club or throw a football, there is no one correct way of getting every job done.

3. **Teams and individuals set their own goals.**
   Rather than having goals set for them, when people set their own goals, they naturally feel the responsibility for meeting them, as well as monitoring the results along the way. When we dictate policies, people lose empowerment. Everyone shares their goals and holds one another accountable for progress and results.

4. **The truth keeps us free.**
   When information concerns someone (or a group) within the organization, don't hide it behind closed doors. Unlock it. People deserve to be kept informed. Jesus taught us that truth sets us free only when we *know* it. Never pull rank or project intimidation to anyone at any skill-set level, including his or her right to speak up on an issue. Information and resources will not be held in control by any one person or subgroup of any size.

Alan Hirsch: Visitors to the headquarters of the Central Intelligence Agency (CIA) at Langley, Virginia, are confronted with this slogan: "You will know the truth, and the truth will set you free" (John 8:32). This is not only a perverse use of Jesus' words but also excludes the precondition of discipleship on which it was given. The fuller text reads, "So He said to the Jews who had believed Him, '*If you continue in My word, then you are truly disciples of Mine*, then you will know the truth and the truth shall set you free'" (John 8:31–32, emphasis added). The freedom promised here is conditional on discipleship! We must be willing to follow Jesus and conform our lives to his if we are to experience the freedom that he brings. Leaders must be disciples if they are to lead others to freedom.

Leadership is an issue of power. In any given group, its essence and outcomes come down to how power is viewed, exerted, released, and respected. When we choose partnership over paternalism, we carry out the "intention to balance power between ourselves and those around us."[7]

The fear leaders have in allowing others to exercise significant freedom is that the job will not be done properly, on time, or with the "branding" that represents the organization. For Holy Spirit–guided innovation to break through, apostolic creativity and entrepreneurship are needed at all levels.

So be ready.

You may nibble your nails and bite your tongue a lot as you learn to let go of control while stewarding a new culture of freedom and innovation that is informed by values you have clearly formed and shaped.

Do not underestimate the power of values. Herein lies the safeguard from the toxic mutations you fear. As a catalyst, your role in stewarding and cultivating culture may be the most important one you play. Culture strategist Brian Zehr defines the following elements of culture creation:

- a unique and distinctive set of core values
- a distinct dialogue (an intentional narrative) and dialect (intentional language) that celebrate and communicate those values
- behaviors and practices that bring those values to life in tangible ways[8]

The most effective cultures powerfully align their core values, narrative, and expected practices in ways that build trust and make it simple for people to participate personally.[9] In particular, your values create culture, as they are the origin of your culture. Values are deeply embedded and shape how you do everything you do. You see them, you hear them, and you feel them. Values are like a magnetic force field surrounding the people and operations of the church, proactively shaping the things to come and correcting the things that go off track. If those values are clear, compelling, and common, leaders and teams can create and innovate endlessly, and the end "products" will still look and feel like your culture—without micromanagement.

Underground Values

Every sister movement in the Underground networks shares the same values. This values statement is known as the Manifesto. These values represent our deepest convictions and bind us together across cultures and continents. Explore the Manifesto at www.kcunderground.org/our-story/#manifesto.

For example, if you value multiplication, you must . . .

- regularly tell stories of disciples, leaders, and microchurches multiplying,
- use multiplying language regularly—phrases like "reproduce at every level," for example,
- and then model simple practices like "everyone has an apprentice."

If you do these simple things, then guaranteed, the value of multiplication will be present everywhere in the living system, without command-and-control tactics.

Hirsch and Catchim write, "We need a new influx of apostolic imagination to dislodge the hierarchical, machine-like metaphor that imbues our more inherited ecclesiologies and that has so captured our imagination. We have to think differently about how we conceive of ourselves if we are to see different results."[10]

First, we must create the right culture and then choose to release control to the nearest places the work is done. This doesn't happen in a vacuum. Along with the elements of culture mentioned, well thought out policies and practices will also be crucial. Among the most rewarding fruits of self-management is the impact it has on the responsibility and ownership throughout the entire organizational culture. It yields quicker responses and higher degrees of accurate answers to needs as they present themselves. Let's look at some key ways our associations can reorganize via self-management.

Potential #2: Highly Trusted

Willie Mays is considered one of the greatest baseball players of all time. Yet he failed to get a hit in his first three major league games. Downcast and distraught with an expectation that he was about to be yanked from the lineup, everything changed when his manager, Leo Durocher, said, "Look, son, I brought you up here to do one thing. That's to play center field. You're the best center fielder I've ever seen. As long as I'm here, you're going to play center field. Tomorrow, next week, next month. As long as Leo Durocher is manager of this team, you will be on this club because you're the best ball player I have ever seen."[11]

Mays started hitting that day and continued to do so for twenty-one seasons, ending up in the Hall of Fame. Such is the role of a good coach or consultant. We all learn through struggles. Leo Durocher knew Willie Mays was talented. Though he oversaw the team, he knew he could never hit like Willie could. He didn't need to tell his player how to hit a baseball. The problem was that the pressure to perform was locking up Mays's natural greatness.

Great coaches and catalysts focus on stirring up inherent strengths and existing capabilities in their players by curating a culture of freedom and trust. The undergirding effect of trust is that it breeds confidence in the one who knows they are being trusted. It results in a relaxed approach that causes talent to do its thing naturally and unforced.

A commitment to trust produces a culture whereby people across the board feel respected and taken seriously. Leadership guru Max De Pree suggests, "Respect demands that we first recognize each other's gifts and strengths and interests; then we must integrate them into the work of the organization."[12] This speaks to a change in paradigm necessary among senior leaders as to how they view their roles. This shift is essential if we are serious about transitioning a rank-based organization to a role-based team of partners. To do so means we transition from controlling to consulting, from calculating to coaching.

Good consultants listen more than they tell. Consultants and coaches focus on the common goals, collect and disseminate necessary information, and work to deliver the needed information and resources into the hands of the ones who are closest to an issue. This role aims to enrich and endow those who already have the skill sets to solve a problem or create new opportunities.

Take Tom Martinez. You know who he is, don't you? Most likely you *don't* know who Tom Martinez was. He was the mentor and coach widely credited with grooming Tom Brady, nine-time Super Bowl quarterback. He is arguably the greatest quarterback of all time. Yet he had a mentor and to this day has a quarterback coach. The great Tom Brady benefits from having a consultant help him with the nuance of his craft. You've probably never heard of Tom Brady's mentor or quarterback coach. Why? Because those guys were never trying to be stars. They know their job is to help Tom Brady be the best quarterback he can be.

This is the mindset we should crave. It brings to life the instructions in Ephesians 4 by equipping the saints for the work of service (see Eph. 4:11–13). The job of a New Testament–believing leader is to help those around them be the best they can be in service of the kingdom of heaven. That means we are convinced that the skill and knowledge for whatever needs to be done are inherent in the team. Advising on peer-based organizations, Jeffrey Nielson writes, "When you trust your people and seek to consult them, not control them, and when you trust the intellectual capital already in the organization . . . you are cooperating with the self-organizing dynamic in organizations."[13]

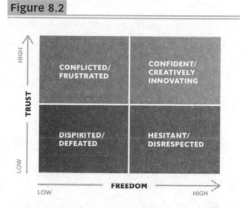

Figure 8.2

We can't expect people to take risks if we demand they get inspection and approval at every step of the process. We must place faith in our coworkers' commitment to stewardship. Do we really believe in their faithfulness to use the organization's time and resources in God-honoring ways that will produce the greatest yield?

Potential #3: Highly Accountable

Self-management, and the green pastures of freedom it brings, is an appealing proposition. But higher degrees of freedom last only with greater degrees of responsibility. Entering these meadowlands means we can no longer hide in the barns of blaming bosses for our own mistakes, laziness, or indifference. To be treated like an adult requires acting like one.

Throughout our research, we have discovered a myriad of groups and organizations that have developed accountability processes that include sound habits and principles. Doug Kirkpatrick shares Morning Star's key principles each worker promises to uphold:

Keeping Commitments

"People are used to having a boss. And they do have bosses in a self-managed environment. They are their own bosses. Beyond that, the mission of the company is their boss—it should guide all their actions on behalf of the company. And even beyond that—each and every commitment that they make and the colleagues to whom they make the commitment is their boss for that commitment."[14] *Integrity* is the single-word definition Morning Star uses to sum up keeping commitments. It sounds simplistic, but this means we do what we say we are going to do. Jesus said, "Let your yes mean yes, and your no mean no" (Matt. 5:37 CEB).

No Use of Force against Other People

There are certainly times command authority is needed. The recent COVID-19 pandemic crisis is a sterling example of the need for stay-at-home directives from national and local authorities in order to starve the virus of human hosts. But when life is going as it should, commanding others doesn't work in a free society. Even family members don't respond well to being ordered around. No one person at Morning Star has unilateral authority to fire anyone. This does not mean that people are not fired. It is how they are dismissed that is different. We will get to the dismissal process later.

As we have said earlier, leadership is an issue of power. Supervisors and superiors have power over others. When we eliminate the rank and title of superiors, we take away the command authority of one person ordering another person what to do.

Mutual Accountability

If a member senses certain actions or attitudes of a fellow worker are in conflict with the overall mission, they are obligated to speak directly to the other person concerning the matter. Placing supreme value on communication at the micro level can often circumvent larger crises or conflicts. Sometimes simple miscommunication or mere assumption leads to wrong perceptions. Seeking and speaking the truth in love is the way of the Spirit of God and should be a guiding rule for our organizations as well as our personal lives.

One can clearly see that the practices of Morning Star reflect the "one another" commands of the New Testament, along with Jesus' counsel on accountability in Matthew 18:15–17 and the pithy wisdom of James on relationships (James 1:19–21; 2:1–13; 3:9–12; 4:1–12). They have operationalized this wisdom into simple processes. We will explore these processes further in the collective intelligence starfish.

Potential #4: Highly Informed

Ori underscores a vital principle of decentralization in *The Starfish and The Spider*: "An open system doesn't have central intelligence; the intelligence is spread throughout the system. Information and knowledge naturally filter in at the edges, closer to where the action is."[15]

If we value freedom, we will value the sharing of truth. Systemically this means we commit to installing a *truth system*. Truth systems are organically open systems. Such systems are a requirement for life and renewal. For instance, the human body shares information freely. The brain doesn't withhold information from the little toe. For a living system such as a church—the body of Christ—when information stops, *formation* stops. And when formation ceases, healthy life begins to seize up.

<u>in</u> + <u>formation</u> = continually forming or developing

The way information flows reveals everything about command and control or freedom and release in an organization. In top-down organizations *top* people decide what lower level people are privy to and when they are allowed to receive privileged information. The conjecture is that employees are only marginally trusted. Organics come into play in control-based organizations. Where you sow distrust, you reap distrust. The atmosphere of such associations is occupied with suspicion and distrust.

In self-managed churches and businesses, everyone is a VIP! Everyone is free to access information. This means financials are available in every sphere of the organization. Frederic Laloux speaks to the importance of such open policies:

- In the absence of hierarchy, self-managing teams need to have all available information to make the best decisions.
- Any information that isn't public will cause suspicion (why else would

someone go through the trouble to keep it secret?), and suspicion is toxic for organizational trust.

- Informal hierarchies reemerge when some people are in the know while others are not.[16]

Alan Hirsch: One of the most fruitful approaches of Christian life and thought is to be found in the principle of "dialogue." When we look back over two thousand years of Christian theology, it is astonishing how little attention it has received. But when we really stop to consider it, dialogue is built into the center of the biblical events, for instance the covenants between God and humanity, in which God grants a certain freedom, an area of independent being, an area where we can freely hear and answer, and an area in which we ultimately cooperate responsibly with God.

Carefully consider the word *communication*. The root of it is commune—which includes community and cooperative. In a genuine community, communication is a two-way street. People are not talked down to, because no one is above another. Anyone is welcome to ask anything about any issue.

I also want you to think about how this keeps your significance from getting blown up into self-importance. For no matter how significant you are, it is only because of what you are a *part* of. An enormous eye or a gigantic hand wouldn't be a body, but a monster. What we have is one body with many parts, each its proper size and in its proper place. No part is important on its own. Can you imagine Eye telling Hand, "Get lost; I don't need you"? Or, Head telling Foot, "You're fired; your job has been phased out"? As a matter of fact, in practice it works the other way—the "lower" the part, the more basic, and therefore necessary. You can live without an eye, for instance, but not without a stomach. When it's a part of your own body you are concerned with, it makes *no* difference whether the part is visible or clothed, higher or lower. You give it dignity and honor just as it is, without comparisons. If anything, you have more concern for the lower parts than the higher. If you had to choose, wouldn't you prefer good digestion to full-bodied hair?

The way God designed our bodies is a model for understanding our lives together as a church: every part dependent on every other part, the parts we mention and the parts we don't, the parts we see and the parts we don't. If one part hurts, every other part is involved in the hurt, and in the healing. If one part flourishes, every other part enters into the exuberance.

You are Christ's body—that's who you are! You must never forget this. Only as you accept your part of that body does your "part" mean anything. (1 Cor. 12:19–31 MSG)

If we suppress the gifts of any member, we suppress the Spirit of God working through the gifts, talents, wisdom, and experience of that person. But when we open the floodgates of information and decision-making, we expose the entire organization to the Spirit's treasure trove of innovation and creativity. Progress along these lines rests on the free flow of information and the freedom for all team members to be able to speak openly and honestly to one another without fear or threat of retribution.

Potential #5: Highly Collegial

Now I myself am confident concerning you, my brethren, that you also are full of goodness, filled with all knowledge, able also to admonish one another. (Rom. 15:14 NKJV)

The language of the New Testament is that the church is a family. The apostle Paul says he is assured that the body of Christ is capable of carrying out the task of admonishing one another. Remember, the letter to the Romans wasn't addressed to elders, senior leaders, or a board or committee. The apostle does not say, "You need senior staff to admonish the workers." He places the responsibility of warning and exhorting one another squarely on the shoulders of the collective community of believers. This raises the bar on expectations of maturity for the "normal" everyday saint.

One of Doug Kirkpatrick's books is titled *Beyond Empowerment* because he believes "employee empowerment implies that one person is transferring power to another person. In the real world, what is given can be taken away. In self-management, colleagues already have all the power they need to make anything happen they want to have happen from the moment they start work. Self-management is beyond empowerment. Self-management is power itself."[17]

Leaders do not empower followers. Rather, leaders create the systemic freedom and cultural conditions for the entire community to exercise their gifts and abilities. The community as a whole has the frontline responsibility for social order and group harmony. Throughout the epistles, verse after verse underscores the responsibility of the brothers and sisters, the servantship community, to rebuke when necessary and edify at all times. The following are but a sampling of such passages:

- Honor one another (Rom. 12:10).
- Build up one another (Rom. 14:19; 1 Thess. 5:11; Heb. 3:13; 10:25).
- Warn and instruct one another (Rom. 15:14
- Provide discipline among yourselves (1 Cor. 5:3–5).
- Bear one another's overwhelming burdens (Gal. 5:13; 6:2).
- Submit to one another (Eph. 5:21).
- Teach one another (Col. 3:16).
- Incite one another to "love and good works" (Heb. 10:24 ESV).
- Confess sins to one another (James 5:16).

Church discipline has been categorized as a leadership function and duty. Scripture says otherwise. It is not to be carried out by a hierarchical few. It is the responsibility of everyday saints, normal people with the Spirit of God in them. Siblings throughout the faith community are called to be accountable to and for one another. This certainly applies to everyone that works in your church staff or faith-based organization.

Mutual oversight is a theme of the New Testament. Hierarchy is not only absent from the narratives of Jesus and the epistles, it is forbidden. This is not to say people don't have responsibilities they must answer for. But in no place do we find the idea of a boss-employee arrangement in the New Testament. What we do see is a commitment to self-discipline, accountability to the group as a whole, and personal responsibility.

In *Leadership on the Other Side*, author and church growth expert Bill Easum shares three essential characteristics for the sustainability of a culture of servant disciples practicing mutual accountability and oversight:

- Competency: those who function as a team must be able to count on the other members of the team to do what they say they will do.

- Consistency: they have to be able to count on the other team members to be there for them.
- Integrity: they have to be able to take team members at their word.[18]

Responsibly mature disciples are faithful servants who need not be evaluated by a centralized office of command and control.

Systems of self-management are sustainable only in cultures of high collegiality. Team members consistently submit themselves to other members, maintaining a humble posture that invites forthright critique from their peers on an ongoing basis while keeping in mind several questions:

- Am I stewarding with integrity the resources I have been entrusted with?
- Is pride keeping me from soliciting advice from others?
- Am I being faithful (giving my best) to my calling?
- Is there someone here who could do what I'm doing better than I can?

Table 8.1

MANAGEMENT	SELF-MANAGEMENT
Limited access to leaders	Open access to anyone
Information guarded	No limits on information
Goals set by higher ups	Goals set by individuals and teams
Limited accountability (to bosses)	Mutual accountability (to all)
Corporate culture	Community culture
Power loaned out	Power acknowledged and permitted

Conclusion

We are now at a pivotal moment in our journey. The movement starfish gave us a definition for church as movement that is inspiring yet grounded, magnificent yet measurable in five points of multiplication, Spirited-empowered yet strategic. We begin with that end in mind.

Alan Hirsch: The issue of movemental structure, what I call organic systems in *The Forgotten Ways*, is somewhat complex and is not the most immediately appealing aspect of movements. But we must be deliberate and design systems that genuinely support and facilitate movement as well as remove what I call the "movement killers" that are lodged in the current system. I am convinced that if we don't pay attention to structure and organizational dynamics, they will most certainly pay attention to us. Anyone trying to lead a church knows how institutional systems can resist (as well as outlast) change. Movements inevitably require a paradigm shift in the way we organize and lead.

The three starfish that followed—the light-load leader, structure, and self-management starfish—create the right leadership culture, a Spirit-empowered culture from which the vision of the movement starfish can rise. But the real test of leadership is that of discipleship. Although we started with leadership culture, that actually flows out of and builds on a disciple-making culture. They are two sides of the same coin.

In the pursuit of the movement starfish, everything rises and falls on our ability to make disciples who make disciples. If a healthy multiplicative, transformative disciple-making culture is in place, a healthy multiplicative leadership culture naturally begins to arise. If both of those environments—disciple-making and leadership development—are healthy, you'll end up producing healthy microchurches, healthy hubs, and healthy networks as well. Disciple-making and leadership development are the basic building blocks of all those larger expressions. Fractals are irregular microshapes or patterns that are repeated in the whole or the macroshape of a thing or organism. As you'll see, it's that same fractal that is reproduced, all the way up into the larger expressions like hubs and networks.

Bottom line, Alan says, "In short, apostolic movement involves a radical community of disciples, centered on the lordship of Jesus, empowered by the Spirit, built squarely on a fivefold ministry, organized around mission where everyone (not just professionals) is considered an empowered agent, and tends to be decentralized in organizational structure."[19]

Now we begin our journey into the creation of that radical community of disciples through what we believe are the two most critical starfish because they help us define and cultivate disciple-making environments and ecosystems.

A Culture for Multiplying Disciples

Section 3 Introduction

In this section of the book, we will explore how to create environments within an ecosystem that will cultivate the transformation and multiplication of disciples. As we look at the inspiring stories of phenomenal apostolic movements in history, all are first and foremost disciple-making systems. On this, Alan remarks, "The rather funny thing is that they never appear to get beyond this—they never move beyond mere disciple making. This is because it is at once the starting point, the abiding strategic practice, as well as the key to all lasting missional impact in and through movements. Whether one looks at the Wesleyan, the Franciscan, or the Chinese phenomenon, at core they are essentially composed of, and led by, disciples, and they are absolutely clear on the disciple-making mandate."[1]

Disciple-making is an irreplaceable core task of the church, which is why it is the second of the six mDNA of *The Forgotten Ways*, following only the lordship of Jesus in order of importance.

The disciple-making ingredients starfish and the disciple-making ecosystem starfish will provide the ingredients, elements, language, and tools for you to design and create your own disciple-making systems.

Starfish #5: The Disciple-Making Ingredients Starfish

Purpose: The disciple-making ingredients starfish helps us discover the five essential ingredients required for creating intentional disciple-making environments (IDEs) that are transformative and multiplicative.

Starfish #6: The Disciple-Making Ecosystem Starfish

Purpose: The disciple-making ecosystem starfish provides a framework of five essential elements needed to design a disciple-making ecosystem that is transformative and multiplicative.

We face a massive dilemma in our day. While we have the language of discipleship everywhere in churches, the practice is far from common or consistent. Dallas Willard claims we have turned the Great Commission into the Great Omission.[2] We have lost the art of disciple-making, let alone disciple-making systems that can scale into a starfish movement. The consumerism of our culture has infected our

A MOVEMENT
**4 Generations of Reproduction
on More than One Strand**

understanding and experience of church profoundly, suppressing and hiding what it means to truly follow Jesus.

It is our prayer that these next two starfish will pull back the veil on what has been hidden and unleash the dormant power that is resident within you.

Remember that in every seed there is a forest.

With both DMMs and MDMs, movement starts with a *mindset*: Make disciples who can make disciples, nothing less. Then *momentum*: Let the momentum begin with you. Personally, make disciples who make disciples. Finally, *movement*: Four generations deep on more than one strand.

CHAPTER 9

The Disciple-Making Ingredients Starfish

Creating Environments and Mixing Ingredients

Jesus can do more with twelve disciples than he can with twelve hundred religious consumers.

—Alan Hirsch

Jesus came to them and said, "All authority in heaven and on earth has been given to me. Therefore go and make disciples of all nations, baptizing them in the name of the Father and of the Son and of the Holy Spirit, and teaching them to obey everything I have commanded you. And surely I am with you always, to the very end of the age."

—Matthew 28:18–20

Figure 9.1

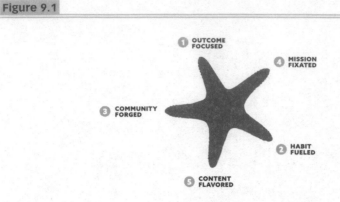

Starfish #5: The Disciple-Making Ingredients Starfish

Purpose: The disciple-making starfish helps us discover the five essential ingredients required for creating intentional disciple-making environments (IDEs) that are transformative and multiplicative.

From Mexico to Alaska, there has been a massive die off of starfish, estimates are in the tens of millions. This is one of the largest mortality events . . . ever observed in the ocean,"[1] states Ben Miner, associate professor in the marine and estuarine program of Western Washington University. Since 2013 a disease has caused starfish to die in record-breaking numbers up and down the US West Coast. Scientists haven't been able to find a smoking gun and aren't sure what causes the disease.[2]

The syndrome known as sea star wasting disease causes starfish to lose limbs and eventually disintegrate, leaving behind the telltale sign of the disease—a pile of white goo. Miner continues, "One of the greatest threats in a massive die-off is that all the adults, which are the only starfish capable of reproduction, are gone. Which means no new babies."[3]

Many, if not most, faith communities in the West are experiencing a similar crisis: a massive fallout of engaged, transformed, reproducing owners of the faith.

Fred Edwords, at *The Humanist*, states, "We're reaching the end of the alphabet—and the end of a religious statistical oddity in the United States. Generation Z, more so than the preceding Generation . . . is demonstrating a telling and permanent downtrend in religious identity."[4] The emptying of organized faith communities is a real phenomenon.

Figure 9.2

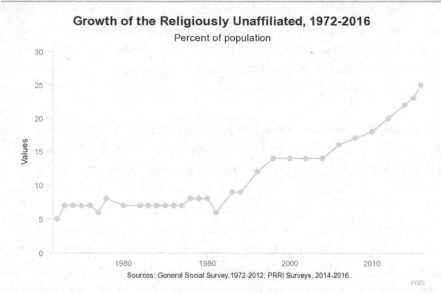

Growth of the Religiously Unaffiliated, 1972-2016
Percent of population

Sources: General Social Survey,1972-2012; PRRI Surveys, 2014-2016.

Scott Thumma, director of the Hartford Institute for Religion Research, predicts, "In the next twenty years, you'll have half as many open congregations as now."[5] In 2017, the Public Religion Research Institute reported a dramatic, rapidly increasing decline that is easy to see when making comparisons over time.[6] In 1986, for example, 10 percent of young adults gave the answer "none" to a PRRI survey asking their religion. In 2016 that figure had shot up to 39 percent.[7] When you pull back the camera lens to include all generations, you discover what may be the most consequential shift in America's spiritual landscape: the rise of the religiously unaffiliated. This trend emerged in the early 1990s, when only 6 percent of Americans identified their religious affiliation as "none." Although this trend is tapering, today one-quarter of Americans claim no formal religious identity, making this group the only growing "religious group" in the US. Furthermore, with the COVID-19 pandemic in full swing at the time of this writing—with churches unable to gather—without a doubt, there will be a culling of congregations that simply won't be viable postpandemic.

If the goal of every faith community is a starfish—the spontaneous reproduction of faith-filled, flourishing disciples—then we are in a crisis. The health and growth of transformative missional movements are directly related to their capacity to make disciples. No disciples, no starfish movement. It's that simple.

But a good news needle is hidden in this data haystack.

When one digs deeper, the rise of the "nones" is not attributable to a decline in the percentage of people who express spiritual and religious enthusiasm, which according to the 2018 General Social Survey at the University of Chicago, is 34 percent, a number that has remained unchanged over thirty years.[8]

Who is converting to the nones? The unengaged middle.

In American faith, we see the same trend that has been growing in the political and economic realms: the middle is dropping out, with sides forming at each end of the continuum. According to the GSS surveyors, the significant drop off is occurring in the faith affiliation group entitled "somewhat strong."[9] These are the folks in our churches who are neither fully engaged nor fully disengaged. As a faith leader, you're likely thinking, "Many of my people fit in that category."

Therein lies the good news. A starfish movement in our faith communities can begin by reengaging and reviving those already within the influence of our faith communities, from the church to the harvest. Within the prevailing model, the congregation becomes the fishing pond from which one can identify and then invite others into an intentional disciple-making environment.

Of course, new disciples must be made from the harvest field as well. In the great DMMs around the world, most of the mobilization is from the harvest. On this, Alan reminds us,

> It is helpful here to remove the role of "discipling" from the confines of the church walls. In the Great Commission we are exhorted to go therefore and make disciples; we believe this to mean that we are called to disciple every person we encounter on the journey of life. Again, another way of looking at it is to "call forth the image of God" within every person. The role of "discipling" will, of course, vary from person to person, depending on our relationship with them and if they have accepted Jesus as their Lord and Savior. We have found the categories "pre-" and "post-conversion" discipleship helpful.[10]

Discipleship is unavoidable. The question is, To whom or to what am I being discipled? First, every human being gives authority to someone or something to be their teacher and lord. Then they become like that someone or something.

Alan Hirsch: The contemporary church is in the habit of seeing the so-called Great Commission as an evangelistic mandate. But where do we see evangelism explicitly mentioned there? Rather, we are to read it quite plainly and simply as a disciple-making and missional mandate—pay attention once again to the language and emphasis: "Go . . . make disciples of all nations . . . baptizing . . . teaching them to obey everything I have commanded you" (Matt. 28:19–20). It's all about sentness and disciple-making and obedience to the lordship of Jesus! Evangelism is implied in discipleship, not the other way around. It is time we changed our approach accordingly. Instead of seeing our mission as simply calling people to "make decisions" and come to church, we need to reframe evangelism in the context of discipleship.

Therefore, the missionary disciple-makers of the KC Underground see every interaction, including with those they've been sent to in the harvest, as a discipleship exchange. When simply chatting with a neighbor about parenting or hobbies, we share, sometimes with overt language and sometimes without, how the lordship of Jesus informs all of life. The harvest is the destination for every follower of Jesus, and we are sent there with one overriding purpose: make disciples.

In the KC Underground, we have seen amazing mobilization of disciples from the harvest field to the church, especially among the incarcerated and the formerly incarcerated. For example, Cory Ozbun, one of the leaders we mentioned earlier, began a Discovery Bible Study (DBS) with a person of peace in the Johnson County jail. That DBS quickly multiplied new disciples, and DBSs multiplied to every single pod in the entire jail, leading to a massive spiritual awakening and numerous salvations. As those people leave jail, they join a microchurch called Share the Hope. Share the Hope has now multiplied DBSs to the jail systems in three counties and birthed three microchurches. That team now has a plan in place to make new disciples by starting DBSs in every Oxford House in our city. We are praying, fasting, and planning for this to become a DMM in our city.

Consider this true story from India. Ravit was thirty-nine years old. He worked hard as a carpenter to provide for his wife, three daughters, and young son. He also farmed their personal small plot of land. Three years ago he attended a DMM training where he rediscovered that Jesus' final command to his followers was to go make disciples. Soon Ravit was putting into practice what he had learned. He worked in the mornings, both in the fields and the shop, and then dedicated his afternoons to ministry.

Ravit never asked for money. When other house church leaders inquired to see if he needed "help," he'd reply, "No, I don't need it. I have my own business and don't need more money." Ravi is part of a larger DMM movement in India. The movement leader describes Ravit as "very wise and bold. He is focused on reaching more places, new villages."

Every one or two months he goes to a new unreached place. Over three years, he has seen nine generations of leaders mentored and new disciples birth 378 house churches! He is not jealous of others' successes but freely shared all he had learned in trainings so that others could also be fruitful.[11]

DMMs like this are *normal* in many parts of the world and are penetrating lostness in historic ways. Let that sink in.

But here in America, in many contexts, we also need to mobilize from the church toward the harvest through MDMs. This book asks the reader to consider a strategy that starts at both ends of the mobilization continuum, the harvest field and the church.

What does it look like when the unengaged middle becomes transformed, multiplying disciples? What does an MDM look like, from the church to the harvest?

Take a look at the whiteboard drawing in figure 9.3. This story has been unfolding in Kansas City for eight years. What started with Brian Phipps, a once-frustrated pastor, has become a movement of disciple-making, with disciples reproducing

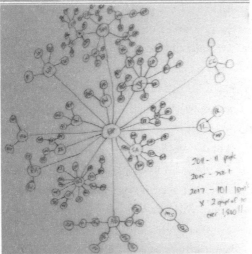

Figure 9.3

to the fourth generation and beyond, on multiple strands. Brian is also one of my (Rob's) best friends, one of the brightest minds on disciple-making I know, and the originator of the first iteration of what we call the *intentional disciple-making environment*. Through our shared work the last six years, we (Brian and Rob) have now expanded it into what you will read in the next six chapters.

Here's how Brian describes

it: "Eight years ago, here I was a pastor, the paid professional holding two master's degrees, having attended over fifty leadership conferences, consumed endless books and articles on discipleship, and yet it had slowly dawned on me, I had never personally multiplied disciples. I had led many small groups and discipleship programs, but the results were discouraging and not reproductive. That was very hard to accept."

He goes on to say, "I did not know what to do differently. So I did the only thing I knew how to do—I repented. With a new humility and earnestness, I returned to the gospels. I prayed, 'Lord, I obey whatever you ask me to do. Please just guide me.' The first thing the Spirit told me to do: 'Put an end date on your current small group.'"

He continued, "For years I had invested my best 'discipleship' energies into people who had no interest in discipling others, which described most of the men in my small group. That had to stop. With excitement, I explained the end date to the group. I shared this vision of becoming disciple-makers, which went over like a lead balloon. You could almost hear an audible 'thud' as the idea hit the ground. Some of the guys were offended that I was ending their group. The rest of the guys didn't think they were up to the task. In so many words, 'Disciple-making . . . isn't that for the religious professionals?'"

Here's what Brian told them: "'I will personally disciple you for one year to help you become disciples who can make disciples.' Sounds simple, right? Well, I didn't even know which people to invite to this new disciple-makers journey! I simply prayed for a few weeks, 'Jesus show me who to invite.' He did. Clearly. Of the original group, five of those guys committed to going on the journey to become disciple-makers. Each of those men invited an apprentice to join them. Jesus had already led me to move from a two-generation disciple-making model to a three-generation model."

Ken was one of those five guys. At that point, Ken's marriage had just taken a significant hit when his wife discovered his pornography habit. During that year of developing character and calling with Brian, Ken's marriage was restored, and his family was transformed. In the last eight years, Ken has made disciples who have made disciples who have made disciples who have made disciples. It literally totals hundreds of people in that "strand" from Brian to Ken downstream four generations and beyond.

Jim, at the beginning of the journey, was depressed and drinking too much. Over the year, Jim broke his addiction by finding what he truly needed in Jesus. Now, there are more than 50 disciples downstream in his disciple-making chain reaction.

One of Jim's disciple-making beneficiaries was a pastor in our area who was in crisis. This leader did not have healthy accountability and was starting to engage in an emotional affair. Jim, "the lay person," discipled "the pastor" in developing his character and calling, which redirected his life and saved his marriage. Now, that pastor is multiplying disciples through his church.

Brian concludes, "I have personally discipled over 120 people in these last eight years. Over thirty percent of those believers were catalyzed into disciple-makers." That may not feel like a great return on investment—only 30 percent. But in starfish movements, slow is the new fast. You can't microwave disciple-making disciples in movements of disciple-making.

In MDMs, we develop disciple-makers in a Crock-Pot, slow cooking over time. Investing in small numbers of people over time, like Jesus did with his twelve. As disciples make disciples, it's addition at first, but eventually multiplication kicks in.

Alan Hirsch: One of the challenges churches wanting to become movements face is to find a way to scale disciple-making. Missional practitioners have found that the formula 8–6–4 is useful. Assuming a common and accessible content (common practices), we suggest that the focus is on the leader of 50—the so-called L-50: Each L-50 commits to discipling 8, the 8 in turn commit to discipling 6 others, and the 6 in turn commit to discipling 4. In this way one L-50 ensures that over 240 people are discipled.

Consider Brian's words carefully:

That 30 percent have similar stories to mine, in their wake. The map you see on that white board, which I drew in 2015, conservatively represents more than 2,500 people who are experiencing transformation in their character and feel a deep sense of personal calling. That story began in 2010 with me and the original five disciples working out at only a 30 percent success rate over five years. Due to the speed up of exponential multiplication, which is now working in our favor, that number has jumped from 2,500 to 4,000 in the last two and a half years!

You're probably wondering, "What is going on under the surface in these stories?

How does that happen? What are the ingredients needed to fuel this kind of transformation and multiplication among ordinary people? How do I, as a church leader, create intentional disciple-making environments of faith?"

This is where the disciple-making ingredients starfish comes in. If we learn to create the right environments—intentional disciple-making environments—with the right ingredients, the power of the starfish can be awakened!

Let us repeat, the health and growth of transformative apostolic movements are directly related to their capacity to make disciples. No disciples, no starfish movement. Over the next five chapters, we will explore the five key ingredients of an intentional disciple-making environment (IDE).

The Disciple-Making Ingredients Starfish

Creating Intentional Environments and Mixing Ingredients

Figure 9.4

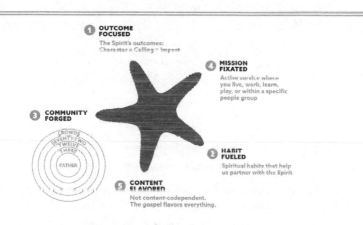

Ingredient #1: Outcome Focused

THE KEY QUESTIONS:

- How clearly can we articulate the outcomes of internal transformation?
- Is our main goal for everyone in our community to experience personal transformation into the likeness of God?" What are the competing distractions to that main goal?
- To what degree are people in our faith community discovering and living into their personal callings?

Ingredient #2: Habit Fueled

THE KEY QUESTIONS:

- Do we effectively help people develop personally meaningful spiritual habits?
- Do our experiential and relational environments make the development of spiritual habits normal?
- How well do we correlate the practice of the spiritual habits to the Spirit's outcomes of transformation in character and calling?

Ingredient #3: Community Forged

THE KEY QUESTIONS:

- Do we understand and engage all five spheres of community required for human flourishing?
- How well do we help people create overlapping social spaces that deepen their engagement in our faith community?
- Do we move people out of the privatized individualism trend and into deep, meaningful faith community engagement?

Ingredient #4: Mission Fixated

THE KEY QUESTIONS:

- How well do we help each person discover that mission involves the everyday spaces where we live, work, learn, and play?
- How well do we help each person own mission personally?
- What resources, processes, and tools do we provide to empower each person to own, apply, and innovate on mission?

Ingredient #5: Content Flavored

THE KEY QUESTIONS:

- Do we have clarity on what the fractal of our faith is? What is our irreducible minimum?
- Do we pass on this fractal of faith in a way that is generous and inclusive?
- Is this passed on in a way that moves beyond intellectual assent to integration into all of life?

Before we examine the ingredients of an IDE, let's remember that disciple-making isn't a microwave activity, it's a slow-cooker lifestyle.

Flash back to the 1980s. I (Rob) remember the day we got our microwave, which came with the much-hyped, space-age promise of time-saving efficiency. Food will be ready in a flash, Gordon! Right away I was ready to strap on my space suit and take off. First I took a hot dog, placed it in a bun, and nuked it for a couple of minutes. Mmm, that bun was as hard as cardboard. Not to be discouraged, I moved quickly to scrambled eggs next and ended up with a rubberized omelet. Delish! The only upside that day was when I discovered that marshmallows blow up when microwaved.

My mom, who was a home economics major in college, never took to the microwave, beyond making popcorn. She preferred slow cooking. Many a day, the Crock-Pot was the instrument of choice. One of her classic meals was porcupines. The imagery might not sound too appetizing, but trust me, they were the pièce de résistance.

Porcupines are meatballs embedded with rice, marinated in an Italian herbs and tomato sauce. She'd tuck those meatballs in the sauce, stick the Crock-Pot on low, and let them simmer all day. Oh, the whole house filled with the most delicious aroma! My stomach is grumbling now as I think about it. Slow cooking those meatballs in the Crock-Pot made them so tender, allowing the sauce to soak entirely through the meatball, saturating every last bite with such flavor.

Jump forward a few decades. After a tumble down the stairs, my wife was bedridden for six weeks postsurgery. We still had three kids to feed daily, as well as some neighborhood children to feed regularly, as that was part of our family rhythm as "missionaries" in our neighborhood. Overnight, I was commissioned with all the cooking duties. In an effort to be efficient, I became "commander of the Crock-Pot." With a little advance planning, I could throw the ingredients into the Crock-Pot early in the morning before work, let it simmer all day, come home after work, and offer up a homemade masterpiece for the family and neighbors. Eventually, we figured out the go-to meals for rotation.

I had no advanced culinary degrees. I didn't need to be a five-star Michelin chef. The best slow cooker recipes were ones that friends shared with me. One of them even had a database of such recipes! It didn't take a ton of food preparation to pull a meal together. And we had some great meals to share. My wife will even brag on my cooking now. But it's not that impressive. Virtually anyone can become a master of the Crock-Pot.

Disciple-making isn't about being the expert. It's about learning and adding back in the basic key ingredients any cook can find, which the people of God have known and practiced for centuries. It doesn't require an advanced degree, a lot of complex preparation, or complicated skills.

Alan Hirsch: One of the few "formulas" I suggest in my writings on movement is the following:

$$MCP + MEE = MM$$

Where . . .
- MCP stands for multiplication church planting (the overt organizational strategy).
- MEE stands for mission of everyone everywhere (the agency of every believer in every context of life).
- MM stands for the missional (or apostolic) movement.

You can't microwave disciples. Forming them takes time, accountability, community, consistency, and practice. As the key ingredients simmer inside those containers, faith-owners are tenderized and transformed by the Spirit. Soon they themselves are ready to share the meal and show others how to make the meal. The culmination of history, as pictured in the book of Revelation, is seen as the wedding feast of the Lamb (Rev. 19:6–9). People from every tribe will be gathered to celebrate the great union of God and humanity. These are the people who have come to own the mission of Jesus to heal, redeem, and restore all things. The authors love to think of millions of people personally owning the mission of universal flourishing, which we believe transcends any one particular faith tradition or denomination.

By the way, I'm positive my mom's porcupines will be on the menu at the wedding feast! Let's now take a look at each of the disciple-making ingredients we want to put into the slow cooker.

CHAPTER 10

Outcome Focused

Disciple-Making Environment Ingredient #1

Figure 10.1

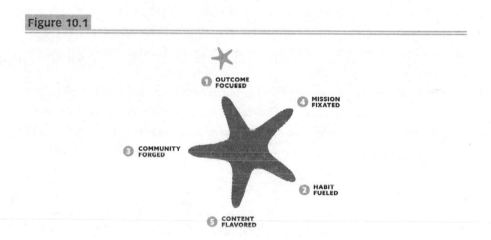

Starfish #5: The Disciple-Making Ingredients Starfish

Purpose: The disciple-making starfish helps us discover the five essential ingredients required for creating intentional disciple-making environments (IDEs) that are transformative and multiplicative.

You've heard it said, "Begin with the end in mind."

Too often, the desired end of most discipleship programs is a "data dump." If we can just open the top of people's skulls and pour in enough good content, mission accomplished. They've been "discipled," regardless of any application or transformation in that person's life.

The outcome of discipleship, however, isn't simply a transfer of information. The goal is transformation by incarnation. The Word becomes flesh and blood in his disciples.

Sheldon Vanauken proclaims in his classic book *A Severe Mercy*, "The best argument for Christianity is Christians: their joy, their certainty, their completeness. But the strongest argument against Christianity is also Christians—when they are somber and joyless, when they are self-righteous and smug in complacent consecration, when they are narrow and repressive, then Christianity dies a thousand deaths."[1]

For a missional movement to survive beyond the initial impulse, the Founder must somehow literally live on in his people. The vitality and validity of their message depends on the willingness and capacity of those disciples to faithfully embody, quite literally, his life. The Founder is actually alive in them, shining through in a gospel-integrated life. In a real way, disciples must become the gospel to the people around them, the embodiment of the real Jesus through the quality of their lives.[2]

What are the required outcomes of this embodiment?

We would like to propose that there are two, which are inextricably linked to the Spirit's work in our lives. In every great movement, the work of the Spirit in each of his people is seen as important not only in the past but also as vital and critical in the present. Transformation begins with a radical reliance on the Spirit of God.

> You, my brothers and sisters, were called to be free. But do not use your freedom to indulge the flesh.... So I say, walk by the Spirit, and you will not gratify the desires of the flesh. For the flesh desires what is contrary to the Spirit, and the Spirit what is contrary to the flesh.... Since we live by the Spirit, let us keep in step with the Spirit. (Gal. 5:13, 16–17, 25)

Each member of the Trinity plays a vital role in our salvation. Biblical discipleship must be trinitarian, or it is not biblical. The Father ordained our salvation. Jesus accomplished our salvation. The Spirit applies our salvation.

In Galatians 5, Paul paints a picture of the Spirit as the prime mover in our transformation. Of course, this is in accordance with the teachings of Jesus in John 16:5–11, where we learn it will be the Spirit that mediates our knowledge and experience of God. The Spirit guides us into "all the truth." He alone "will make known" to us what he has received from Jesus himself, who has received "all that belongs to the Father."

In other words, our discipleship is birthed in the Spirit but also maintained in the Spirit. By the Spirit alone do we enter into the experience and knowledge of the life of God. While cognitive knowledge is very much involved in our discipleship, growth into the "deep things of God" (1 Cor. 2:10) is fundamentally a supernatural endeavor that will not be achieved apart from the ongoing work of the Spirit.

Paul clearly highlights two major classifications by which the Spirit is at work in us: fruit of the Spirit (Gal. 5:22–23; Rom. 8:5–17, 26–29) and gifts of the Spirit (Rom. 12:6–8; 1 Cor. 12:8–10, 28–30; Eph. 4:11–13; 1 Peter 4:11).

These are the two nonnegotiable outcomes of the Spirit's work in us, upon which all our disciple-making efforts should focus—fruit of the Spirit and gifts of the Spirit. We refer to them as character and calling.

Outcome #1: Character (Fruit of the Spirit)

What does Spirit-inspired character look like? In other words, what is God like? Thomas Keating states, "The chief fruit of Old Testament spirituality was a long-term education that gradually weaned the Chosen People away from their narrow concept of God as one among many other Near Eastern gods to the Transcendent One. The monotheistic God is the great gift of Israel to humanity."[2]

Unlike the fickle and cruel pantheon of tribal gods the ancient world and archaic religion sought to appease, this God described himself to Moses this way:

The LORD passed before him, and proclaimed,

> "The LORD, the LORD,
> a God merciful and gracious,
> slow to anger,
> and abounding in steadfast love and faithfulness,
> keeping steadfast love for the thousandth generation,
> forgiving iniquity and transgression and sin." (Ex. 34:6–7 NRSV)

This view became the faith fractal that Israel used to summarize the character of God. Five marvelous dimensions describe the core of what we can become: merciful (in Hebrew, *rhm*), compassionate/gracious (*hnn*), steadfast and unconditional in love (*hsd*), relentlessly faithful (*'emeth*), and forgiving (*ns'*).

The ultimate goal of mature spirituality is to reflect the image of God.

Philosopher Ken Wilber articulates this goal when he describes what he sees as the two transcendent shared outcomes of religion:

> Religion itself has always performed two very important, but very different, functions. One, it acts as a way of creating *meaning* for the separate self: it offers myths and stories and tales and narratives and rituals that, taken together, help the separate self make sense of, and endure, the slings and arrows of outrageous fortune. This function of religion does not usually or necessarily change the level of consciousness in a person; it does not deliver radical transformation. . . .
>
> But two, religion has also served—in a usually very, very small minority—the function of radical transformation and liberation. This function of religion does not fortify the separate self, but utterly shatters it—not consolation but devastation, not entrenchment but emptiness, not complacency but explosion, not comfort but revolution—in short, not a conventional bolstering of consciousness but a radical transmutation and transformation at the deepest seat of consciousness itself.[4]

Many seek only the first outcome of faith, a sense of meaning and comfort. But true disciple-making requires that we move beyond the egocentric goals of comfort toward the greater heights of radical transformation.

Alan Hirsch: The true following of Jesus (discipleship) requires some form of profound conversion, one that implies engagement of our whole being with the whole of reality, with God at its center. More specifically, conversion requires that we give the whole of ourselves irrevocably to the whole of God in a way that involves the whole of creation. Everything changes!

That is why Jesus said, "Blessed are the poor in spirit" (Matt. 5:3). Recognizing our own poverty and brokenness is the beginning of this journey. The greatest DMMs globally always spark most readily among the marginalized, simply because they are already "blessed" with a deep awareness that "something has to change"! The "poor and weak" are vastly more self-aware than the "rich and powerful," who have been lulled to sleep by affluence, success, and comfort.

Periodically, an event like the COVID-19 pandemic or 9/11 will shake millions of people simultaneously from their spiritual slumber. Usually, however, it is the everyday experiences of pain, loss, defeat, failure, bankruptcy, addiction, and the like that make us aware of our desperate need for transformation in our character.

Of course, Jesus is the ultimate, complete, and total revelation of God's character to us. Jesus is like God, but more to the point, God is like Jesus. God chose to make himself known, finally and ultimately, in a real, historical man. Don't settle for inferences and guesswork. You want to know God's character? Go to Jesus. Hebrews 1:1–3, which happens to be my (Rob's) favorite passage in the Bible, says,

> In the past God spoke to our ancestors through the prophets at *many times* and in *various ways*, but in these last days he has spoken to us by his Son. . . . The Son is the *radiance of God's glory* and the *exact representation of his being*. (Heb. 1:1–3, emphases ours)

Previous revelations reveal approximations of God's character; Jesus alone reveals the exact representation of God's character. Only Jesus reveals exactly what God is like in his *very essence*, in his *innermost heart*, and in his *eternal nature*.

The fruit of the Spirit is perhaps the clearest, briefest, multidimensional picture of Jesus' character in the New Testament.

> The fruit of the Spirit is love, joy, peace, patience, kindness, goodness, faithfulness, gentleness, and self-control. Against such things there is no law. (Gal. 5:22–23 NIV 1984)

The first outcome of true disciple-making is this: *We become like Jesus in our character.* Our very soul is the soil from which blooms the fruit of the Spirit. "Those God foreknew he also predestined to be conformed to the image of his Son" (Rom. 8:29).

Alan Hirsch: We need to be very concerned with the culture of celebrity that exudes from many popular Christian leaders in the West. Aside from the contrived "heroism" that is embodied in such forms of leadership, it looks more like it is an illegitimate attempt to steal glory from Jesus himself. The celebrity is a mere slave to the crowd. He or she needs the crowd as much as the crowd needs the celebrity. But this is clearly not Christlike leadership! The false

> heroism of celebrity is way too codependent, narcissistic, and parasitical to be viewed as an extension of discipleship—adherence to Jesus. Christlike character and content are required for leadership in Jesus' church.

Paul does not call these characteristics the traits of the Spirit, the components of the Spirit, or the aspects of the Spirit. He says, "The *fruit* of the Spirit." How does this fruit grow?

In the New Testament, the guiding metaphors are organic. In our time, the guiding metaphors are mechanical. On this side of the Industrial Revolution, we manufacture things. That metaphor dominates the way we think about change. Think of how many times you've said things like, "I've got to *make* this happen."

This attitude is profoundly important as it applies to developing the fruit of the Spirit. Paul deliberately uses the word *fruit* because he is invoking a metaphor of botanical growth. That speaks to not only the product of change but also the process of change. This type of internal, spiritual transformation is not simply made through our own efforts.

The difference between mechanical and organic change is the difference between *striving* and *yielding*.

You can restrain your character temporarily through striving, like squeezing a foam ball to a smaller size. But you didn't really change the ball; you just restrained it. As soon as you let the pressure off, it snaps back to its original shape. That's standard operating procedure: "I will *strive* and *make* the change happen." But when my willpower runs out, my old character returns.

All you get from striving is a morally restrained heart, not a spiritually transformed heart. Striving for a morally restrained heart is like eating manufactured wax fruit rather than feasting on fresh organic fruit. They may look the same on the outside from a distance, but they sure taste different.

Instead of the striving experience of "squeeze and snap back," which leads to frustration, we can discover the yielding experience of "remain and respond," which leads to transformation. We find this power source in the Spirit, which makes the person of God in Jesus Christ fully available to all those who believe.

> I am the vine; you are the branches. If you remain in me and I in you, you will bear much fruit; apart from me you can do nothing. (John 15:5)

Remain in me.

In other words, stay in the Spirit, walk with Spirit, and spend your day aware that the Spirit is available to you. If you do, the fruit of radical, internal transformation—mercy, compassion, love, joy, faithfulness, wisdom, patience, kindness, goodness—will slowly grow.

Think of how fruit grows in nature. Some elements the plant can simply open up and receive: sunlight, water, and oxygen. No one has ever heard an apple tree grunting with effort to produce fruit.

Transformation begins with *receiving* what the Spirit is giving.

Jesus is speaking kingdom of heaven language. Often we hear others say something along the lines of, "We've got to expand the kingdom." Or, "We are building the kingdom." The sentiment is certainly well meaning, but it is also misleading. We don't expand or build God's kingdom. No place in the New Testament will you read of such an idea. But we do "receive" and "enter" the kingdom. That is language we hear Jesus use time and again.

First we must receive what the Spirit is giving. Then we must *respond to what has been given. Receive and respond.*

For a truly productive harvest to be realized, a gardener must learn to respond—or cooperate—with these forces by mindfully engaging in age-old practices that are essential. One must learn to tend the garden and weed out that which threatens the slow-growing harvest.

When it comes to experiencing radical transformation in our character, we "remain" by first trusting that God is gracious. The Spirit will provide the light and oxygen our souls need to grow. Secondly, we remain by practicing the ancient habits of soul gardening that keep us connected to the Spirit. As we remain, the Spirit will guide us and prompt us to new action or explorations of new avenues, then we respond with engagement and obedience to that prompting. We will explore these habits in the next ingredient of intentional disciple-making environments.

Along the way, we are transformed in character, which is the first essential outcome we must focus on. Additionally, along the way, that responsive life leads to a discovery in calling, which is the second outcome focus.

Outcome #2: Calling (Gifts of the Spirit)

Whereas our character involves our becoming, our calling involves our doing.

> We are God's workmanship, created in Christ Jesus to do good works, which God prepared in advance for us to do. (Eph. 2:10 NIV 1984)

According to Ephesians 2, every follower of Jesus receives a sacred summons, what is commonly referred to as a calling. However, this term has been used almost exclusively for pastors, missionaries, or other leaders in vocational ministry. This tragedy has not simply squelched the potential impact of the church in America—it has put the church in a choke hold.

It is time for every person to pursue, locate, and make the greatest possible impact through their personal calling. I believe Jesus has *called* every follower of Jesus in a unique way so that when all the followers of Jesus are active in their calling, every need in every community could be met.

Do you see how much is riding on this? As meaningful as volunteering can be inside the programs of the centralized church, God's vision is ultimately to fill everything in every way with all that Jesus is. Volunteering alone won't ever get us to gospel saturation, only calling will.

Once again, remember the vision of gospel saturation from Ephesians 1:22–23, where Paul declares, "God placed all things under his feet and appointed him to be head over everything for the church, which is his body, the fullness of him who fills everything in every way."

Paul says that *Jesus is filling everything in every way.* He is big enough to fill every need, big enough to be the solution to every problem, big enough to redeem every mistake, big enough to restore everything broken. The Spirit wants to see your entire city, every corner of culture, saturated with all that he is: love, joy, peace, patience, kindness, goodness, and so on.

Is that the kind of city you want to live in?

Where there is isolation, we bring community, because our God is divine community.

Where there is poverty, we bring abundance, because our God is the God of abundance.

Where there is violence, we bring peace-making, because our God is peace.

Where there is racism or misogyny, we bring equality and dignity, because God's image is stamped on every single one of us.

Where there is disease, we bring healing, because our God is a healer.

Alan Hirsch: When disciples pray "Your kingdom come, your will be done," we acknowledge that the current government and all purely human ways of ordering a society are insufficient and can't bring in the just and holy society we long for. The prayer is not that we may come into the kingdom, but rather that the kingdom, the Wholly Other, may come to us and become operative within our order. In praying this, we don't believe the current social order will simply go on evolving from within until at last altruism triumphs and greed is dethroned; nor indeed does history support this view. Rather, we want to bring the God whom we worship—his beauty, his sovereignty, his order—into the very texture of our lives. We long for the rule of God exemplified in the person and work of Jesus.

Directly after the temptations of Jesus in the wilderness (Matt. 4:1–11), he entered the synagogue in his hometown of Nazareth to publicly announce his ministry. Scholars often refer to this as his kingly inaugural speech. Here Jesus gives a glorious definition of the gospel of the kingdom.

The scroll of the prophet Isaiah was given to him. He unrolled the scroll and found the place where it was written,

> "The Spirit of the Lord is upon me,
>   because he has anointed me
>   to proclaim good news to the poor.
> He has sent me to proclaim liberty to the captives
>   and recovering of sight to the blind,
>   to set at liberty those who are oppressed,
> to proclaim the year of the Lord's favor." (Luke 4:17–19 ESV)

This is our first overview of the gospel, and it has more to do with life on earth than life in heaven. Jesus' declaration has five distinct aspects. Any expression of the gospel that lacks one or more of these components is incomplete.

1. Jesus calls his gospel "good news to the poor." It is good news for *those suffering economic defeat.*
2. He proclaims "liberty to the captives"—that is, freedom *for those held captive to social and political systems and power structures.*
3. He announces "recovering of sight to the blind." Throughout his earthly ministry, we see Jesus restore vision both to the *physically* blind and the *spiritually* blind.

4. He is sent by the Father to set free *the morally and spiritually bruised and oppressed.*

5. He proclaims "the year of the Lord's favor," a reference to the Jewish custom of Jubilee, which means *a new beginning* for those who were enslaved and a *restoring of inheritance* for those who had lost what was once rightfully theirs.[5]

How will he do that? Through us. This was the inauguration of the good work that Jesus later commissioned his disciples to carry on.

> "*This gospel of the kingdom* will be proclaimed throughout the whole world as a testimony to all nations, and then the end will come." (Matt. 24:14 ESV, emphasis ours)

In Ephesians 1:23, we are described as "his body, the fullness of him." We are invited to be his body, his hands, and his feet in action on the ground. We are invited to be the fullness of him, making that fullness tangible where we live, work, learn, and play.

In other words, God's people have been mobilized to fill every corner of culture for the purpose of making the love, joy, beauty, and shalom of God tangible. Discovering and living into your personal calling is the way you find your part in that masterpiece. Each of us has a one-of-a-kind "masterpiece mission." As we each discover and live into it, alongside others, those mosaics make up the masterpiece, and the fullness grows with each person who discovers and lives out their calling.

Unfortunately, the opposite is true. Every time a person is unaware of or unengaged in their masterpiece mission, the tank is emptied of that part of the fullness. Individually, without knowing our personal calling, we feel "empty," lacking purpose, significance, and meaning. Corporately, our faith communities, cities, and world feel empty, lacking the fullness that God intends to fill up the needs and emptiness that vex and oppress us.

There are two types of people in the world: those who know their masterpiece mission and those who don't. Most people settle for life in the second category, which contributes to an aching sense of purposelessness. No wonder we see so little effect in our culture.

Currently, many churches have a process to activate volunteers into their programs. As helpful as that is, it doesn't necessarily help every believer know their unique personal calling. Volunteering is a good beginning, but it is not the end zone.

It's time for every faith community to have a personal calling discovery and deployment process. That discovery process may begin with volunteering in the programs of a faith community but will ultimately emphasize the end zone of engagement in personal calling where you live, work, learn, and play. When that happens, our faith communities cease to be cul-de-sac congregations and start operating like the hubs in Jerusalem or Ephesus, launching people and communities out on mission all over our cities and regions.

Helping ordinary folks discover and then be deployed into their calling is an essential part of disciple-making. There are many ways to do gift assessment and calling discovery. In Kansas City we have created a calling discovery and development process.

We call it GPS.

With the invention of the global positioning system, navigation has been revolutionized. The signals from the satellites triangulate your exact position and then can provide clarity on how to get to your destination. Wouldn't it be great if there were a GPS for the soul? What if there was a spiritual technology that could help you locate your unique calling? There is.

We want every disciple to learn about the God-given "soul-technology" of GPS—their gifts, passions, and story. Our calling is primarily expressed as we discover, develop, and deploy our *gifts* in our area of *passion* as we allow Jesus to write our *story*.

Gifts (Rom. 12:6–8; 1 Cor. 12:8–10, 28–30; Eph. 4:11–13; 1 Peter 4:11)

We are all born with natural gifts. These gifts are the product of God's common grace given to all people (Ps. 139:13–16; Gen. 1:27; James 1:17). Our natural abilities come with an invitation to cocreate with God, "fill the earth and subdue it" Gen. 1:28), so there will be order and flourishing in the world.

For those who have received amazing grace, we have also received spiritual gifts at our second birth. Our natural abilities can create wonderful things, but it is through our spiritual gifts that we discover a divine power to make disciples, strengthen the church for its mission, fight demonic evil, and fully manifest the kingdom in healing and power. Through the Holy Spirit and our spiritual gifts, God empowers his church to bless the world at large. Through our natural gifts we join God as cocreators in making culture and society a place of universal flourishing for all people.

It was he who "gave gifts to people" . . . to build up the body of Christ . . . so we shall all come together to that oneness in our faith and . . . become mature. . . . Then we shall no longer be children, carried by the waves and blown about by every shifting wind. (Eph. 4:11–14 GNT)

Passions (Eph. 4:11–13; Ps. 37:4; Gal. 2:8; Prov. 4:23; Ezek. 36:26; Matt. 22:37)

As we discover our God-assigned passions, we will begin to shift from a sense of feeling lost to gaining direction about our place in life. While our gifts outline some of that direction, when we add in an understanding of our passions, we tap into the power source that internally motivates us to pursue our calling. Gifts show us *what* we can do; our passions show us *where* and *with whom* we should use our gifts. Our passion involves a blending of interest in certain groups of people, certain causes, and the particular motivation (Eph. 4:11–12) that fuels us as we look at the world.

> Delight yourself in the LORD,
>> and he will give you the desires of your heart. (Ps. 37:4 ESV)

Story (Rom. 8:28; Phil. 1:8; 2 Cor. 3:3; 4:1; 9:13; Prov. 4:13)

Second Corinthians 3:3 (NKJV) tells us, "Clearly you are an epistle of Christ . . . written not with ink but by the Spirit of the living God." Your story isn't just a list of facts and events. It's a weaving of those facts and events into a narrative that has meaning, one that connects with God's larger story. There is an arc to your story. Do you know how to read it? There are primary themes to your story. Are you aware of them? That arc and those themes will lead you to discover your calling.

With the signals of your gifts, passions, and story, you will be on your pathway of personal calling. You can discover more about GPS in a book I (Rob) cowrote with Brian Phipps called *Find Your Place: Locating Your Calling Through Gifts, Passion, and Story* or by visiting www.giftspassionstory.com, where you can find resources to help with full implementation in your context. We also highly recommend resources like *Younique* by Will Mancini and Dave Rhodes, *More* by Todd Wilson, and *The Call* by Os Guinness.

We must focus on the Spirit's outcomes if we are to see transformation in disciple-making. The result of focusing on these Spirit's outcomes is *impact*. As disciples allow the Spirit to cultivate his character in them, and as they allow the Spirit to demonstrate his power through their calling, their character and calling will create impact in them and through them for good.

The Impact Equation

Here's a simple way to remember the ingredient of outcome focused. We call it the impact equation, developed by the aforementioned Brian Phipps. The relative impact of developing character and calling can be seen by doing simple math through our impact equation, and that math is very telling.

If a person's character is relatively low, perhaps a 3 on a scale from 1 to 10,

Character × Calling = Impact

and they have never even heard that Jesus has a calling on their life, perhaps a 1 on a scale from 1 to 10, then the relative impact they can expect to have is only 3 on a scale of 1 to 100. Here is the math:

$$3 \text{ (character)}$$
$$\times 1 \text{ (calling)}$$
$$3 \text{ (impact)}$$

If this person engages with a disciple-making experience that focuses on developing both character and calling, look what happens when their character goes up slightly and their calling takes a quick jump because they engage a calling discovery and assessment process like GPS.

$$4 \text{ (character)}$$
$$\times 3 \text{ (calling)}$$
$$12 \text{ (impact)}$$

As you can see, small steps can lead to significant impact. Impact, in turn, becomes the fuel that inspires more character and calling development. This person, perhaps for the first time, is living on purpose. They want to protect and deepen that experience, so they accelerate the pursuit of character development. In turn, God honors that focus with more power through their calling. This changes the math even more:

$$6 \text{ (character)}$$
$$\times 5 \text{ (calling)}$$
$$30 \text{ (impact)}$$

Their impact is now ten times greater than the original score and more than doubled from the second score. You know what else has increased significantly? The fuel of internal motivation for further development. Why? They are now experiencing the fully-alive life (John 10:10) Jesus promised. Over time, as character and calling increase, so does impact *and* internal motivation! Our experience based on thousands of disciples made here in Kansas City is that an intentional focus on the Spirit's outcomes within the context of community can lead to incredible increases in both character and calling.

Ingredient #1: Outcome Focused means Character × Calling = Impact!

As the next five chapters unfold, we want you, as a church leader, to consider your current disciple-making environments and systems. Consider grabbing a journal and jotting your answers to these questions.

- To what degree is the goal of our disciple-making that of personal transformation into Christlike character?
- Are our disciples experiencing growth in their character from the inside out through the Spirit or temporary change through restraint and willpower?
- Do we clearly articulate the Spirit's outcomes as the focus of our disciple-making?
- Can the average disciple clearly articulate the outcomes?
- To what degree are disciples discovering and living into their personal calling?
- What does your calling discovery process look like? What assessments do you use?
- What does your calling deployment process look like?
- Pray and ask the Spirit to help you identify one next step.
- Write an "I will . . ." statement to summarize that step.
- Whom will you share your "I will . . ." statement with?

CHAPTER 11

Habit Fueled

Disciple-Making Ingredient #2

Figure 11.1

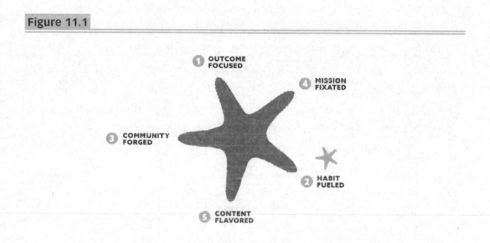

Starfish #5: The Disciple-Making Ingredients Starfish

Purpose: The disciple-making ingredients starfish helps us discover the five essential ingredients required for creating intentional disciple-making environments (IDEs) that are transformative and multiplicative.

You have heard it said that practice makes perfect. Not true. No one reaches perfection. However, one change will make that phrase more accurate.

Scripture Memorization and Meditation: How It Works

My (Lance's) best friend, Johnny, and I had been to a Texas Rangers baseball game. On our way out of the ballpark, we hit some heavy traffic. My new Jeep CJ-7 sparkled. The top was off so we could fully enjoy cruising on that pleasant summer night. We stopped at a red light, and another Jeep with four guys around our age pulled up next to us. Without provocation, the driver looked over at me and yelled, "Your Jeep looks like ——!"

Pause the story.

Johnny and I had been buddies since we were toddlers. Over the years, he had seen me in plenty of fights. When the other Jeep guy insulted my ride, Johnny was certain we'd be pulling into the next parking lot for a rumble. But something different was going on in my mind and soul. As a new disciple, I had spent the previous three months reading the book of Proverbs over and over. When the insult was launched, surprisingly, Proverbs 15:1 popped into my mind: *A soft answer turns away wrath, but a harsh word stirs up anger.*

As the insult landed like a hand grenade, all eyes were on me, waiting for a response. My mind was gently repeating the Proverb. Out of my mouth came a calm reply: "Why would you say something like that?"

If I had thrown a bucket of ice-cold water on the other guy, he would not have looked more shocked. He was stunned into speechlessness, as were his buddies and Johnny. Guess what? So was I! After several seconds of silence, he sheepishly said, "Nice Jeep. How do you like it?" I told him, "Oh, yeah!" He replied, "Have a great night" and turned right as the light went green.

Scripture meditation, empowered by the illumination of the Holy Spirit, had rewired my neural pathways, making new ways of being and living possible.

Practice makes permanent.

Our practices literally create new neural pathways.

Alan Hirsch: Sociologists have pretty much proved that the vast majority of our daily practices have been birthed out of the deep habit patterns (called *habitus* by Paul Bourdieu) embedded into a given culture. These habits (good and bad) will dictate most of our actions unless we deliberately engage in a counterformation process that shapes us to be more Christlike. Discipleship must change the habits we simply inherit and mold them into holy habits. What starts as a discipline becomes a deliberate habit and then turns into an inbuilt reflex.

Neurologist Curt Thompson, author of *Anatomy of the Soul* says,

Anytime we think about changing the course of our mind, we're talking about neuroplasticity. We're talking about changing the way our neurons are firing. One of the most important elements of helping neuroplasticity flourish is activating it through the use of attention. I like to describe attention as being the engine that pulls the rest of the train of the mind. There's nothing that we do throughout the day that does not, in some way, shape or form, involve a shift in attention from one thing to another to another. That attentional change is crucial—if my life is going to be different, I'm going to have to change the focus of my attention and in so doing, activate neuroplasticity. If I want my brain to change, I need to change the focus of my attention.[1]

Practice is a form of attentional and intentional change.

Practicing something regularly will make it a permanent habit, which can either benefit us or break us. Whether that's a healthy pattern or a destructive pattern, we become what we practice. Practice makes permanent.

Spiritual Habits

A spiritual habit involves figuring out how to meaningfully engage a practice or repeated set of behaviors that helps you both connect with the Spirit and cultivate your spiritual development, which nurtures holistic well-being (relational, emotional, intellectual, and physical).

Consider the spiritual habit called contemplative prayer. During contemplative prayer, one remains silent in prayer, with the hope of moving beyond language to experience directly the mystery of God's presence. Naturally, our thoughts drift toward the things we are anxious or preoccupied with. Therefore, disciples are encouraged to pick a meaningful word or phrase—perhaps one of God's names, like "I Am," or a word that is symbolic, like shalom—that they return to as a reminder to let anxious thoughts go, to find a way to return to the center, and simply to be in God's refreshing presence. Mindfulness of your breathing is another important piece of this spiritual practice. The average human breathes twelve to fifteen breaths per minute. In contemplative prayer, we intentionally slow down our breathing to six to eight breaths per second.

In so doing, we practice slowing down and focusing our attention and intention on our breathing and the always-available presence of God. We practice how to disengage the mind chatter that usually dominates all our attention. We transcend our own judgments, defenses, and the other skipping records in our minds. This practice also lowers the blood pressure and heart rate. This will reduce anxiety because anxiety is a mixture of preoccupation with future states along with high-tension physical states.

If a disciple allows this habit to fuel their heart, mind, body, and soul for fifteen to twenty minutes once or twice a day for six weeks, they will have radically enhanced their attentional muscle: the ability to separate from mind chatter to a place of rest and clarity. Almost without knowing it, they are practicing the virtues of peace and discernment. In these moments, the Spirit is working in them to transform them from the inside out.

This may seem extremely esoteric and unpractical to some, but it is profoundly practical. How so? Consider the following.

Imagine you're in conflict with your teenage child, a spouse, or a coworker. The situation, the energy level, and the language are escalating. Underneath this high-stakes conversation is an easily triggered minefield ready to blow up the relationship. Your temper is rumbling, and you're about to blow like Mount Vesuvius.

You've been there before. Maybe recently. Maybe today!

Situations that feel dangerous activate neural networks in the lower brain that then lead us to automatic behaviors like fight or flight with very little higher brain function.

Who is more prepared to handle that situation with peace and discernment, the unpractical praying person or the practical nonpraying person? Whose brain is going to have the better chance of operating out of higher brain function instead of devolving to the reptilian brain?

The unpractical praying person has been practicing through prayer how to focus their attention, how to disengage their own mind chatter, how to lower their breathing rate, how to lower their muscle tension, and how to be open to the Spirit's presence and wisdom as their source and strength.

Can you see how practical prayer is? Can you see how holistic the impact is?

Patience, mercy, and discernment don't just pop into existence in such trying situations. They must be practiced, and contemplative prayer is one way to do that.

When we arrange our lives around these life-giving spiritual habits, transformation happens.

Work In, Work Out

Paul describes the habit-fueled life this way in Philippians 2:13 (NIV 1984): "It is God who works in you to will and to act according to his good purpose." In other words, I can't change myself all by myself. I can modify my behavior, but only the Spirit of God, my faith fractal, and amazing grace can change a heart.

As a follower of Jesus, I know God *works in* me by grace through the gospel

But I'm not passive either. I don't just tread water. Paul says in Philippians 2:12, "Therefore, my dear friends, as you have always obeyed—not only in my presence, but now much more in my absence—continue to *work out* your salvation with fear and trembling" (emphasis ours).

While *God works in* me, *I work out* through spiritual practices.

God works it in. I work it out.

Many have misread this verse and assume people must earn their salvation through good works. But that is totally out of line with what Paul's intent. We know from the entirety of Paul's teaching, salvation is God's work from start to finish, accomplished through Jesus' life, death, and resurrection. Paul is not asking people to earn their salvation in this verse, but rather to own their participation in their ongoing transformation. Grace can't be earned. Grace, however, does energize effort. As God works in us, his grace energizes our efforts to work out.

Paul articulates a revolutionary new approach to the habits Jesus embodied. No longer do we see these habits or good deeds as the end in and of themselves, which we muster up to please God or earn some new standing before him. No longer do we measure our goodness by the quantity of external religious behaviors.

The goodness Jesus is most concerned with is our internal character transformation.

By grace, we can become qualitatively different people internally. With this as the end goal, spiritual habits become our way of cooperating with God by responding to his grace. They move us into a flow where we are doing life with God and abiding in him. In this way, we place ourselves in a space where we see God moving and grace flowing, and we join in!

These activities are a way of raising the sail so we can catch the wind of God. These activities are a way of keeping the radio tuned in so we can always hear the divine music and join the dance. These activities are a way to put our boat in the river and start rowing. But there is a current underneath us that is already and always flowing.

Alan describes it this way in *The Forgotten Ways*,

Our mystical union with Christ and his indwelling with us lies at the very center of the Christian experience of God—this is seen in all of Paul's teaching about being "in Christ" and he in us, as well as John's theology of "abiding in Christ." All the spiritual disciplines therefore aim us toward one thing: *Christlikeness*. We heed the words ascribed to Mother Teresa: "We must become holy not because we want to feel holy but because Christ must be able to live his life fully in us."[2]

Alan Hirsch: It is useful to think of the process of our discipleship in terms of (1) imitation of Christ, (2) conformation to Jesus, and (3) ever-increasing transformation into his likeness. A metaphor for these processes is that of *attunement*. When for instance two guitars both are tuned to perfect pitch, when the one is played, the strings on the other will vibrate in perfect tune without any touch. The aim is that the individual believer, and with him or her the entire body of Christ, will increasingly be in tune with Jesus and so look, think, act, and sound like Jesus.

H2O

Brian Phipps summarized engaging spiritual practices with the phrase "habits to outcomes" (H2O). When these spiritual practices become habits and are engaged as a means to partner with the Spirit toward the Spirit's outcomes, it will naturally lead to transformation in both character and calling; Christ will be fully alive in us.

All IDEs will introduce people to these practices. More than that, IDEs equip people *to orient their entire lives* around these practices until they become habits. Along the way, every disciple is reminded, again and again, it's not about "checking the list." It's all about H2O, habits to outcomes.

Jesus' life is the ultimate example of the habit-fueled life with a focus on the Spirit's outcomes.

In other words, Jesus engaged in certain practices, and he built the rhythms of his life around these practices. He engaged in solitude by seeking retreat in creation. He rose early to be alone with his Father in prayer to be reminded of his identity. He immersed his mind in the Scriptures to remember the story he alone could fulfill. He engaged in multiple levels of community on mission that provided the support and accountability he needed. He lived to bless others by listening to them, eating with them, serving them, and teaching them. Jesus practiced the habit of work and rest.

Jesus' practices became his habits that fueled the rhythms of his days, weeks, and years. If Jesus felt like he needed to lead a habit-fueled life and he was the Son of God, how about us?

Examples of IDEs

Developing these practices is awkward at first, like learning to ride a bike. We are wobbly and inconsistent. It takes training wheels (time, supportive folks to help hold us up, and practice) for these to become life-giving habits. As with any apprenticeship, you can't learn all the practices at once, as they build on each other. Therefore, we have created four IDEs that vary in length from three months to twelve months to allow for this kind of incremental development. This slow play also allows for these to truly become engrained, lifelong habits. People join a guided cohort of about twelve folks plus a guide. There is a weekly huddle, supported by the daily online engagement. Here's a quick summary:

> *Followers Made*: A six-month experience to discover character and calling, equipping you to be a disciple and make disciples.
> *Leaders Made*: A ten-month experience to discover servant leadership and what it means to lead a community on mission.
> *Missionaries Made*: A three-month experience to develop a lifestyle around

five incarnational rhythms that equip you to live as a missionary where you live, work, study, shop, and play.

The Microchurch Learning Community: A twelve-month experience that equips you step-by-step in planting a simple form of church—an extended spiritual family living on mission together—where you live, work, study, or play.

Along the way, participants learn to practice a given set of habits in community. They are equipped to empower others to do the same. We keep the bar high. People in our IDEs evaluate themselves on the level of transformation they are experiencing in their character, their calling, and the habits associated with each.

There's even a dashboard inside a web app, along with all the tools they need to practice the spiritual habits. Each member of that disciple-making community has access to an online portal where all the resources—the Bible, a journal, the huddle guides with the H2O focus for the week, equipping videos, and more—are seamlessly integrated. They can also see how others are doing and practice community by commenting, discussing topics, logging prayers, and more.

As people build trust within the cohort, they can make their dashboard and journals public to others in the group, which engenders support, encouragement, and accountability. If we truly want to empower others, then we will embrace the parallel values of accountability and support. Through the Disciples Made training, we've seen what started with a handful of folks, mostly the unengaged middle, become an MDM of thousands of transformed, reproducing disciples.

Earlier in this book, we mentioned the rapid rate of multiplication in microchurches this last year in the KC Underground. We didn't organize these microchurches on the backside of weekend services at a large church. These were folks commissioned as missionaries to make new disciples in new contexts. Those loving missionaries saw new disciples emerge in new contexts and formed new extended spiritual families. If you've ever attempted this way of life, you know it is costly and not for the faint of heart. As we have reflected on such an encouraging level of multiplication of disciples and microchurches this year, we attribute it to three things: extraordinary prayer and fasting, an increased focus on how to hear the voice of God, and participation in one or more of the four IDEs just listed. They are learning the ways of Jesus in community on mission with a focus on the Spirit's outcomes.

Alan Hirsch: The aim in developing communities of practice is to embed discipleship practices into the rhythms and life of the entire community. To distill one's own version of practices, leaders can follow this process: (1) identify core values that are passionately believed in, (2) ask what would this value look like if it was embedded in an observable practice, (3) brainstorm many possible practices for the core value, (4) choose a practice that can be experienced as broadly as possible in all of life (in other words, not just a churchy activity), (5) develop a memorable acronym, and (6) bake the practice into the culture of the church—expect conformity to it to some degree.

Spiritual Habits of the Kansas City Underground Church

Through IDEs, equipping gatherings, and participation in the life of a microchurch, disciples learn to integrate these spiritual habits into everyday life.

- **Daily Scripture engagement**, with a bias toward self-discovery, immediate application, and sharing with others. We use a method called Discovery Bible Study.
- **A daily combination of two forms of prayer, contemplative prayer and missional prayer.** Contemplative prayer emphasizes listening and silence. Missional prayer is praying for and with others.
- **Healthy accountability with a triad and a group of twelve trusted companions.**
- **Active service** where you live, work, learn, play, or among a specific people group.
- **Journaling.**
- **Sabbath** (planning for daily, weekly, and annual work and rest rhythms).
- **Gospel fluency**, learning to speak and apply the gospel to the deepest needs in ourselves and others.
- **Relational rhythms in all five social spaces** (crowds, social, personal, intimate, and divine).
- **Calling discovery and optimization** through calling assessment and feedback (GPS).

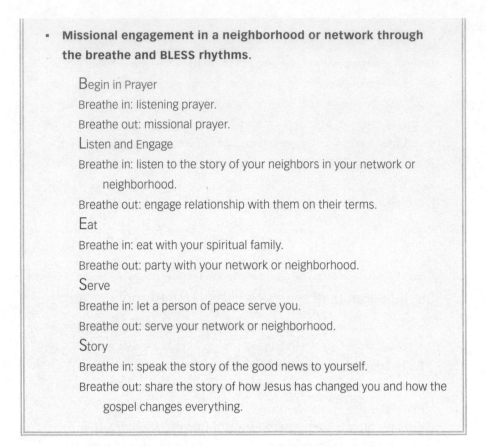

- **Missional engagement in a neighborhood or network through the breathe and BLESS rhythms.**

  Begin in Prayer
  Breathe in: listening prayer.
  Breathe out: missional prayer.
  Listen and Engage
  Breathe in: listen to the story of your neighbors in your network or
      neighborhood.
  Breathe out: engage relationship with them on their terms.
  Eat
  Breathe in: eat with your spiritual family.
  Breathe out: party with your network or neighborhood.
  Serve
  Breathe in: let a person of peace serve you.
  Breathe out: serve your network or neighborhood.
  Story
  Breathe in: speak the story of the good news to yourself.
  Breathe out: share the story of how Jesus has changed you and how the
      gospel changes everything.

Throughout the history of the church, there have been a myriad of intentional communities. For example, John and Charles Wesley were pioneers in the eighteenth century with their *classes*. These were close-knit gatherings of around a dozen men and women who came together weekly for personal spiritual recalibration and growth. Within the classes, there were bands, which were groupings of three to four gender-specific groups, where support and accountability went deeper. Our IDEs are yet another embodiment of this relational way of disciple-making, which are designed after the example of Jesus.

We share these IDEs as an example and embodiment of the things we teach. Each of these experiences blends all five ingredients of the disciple-making ingredients starfish into a relational environment for the purpose of disciple-making. As you discover all these essential ingredients, we hope you will be inspired and equipped to adapt and inform your current efforts and environments to become IDEs. Or you may be led to create new IDEs altogether.

Intentional communities are those that intentionally *practice* the faith. These groups agree on practices or habits that better equip the members to shine in the world around them and to "gospel" the community they live in. Like a salsa dance, these aren't linear steps. They do not bow to hard-and-fast rules. These moves dance to a rhythm that provides a bit of order and direction for living, while allowing for improvisation. To fixate into rigid rules would be to degenerate into dead religious policies of duty.

The most successful intentional communities are ones that commit to a set of soul-feeding and practical missional habits. This is a way for each member to live out the apostolic commandment to "*provoke* one another to love and good works" (Heb. 10:24 WEB, emphasis ours).

We ask you, as a missional leader, to pause and consider these habit-fueled questions:

- Do we help disciples develop personally meaningful spiritual habits?
- Do we help disciples develop sacred rhythms that feed their minds, bodies, and souls?
- Do we help disciples connect the practice of their habits to the Spirit's outcomes?
- Do we create relational environments and mentoring relationships that allow people to apprentice themselves to others as they learn spiritual practices?
- If so, how effective are they? What degree of transformation and multiplication do we see?
- Pray and ask the Spirit to help you identify one next step.
- Write an "I will . . ." statement to summarize that step.
- Whom will you share your "I will . . ." statement with?

CHAPTER 12

Community Forged

Disciple-Making Ingredient #3

Figure 12.1

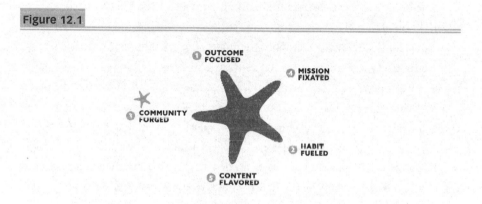

Starfish #5: The Disciple-Making Ingredients Starfish

Purpose: The disciple-making ingredients starfish helps us discover the five essential ingredients required for creating intentional disciple-making environments (IDEs) that are transformative and multiplicative.

Thus far, we've said if we desire to see the vision of the movement starfish released, that begins with transformed disciples who multiply. Every missional movement always begins and ends with disciple-making under the lordship of Jesus. For that to happen, an intentional environment with the right ingredients must be in place. Consider that all greenhouses rely on five key ingredients for flourishing plant multiplication: heat, air, water, light, and soil. Similarly, intentional disciple-making environments, which are greenhouses for disciples, contain five key ingredients.

Ingredient #1 was a focus on the Spirit's outcomes, through transformation of our character and deployment into our personal calling. The venerable Jewish rabbi Abraham Joshua Heschel said, "The higher goal of spiritual living is not to amass a wealth of information, but to face sacred moments."[1]

Ingredient #2 was to arrange our lives around spiritual habits that fuel the flow of God's transforming grace in us. He works in us, and we work out through spiritual habits. Through spiritual habits we learn to abide with Jesus, which leads to the Spirit's outcomes. We call this H2O, habits to outcomes.

Underneath all disciple-making, enabling the Spirit's outcomes and empowering the spiritual habits, is the gospel, the irreducible content of our faith: Jesus is Lord. Ingredient #5, being content flavored, means that the gospel must flavor and inform every area of our life and discipleship. More on that later.

The impact of those three ingredients, however, can't be fully realized without the addition of the other two ingredients: community forged and mission fixated.

Consider the following metaphor to understand why these are so essential.

Community and mission are the container in which outcome-focused, habit-fueled, and content-flavored living must be held for transformation to take place. The first three are like water, and the other two like a bowl. You can pour out those three, but without the bowl of community on mission to catch it, the water simply spills, and our thirst is never quenched. The container of community on mission catches what is being poured out so it can be truly caught and then ingested. Only then will our thirsty souls be filled. Spiritually transformed, multiplying disciples are forged in community that is fixated on mission.

This unique combination of mission and community is what Alan refers to as *communitas*. It is "the kind of community that is able to integrate adventure and movement, a community that experiences a *togetherness* that happens only among people inspired by the vision of a better world and attempting to do something about it. The name we gave to the communal phenomenon that forms in adventurous mission and liminal discipleship is *communitas*."[2]

The fire, trial, sacrifice, and adrenaline rush of mission fundamentally restructures the nature of preexisting relationships.

Friendships emerge from mere associations, and *comradeship* evolves from preexisting friendships. Being immersed in a communitas, participants experience an almost mystical *togetherness* that occurs only among a group of people engaging in a task bigger than itself. A different genre of love emerges . . .

The bonding is deep; people get to *need* each other, they get to know and rely on each other . . . to overcome the liminal challenge in whatever form it is experienced. . . .

We cannot shake the impression that the church Jesus built was meant to experience this form of togetherness . . . and lots of it. . . . Mission propels us out of self-concern to other-concern, from holy huddle to venturing out into God's world. And mission, encapsulating as it does the purpose of the church, has always been vital to the equation of ecclesia that Jesus intended in the first place—it goes to the reason of why we exist at all![3]

No one becomes a transformed, multiplying disciple apart from communitas.

Alan Hirsch: I remember talking about the need for innovation at a gathering of denominational leaders. At the end of the talk, two or three of these leaders literally cornered me and stood over me, saying, "Alan, you're saying that we can all be innovative, but we can't all be innovators, can we?" Their body language indicated that they wanted me to say, "No, of course not. We can't all be innovators." Instead, I said, "We can't all be innovators—*unless* our lives depend on it. If our lives depend on it, I suggest we all can be very innovative indeed." My point was taken, and they backed off.

Healthy communitas will function as an extended family on mission, where one can be apprenticed and also apprentice others. Discipleship is best seen as an apprenticeship to Jesus. Others also mediate this apprenticeship, as in Paul with Timothy and Timothy with other reliable people whom he apprenticed. Fundamentally, an apprenticeship is a journey toward mastery in a given area. In Jesus, we are being apprenticed into the fully alive life (John 10:10).

You don't want to apprentice yourself to me (Rob) on anything having to do with mechanics. Want to learn how to fix a carburetor? Watch YouTube; don't ask me! If you ask me about a carburetor, I'll reply, "Is that near the flux capacitor?" If you explored my garage, you would find a handful of tools, all of which were given to me by my thoughtful brother-in-law. However, I do know a couple of guys who can fix anything mechanical, top to bottom. Their garages? It's like an episode of Fast N' Loud or Counting Cars. Want to fix a car? Apprentice yourself to them.

As with any other pursuit, transformation is an apprenticeship that requires us to come alongside someone who is further down the road, and we do the same for another. First we imitate them as they practice the craft in front of us. Paul said, "Follow my example, as I follow the example of Christ Jesus" (1 Cor. 11:1).

As disciples, we are willing to be a beginner again and again as we discover more areas needing transformation in our lives. We are always students who need teachers. We are always players who need coaches. Communitas, an extended spiritual family on mission, provides a relational network broad enough and deep enough to help me find teachers in the areas in which I need apprenticeship. Information is not enough. We must see it embodied, and then we can imitate.

Then we do the same for others. As we move forward, we are also always teachers who need students, coaches who need players. Again, others' transformation requires imitation, which requires relationship with me in a given area. Actually, it requires a whole framework of relationships made up of interwoven relational connections. One-on-one discipleship is not enough. No one person can model all the needed areas of growth for me. Disciple-making is a team sport.

If you were able to clear all the surface dirt away in your local forest, you would discover the wood wide web. Beneath the surface of the forest, the trees aren't in competition; they are interconnected, their roots intertwining into a network. Believe it or not, the trees communicate and share information through this network. They even eat together by sharing nutrients. Large trees like redwoods have shallow root systems. Storms with heavy winds could easily bring these giants crashing to the ground. Yet it rarely happens because redwoods grow in clusters. They grow together, their roots intertwining, providing support for one another against the storms. They stand and grow together. We are all too shallow to grow alone. Transformation is forged in communitas.

The key words that describe most relationships in our culture are *scattered*, *busy*, and *temporary*. We attempt to navigate our relationships in many different networks (our neighborhood circle, our workplace circle, our church circle, our school circle, our hobbies circle, our friends circle, and the list goes on); we just can't keep all the plates spinning! In the end, our relational world feels wobbly and thin. At best we have just enough bandwidth to exist in each of these different contexts. At worst we're frustrated, burned out, and exhausted.

Intentional disciple-making environments will equip people over time to first order their relational world in a particular pattern and, secondly, to do so within the context of mission, mostly in one relational network.

To describe this way of ordering our relational world, we will cross over into a field of study called proxemics. Proxemics is the study of human spatial requirements and the effects that density has on behavior, communication, and social interaction. This field sets on the foundation laid by the pioneering work of sociologist Edward Hall, encapsulated in his opus, *The Hidden Dimension*. Later, author Joseph Myers applied and expanded this thinking to the process of belonging, in *The Search to Belong*. Bobby Harrington and Alex Absalom, in *Discipleship that Fits*, bring additional clarity on faith integration in each relationship sphere.

Harrington and Absalom, building on the work of Hall and Myers, suggest that there are five social spaces required for human flourishing and spiritual transformation. You can see the summaries in table 12.1.

Table 12.1

CONTEXT	SIZE	FOCUS	DISTANCE
Public	100s	Engaging with an outside resource	12'+
Social	20–70	Sharing snapshots that build affinity	4'–12'
Personal	4–12	Revealing private information	18"–4'
Transparent	2–4	Living in vulnerability and openness	0"–18"
Divine	Alone with God	Being with your Creator and Redeemer	Inner world

These five social contexts comprise the levels of communitas that forge disciples. Each of these social contexts has a different type of focus and benefit. Each social context is necessary in the spiritual development of an individual disciple, as well as an extended spiritual family.

Here is something that is fascinating: Jesus perfectly models nesting these five *overlapping* social contexts, one within the other, like those Russian nesting dolls. Jesus interacts with different sized groups of people at different times, for different purposes, and to different depths. Notice the circles of Jesus' relational world. He announced and demonstrated the presence of the kingdom of God with the *crowds* through his teaching, healing, and compassion.[4] We see *seventy-two* people following Jesus, attending parties, weddings, and other social events. Eventually, he sent the seventy-two out together on mission.[5] Jesus also called *twelve*, and they followed him around daily.[6] Out of these twelve, Jesus had *three* he was closest to: Peter, James, and John.[7] Of course, at the very

Figure 12.2

center of Jesus' relational world was his Father. Jesus said, "I and the Father are one" (John 10:30) and "The Son . . . can do only what he sees his Father doing" (John 5:19). No relationship mattered more to him.

In the *divine space* with his Father, Jesus found his identity and destiny, sharing everything. In the *transparent space* with the three, they shared deep vulnerability, openness, and intimacy. In the *personal space* with the Twelve, his team, they didn't have the same depth of openness as in the transparent space, but private information was shared inside the support, challenge, and closeness of that group. The seventy-two were his tribe in the *social space*, a bigger extension of this extended family on mission. The crowds, or *public space*, were where Jesus' tribe, twelve, and three all nested inside one another, living on mission and sharing experiences and resources, from meals and miracles to information and inspiration with hundreds and even thousands.

Consider the following observations about this multilayered understanding of disciple-making communitas.

We Need All Five Social Contexts

Every disciple needs all five spaces because each is conducive to nourishing a certain aspect of flourishing and multiplying disciples. The full flourishing effect of communitas is realized when all five social contexts are normative. We must engage all these social contexts as disciple-makers. Furthermore, if you consider any successful enterprise, they organize around these social spaces. For example, a football game contains all four "human" social spaces: the crowd in the stands, the entire team (the seventy-two), the players on the field (the Twelve), and the coaches (the three). Once you notice this pattern, you will discover it everywhere around you—in the marketplace, the military, in education, and in every successful human endeavor.

Alan Hirsch: I currently live and serve church planters in New York City. It has been wisely noted that NYC, and particularly Manhattan, is a church planters' graveyard. It is tough going, partly because of the cultural resistance to the gospel but also because the city is inordinately expensive, and renting space to hold services is therefore difficult. Part of the problem is that most church planters, assuming the model used in more churched America, think they have to plant a worship service (public space) rather than leveraging the other social spaces effectively. But I am convinced that the idea of using the five social contexts, and especially majoring on the social space (what I call the party level), is a significant key to evangelizing NYC—as well as your city.

The More We Can Overlap the Circles, the Better

The more we can overlap the circles, the more cohesive and powerful our experience of communitas will be. If we try to develop our *personal space* (4–12) in one relational network and our *social space* (20–72) in another, we'll quickly find our relational world stretched too thin. As with a Russian nesting doll, each of these relational spaces nests inside the other. The more these overlap and nest inside one another—within in one mission context, within one extended spiritual family—the more depth, meaning, and transformation we will experience. This is the way Jesus did it. Do we think we can improve on his example? As discussed early in the book, the early church continued in this pattern that Jesus modeled for them: "Every day they continued to meet together in the temple courts. They broke bread in their homes and ate together with glad and sincere hearts, praising God and enjoying the favor of all the people" (Acts 2:46–47).

We Must Intentionally Develop Diversity in Our Relational World

Within the four human social contexts, Jesus had connections with people at all levels of spiritual interest, with various worldviews, and with different lifestyles. He invited everyone to experience life within the kingdom. Even among his Twelve, Jesus had a surprising range of people, from fishermen to a tax collector to a political zealot. Think spicy curry, not plain vanilla. He invited people to belong long before they believed the same things as him.

The Closer to the Center, the More Important It Is to Have Shared Mission and Values

We find that the closer people moved toward the center circles of Jesus' world, the more they shared an increasing alignment with his mission and values. Jesus was selective, particularly about the Twelve and three. The Twelve and the three demonstrated a willingness to drop everything and learn the way of Jesus. Like us, they were a jumble of beliefs, ideas, personal histories, and bad habits. Even so, they knowingly pointed their feet toward Jesus and intentionally followed him in all of life. As we develop our personal and intimate relationships, issues like shared values, shared mission, confidentiality, communication, trust, and expectations become increasingly important to clarify. We usually become like the people we share the deepest bonds with.

In the KC Underground, the overlapping, nested development of all five relational spaces happens in a gradual process as people move through the different IDEs we described earlier. We come alongside our missionaries to help them rethink and then rebuild their relational circles in one particular neighborhood or network, the one to which they have the greatest sense of mission and presence. That is the context in which they own the faith and share their faith with others. Typically we find that forming this kind of multilayered communitas in one mission context, even when one is intentional, can take six to twenty-four months to emerge. Once it is formed, this is one of the most countercultural ways to live in America and, perhaps, the greatest apologetic for the gospel. The gospel presence of an extended spiritual family on mission is, in the authors' opinion, the most compelling witness to be offered to our current culture.

Our family (Rob and Michelle) has seen this develop in our neighborhood, but it was a slow process. We lived as missionaries for twelve months, slowly seeing neighbors who were strangers become acquaintances, and those acquaintances eventually becoming friends. About eighteen months in, one of our neighbors gave her life to Christ, which set off a spiritual chain reaction in our neighborhood. Over a couple of years, we have intentionally overlapped and nested our relational spaces in this context. Now we have an extended spiritual family living on mission together.

We can't imagine a better way to live or a more compelling witness.

Labor Day is party day in our neighborhood. Last year two new neighbors, a young couple who had moved in the month before, were invited to the festivities by Lori. Lori lives directly across the street from them. She was the first neighbor who opened her soul to us and Jesus.

The party was nothing fancy, just BBQ (it's Kansas City!), a potluck, a Spotify playlist, and conversation. Our microchurch, made up mostly of people in our neighborhood, was behind the party coming together. Over time that extended spiritual family has transformed the culture of our neighborhood.

The new young couple, Mikaela and Tyler, lingered until every other person had left. We loaded them down with a bunch of leftovers. Right before they exited, Mikaela paused and remarked, "I've got to say something. You know how you hear about the forties and fifties in America, where neighborhoods functioned like big families, where everybody knew each other, raised their families together, had an open-door policy? We feel like we climbed into a time machine and moved into one of those neighborhoods! Was it like this when you moved in?"

I explained somewhat sheepishly, "Not really. When we moved in, community was basically the 'courtesy wave' as you pulled into your driveway." She asked, "What happened?" I responded, "Well there's a group of us here now that value our neighborhood deeply. Here's why. When Jesus said, 'Love your neighbor,' we think he meant your actual neighbors."

Mikaela laughed out loud, "I get it! Like, it's not just a metaphor. You're supposed to love the people you actually live by, not just some metaphorical neighbor." I chuckled and responded, "Some of us here are very committed to treating each other like family because we believe Jesus calls all of us to be brothers and sisters. We've been doing that for a few years, and it has really changed the culture of our neighborhood."

She smiled and said, "That is so cool. When's the next party?"

A little over a year and a half later, Tyler and Mikaela have now opened their home to host neighborhood parties and Discovery Bible Studies. Over time, gradually, via many dinners and parties, the conversations became profoundly spiritual. After a Chiefs NFL playoff game party, as the conversation overtook the viewing of the game, Mikaela said point-blank, "I want a relationship with God like you two have." That was a turning point. Mikaela and Tyler have been growing as disciples of Jesus in amazing ways, including their friends and family in the life of our microchurch. They are now owners of their faith and cocreators of our communitas. In fact, as I write this, we are but a few hours from our microchurch gathering. Guess who is leading the gathering. Mikaela.

Through intentional living, these different social contexts now overlap in our neighborhood. At the heart of it is a vibrant microchurch on mission together. Through the KC Underground, we are equipping others around the city to do the same. We are a family of extended spiritual families. I could tell you similar stories where these spiritual extended families are emerging in other networks and neighborhoods, from Kansas rodeo riders to Algerian refugees.

Now more than ever, people long for this. The convergence of technology and the breakdown of the family have created an unparalleled need for communitas, perhaps like never before. George Friedman, who is considered one of the most accurate geopolitical forecasters and futurists of his generation, describes in his latest book, *The Storm Before the Calm*, the current crisis of community and the massive backlash he sees coming.

> Social media . . . is a place of anonymity where you can reinvent yourself many times. It is a place where you can be heard but not known. And this is its mortal problem. In the end, for all of the distance the microchip has made possible, human beings must know whom they are speaking to. This is not a very profound truth, but it is the truth that the believers in social media have missed. . . . Today, when you walk into a bar, there are no debates or seductions under way. Men and women sit looking at their phones.
>
> But here there is an oddity. Television absorbed you. The cell phone connects you. Granted it is a strange and unprecedented way, as the rise of texting has superseded the prime purpose of the phone—a conversation hearing another person's voice. But as distorted as the connection might be, the phone, and its obsessive use, speak to the craving we have for other people. It is a caricature of human relationships, but a hunger for them as well. . . .
>
> It has become so thin in its efficiency that it cannot sustain the emotional needs of a human life. What will actually happen is the transcendence of the microchip culture and an aggressive reassertion of community, not perhaps with the old rituals, but with a culture that has at its center the avoidance of loneliness. The self-imposed loneliness of the microchip cannot sustain itself in human relations. It imposes rituals as all things human do. But they are rituals that may be addictive but can't be satisfying. In this, there will inevitably be a return to the past. Or more precisely, moving the computer into its limited place re-creates the past. . . .
>
> The children of what are called millennials will be the ones who revolt against the previous generations' rootlessness. They will be the ones who find computers and the Internet old-fashioned and creating powerful family ties modern.[8]

He goes on to explain in the book that there will be a massive rise in the longing for new families, an insistence on being "rooted." They will look for what he calls "ritualized relationships" that create an "element of predictability in people's lives."[9]

These rituals will form "traditions [that] . . . reach back to the past. It is also in the nature of those honoring traditions to want to universalize their principles and rituals, first through persuasion and then through law. In other words, the new rituals, to some extent mimicking the old."[10]

There is a growing pent of demand, of historical proportions, for the exact type of community that we have described as a critical ingredient in disciple-making. Just as Jesus promised, our greatest apologetic—as the cultural groundswell rises over the coming decades—will be communitas, extended spiritual family on mission. For he said, "By this everyone will know that you are my disciples, if you love one another" (John 13:35), and Jesus is always right.

Alan Hirsch: The great missiologist Lesslie Newbigin once pondered on what was the best way to make the gospel credible. He concluded that the key factor is that of the Christian congregation. He suggested "that the only hermeneutic of the gospel is a congregation of men and women who believe it and live by it. I am, of course, not denying the importance of the many activities by which we seek to challenge public life with the gospel. . . . But I am saying that these are all secondary, and that they have power to accomplish their purpose only as they are rooted in and lead back to a believing community."[11]

As a church leader, pause to consider the following community forged questions:

- How well do disciples in our context understand and engage all five spheres of community required for flourishing?
- Do we equip people to overlap and nest these social spaces within the context of mission?
- How well do we move people out of the privatized individualism trend into deep, meaningful extended spiritual families on mission?
- Pray and ask the Spirit to help you identify one next step.
- Write an "I will . . ." statement to summarize that step.
- Whom will you share your "I will . . ." statement with?

CHAPTER 13

Mission Fixated

Disciple-Making Ingredient #4

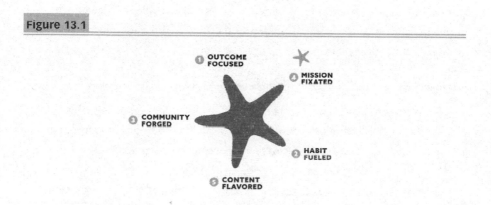

Starfish #5: The Disciple-Making Ingredients Starfish

Purpose: The disciple-making ingredients starfish helps us discover the five essential ingredients required for creating intentional disciple-making environments (IDEs) that are transformative and multiplicative.

"As the Father has sent me, I am sending you." (John 20:21; cf. 5:36–37; 6:44; 8:16–18; 17:18)

Flung and Plunged

The people who have been captivated by the vision of the movement starfish are people who understand at the most fundamental level that we are a *sent* people.

This sending impulse originates in the very heart of God, thrusting us outward with each pulsing heartbeat into lostness and into the margins, where brokenness and alienation abound.

Jesus, leaving heaven, plunged himself fully into the soil of the lost and least.

Every disciple must take the same plunge.

Jesus broadcasted that being in the kingdom is like a seed being sown. Indeed, the Spirit is casting his people out on mission.

Every disciple must be flung.

IDEs must be mission fixated: mission is the context for disciple-making.

Mission is the natural habitat for a disciple. If you pull a starfish from its natural habitat, eventually it will begin to die, slowly harden, and at best become a souvenir. At that point the starfish is a mere token to place on the shelf as a reminder of what it once was—alive and reproducing. Outside of mission, disciples harden and become souvenirs sitting in services and small groups, at best dim reminders of what they were meant to be—agents of mission and healing.

> **Alan Hirsch:** In a remark ascribed to Gordon Cosby, the pioneering leader of the remarkable community Church of the Saviour in Washington, DC, he noted that in over sixty years of ministry, he had observed that no groups that came together around a nonmissional purpose (e.g., prayer, worship, study, etc.) ever ended up becoming missional. Only groups that set out to be missional (while embracing prayer, worship, study, etc. in the process) actually got around to doing it. If evangelizing and discipling the nations lie at the heart of the church's purpose, then mission, not ministry, is the true organizing principle of the church. Experience tells us that a church that aims at ministry seldom gets to mission, even if it sincerely intends to do so. The church that aims at mission will have to do ministry, because ministry is the means to mission.

Missional (Flung)

On the centrality of mission, Alan states, "The church's true and authentic organizing principle is mission. When the church is in mission, it is the true church. The church itself is not only a product of that mission but is obligated and destined to extend it by whatever means possible. The mission of God flows directly through every believer and every community of faith that adheres to Jesus. To obstruct this is to block God's purposes in and through his people."[1]

Therefore, the degree to which they are fixated on mission is the degree to which effective disciple-making happens. It is a necessary ingredient for intentional disciple-making.

Yet many of God's people, and those who lead them, see mission as an extra activity added on to the programs of the organized church. One can volunteer at the soup kitchen or do a light construction project in a foreign locale once a year. Although intentions are good, this definition of mission as an occasional activity, usually known as missions, subliminally defines mission as a specialization reserved for professionals and, of course, the occasional volunteer. This mindset disempowers millions of ordinary folks and keeps people from seeing that they have been flung and plunged already, where they live, work, learn, and play. The Spirit is prodding his people to awaken to mission in their everyday life.

Mission reaches down to our deepest understandings of who God is, why we are here, and how we are to live. Mission is not an add-on. Mission is not a department. Mission isn't something we volunteer for a few hours a month. Mission is not something reserved for the elite or the paid professionals. Mission is the sweeping force that runs through everything we are and do.

Ultimately, mission is not first about activity. Mission is first about identity: God's identity and ours, as his offspring. Mission starts by understanding that we serve a God who is a missionary. By his very nature, our God is a *sent one* who left his throne on mission to redeem humankind and all of creation through Jesus. It's this simple: The Father sent Israel. The Father sent the Son. The Father, Son, and Spirit are sending the church. If God is a missionary God, then as his offspring, we are a missionary people.

Furthermore, mission is not something outside of God. Mission is woven into his very nature. Mission is the heartbeat of God. This is the reason God left his throne on mission. This heartbeat-mission is what drives all redemptive history.

The New Testament describes the heart of God this way in 2 Peter 3:9: "The Lord is not slow in keeping his promise, as some understand slowness. Instead he is patient with you, not wanting anyone to perish, but everyone to come to repentance."

That's God's heart, that none should perish. That phrase pounds like a repeating heartbeat at the center of God's being. That's his heart for you and for every single person you will see today. The pulse pushes and even flings us *outward* toward those who don't yet know how much they matter to Jesus.

Incarnational (Plunged)

At a time when alienation from God dominated human history, through the covenant with Abraham and later with Israel, the Father *himself* came to humanity. Perhaps the most remarkable aspect of Yahweh's covenant with Israel was the gift of his presence. "I am going to come to you" (Ex. 19:9). God sent himself. This *downward* impulse is the essence of what it means to be incarnational.

Leading Exodus scholar John I. Durham sees this gracious act of coming down as the most important event not only in Exodus but arguably the whole Old Testament. He proclaims, "The Sinai narrative has been determined by a single factor . . . the gift of Yahweh of his presence to Israel."[2]

Of course, we Christians believe Jesus is the fullest expression of the incarnational missionary presence.

> The Word became flesh and blood,
>> and moved into the neighborhood. (John 1:14 MSG)

Jesus didn't send us an email offering us salvation. He didn't volunteer for an hour and head back to heaven. He moved into the neighborhood. He became one of us, lived with us, loved us, served us, suffered with us, and died for us to redeem us.

Jesus paints a sevenfold image of his mission when he quotes the prophet Isaiah,

> The Spirit of the Lord is on me,
>> because he has anointed me
>> to proclaim good news to the poor.
> He has sent me to proclaim freedom for the prisoners
>> and recovery of sight for the blind,
> to set the oppressed free,
>> to proclaim the year of the Lord's favor. (Luke 4:18–19)

We are invited to join him in that mission to bring this type of wholeness and healing to the earth, *through our presence.* The mission will always embody itself incarnationally within the everyday context of the disciple.

Mission is the "what," and incarnation is the "how."

Combine those and you have what Alan describes as the *mission-incarnational impulse*, one of the six essential mDNA of apostolic genius. "The missional-incarnational impulse is, in effect, the practical outworking of the mission of God (the *missio Dei*) *together with* the New Testament teaching of the incarnation of God in Jesus. It is thus rooted in the very way that God has redeemed the world and in how God revealed himself to us."[3]

A movement of "ordinary" disciples living out their missional-incarnational impulse in their everyday world in their city will be exponentially more powerful in making new disciples in new context than all the weekend services of all the churches in that city.

The same Spirit that raised Jesus from the dead, which toppled the hold of Satan in this world and shook the very foundations of history, resides in each one of us, waiting for us to be kindled to life. Dry bones rattle, stand, and are enfleshed when disciples become mission fixated and incarnationally activated.

Mission is not meant to be a category of activity that we try to fit into the discretional time slot in our lives as a "volunteer" who serves on the weekends or a "member who brings a friend to church." It is all of life. When volunteering or bringing a friend to a weekend service is the overflow of a mission-fixated, incarnational lifestyle, it's beautiful. When it is a substitute, we've settled for a domesticated version of Christianity that will never change the world.

One of the biggest challenges President Lincoln faced early in the war was his do-nothing generals. The first year on the battlefield was marked by inactivity and frustration. The Union generals refused to directly engage Confederate troops for various reasons—not enough training, not enough resources, too many enemy combatants, the terrain was disadvantageous, and the list went on. When George McClellan took over command in 1861, he was greeted as a savior, and Lincoln had high hopes. After the troops had suffered a humiliating and costly defeat at Bull Run, McClellan stepped in and seemed to understand the necessities of the new kind of war they were fighting. He trained and drilled the troops to no end, restoring the confidence of the troops in the process.[4]

But when the spring of 1862 came, Lincoln found himself once again in the same spot. McClellan would not lead the troops into battle. He was constantly preparing but never moving the troops into the battlefield. According to him, the troops were never quite ready. He refused to engage the fight.

In exasperation, Lincoln reportedly remarked, "If General McClellan doesn't want to use the army, I should like to borrow it." He had to repeatedly write and urge McClellan to move his army, which cost valuable time and allowed the enemy to effectively check McClellan's advances.[5]

Alan Hirsch: In 1519, with some six hundred men, sixteen or so horses, and eleven boats, Hernán Cortés landed on a vast inland plateau now called Mexico. They had come from Spain to the New World in search of some of the world's greatest treasure. But with only six hundred men with no protective armor, conquering an empire so extensive was a highly unlikely affair. Instead of charging through cities and forcing his men into immediate battle, Cortés stayed on the beach and awoke the souls of his men with emblazoned speeches ingeniously designed to urge on the spirit of adventure and invoke a thirst for lifetimes of fortune among his troops. His orations bore fruit, for what was supposedly a military exploit now took on an extravagant romance in the imaginations of the troops. Ironically, it wasn't the eloquent "preaching" that led to the ultimate victory of those adventurers; it was just three words that would change the history of the New World. As they marched inland to face their enemies, Cortés ordered, "Burn the boats!" They destroyed the boats, and thereby eradicated any possibility of retreat from the minds of the troops. They had to commit themselves unwaveringly to the cause—win or die. Retreat was no longer an option.

I wonder if God feels the same way about faith communities that have people constantly training and educating at services and in small groups but rarely engaging mission. The mission is what the training is for!

Mission and maturity go together when it comes to disciple-making. You can't have one without the other. Mature soldiers start with basic training, but real maturity is forged in the battlefield, while engaging mission. Mature soldiers are battle tested and battle hardened. Shared mission in the same context provides the proximity and pressure needed to make transformed owners of the faith. That's why we advocate so strongly for people to drill down deep and attempt to build all their social contexts in mostly one setting: live, work, learn, or play.

Just to be clear, you don't have to go somewhere else to find that context of mission. You already are in it. The mission of God isn't first about crossing oceans, jungles, and deserts; it's first about crossing the room, leaning over your fence, crossing the street, going beyond the cubicle wall at work, or perhaps crossing the gym where you work out in the morning. You can be on mission without leaving your zip code. Mission starts where you live, work, learn, and play. Yes, it also includes crossing ethnic, socioeconomic, geographic, and other cultural barriers that will take you to places you never imagined. But it starts where *God has already sent you.*

God is already on mission in that place every day. We must turn on the mission light by awakening people from an insular lifestyle that keeps us looking at our neighbors as strangers or keeps people so caught up in the ghetto of religious programs that they have no time to live with the people God has sent them to as agents of healing.

We accept that people often start with a lack of clarity on their primary place of sentness. They will need help discovering and clarifying their missional focus. Over time, through experiences like Followers Made and Missionaries Made and tools like The Missionary Pathway, a map that defines the various stages a gospel-planting, disciple-making missionary goes through, people can gradually refine and clarify their missional focus.

Occasionally, people will have an intuitive sense of awareness about where they have been sent on mission. But for most, as they walk through our various IDEs and other equipping experiences, they become increasingly focused on the Spirit's outcomes, practice the habits, move deeper into community, and gradually gain clarity on the context in which they are to be mission fixated. Over time, we continue to ratchet down until there are crystal-clear answers to these questions: To whom have you been sent? What is your calling?

Then, once you know the answers, go down. Go incarnational. Go deep. You can't be a good missionary in multiple contexts because the incarnational impulse pushes us to go deep, not wide.

Whom are you called to live with, love, serve, suffer with, and even, if need be, die for? God has already placed you in a network of people or a neighborhood. Just as Jesus was, we are called to be "one of" those whom we are sent to and get involved in a deep way. From involvement we move to identification. Whom does Jesus identify with in the following passage? "Then the King will say to those on his right, 'Come, you who are blessed by my Father, inherit the kingdom prepared for you from the foundation of the world. For I was hungry and you gave me food, I was thirsty and you gave me drink, I was a stranger and you welcomed me, I was naked and you clothed me, I was sick and you visited me, I was in prison and you came to me.'" (Matt. 25:34–36 ESV)

Jesus has identified so completely with the hungry and thirsty in the hood that when we help them, he says we are doing that for him. We are to identify with the people we are sent to. No matter what people group God sends us to, when we go out on mission, we'll find he's already out there on mission, helping his family, serving, living as "one of." That's where he expects to see us.

Joining God in his mission to redeem means continually asking this question: To whom have I been sent?

That's where simple training tools like the breathe and BLESS rhythms described earlier empower ordinary people to do everyday activities consistently with missional intentionality. Those small interventions inside a laser focus on one particular community over time equal a big impact. Our role as faith leaders is to help people discover their areas of passion and calling, then equip them to engage that part of God's mission.

Here are some questions for you to pause and consider:

- How well do we help each disciple discover that mission involves the everyday spaces where they live, work, learn, and play?
- Do we have a standard set of missionary rhythms we teach every disciple? If so, how effective are they?
- Do we have a framework for what the missionary journey looks like at various stages?
- How well do we help each disciple listen to the Spirit and discern their primary place of sentness?
- What resources, process, and tools do we provide to empower each person to own a missional focus, build a missional team, and innovate strategies on mission?
- Pray and ask the Spirit to help you identify one next step.
- Write an "I will . . ." statement to summarize that step.
- Whom will you share your "I will . . ." statement with?

CHAPTER 14

Content Flavored

Disciple-Making Ingredient #5

Figure 14.1

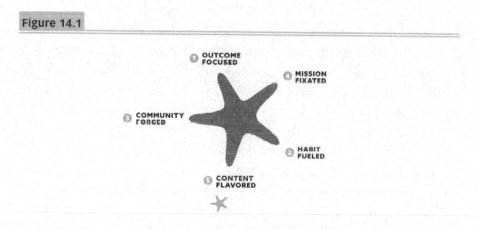

Starfish #5: The Disciple-Making Ingredients Starfish

Purpose: The disciple-making ingredients starfish helps us discover the five essential ingredients required for creating intentional disciple making environments (IDEs) that are transformative and multiplicative.

In the Western religious experience, content and doctrine are king. Much of what is labeled "discipleship," "confirmation," or "training" in the church is just a data dump. We are content focused, fueled, and fixated. The emphasis is on transferring content, with little concern for whether people are actually transformed or multiplying. Content-codependence is the diagnosis. Our addiction to "content" enables immaturity and underachievement in disciple-making.

Knowledge Is Not Enough

As church leaders, we know what it's like to slave over sermons, small group curriculum, classes, and the like, earnestly believing that if we can just get the *right content* into people, they will change. I've been there, thinking, "This weekend series is going to be a game changer. This forty-day church campaign is going to be a game changer...." ad nauseam.

This is simply not true.

The most content-focused, theologically trained people in Jesus' day were in fact his worst enemies. Many of the cruelest, most bigoted, and destructive people are those who are religious zealots, completely sold on the supremacy of their religious belief.

Alan Hirsch: When Jesus the eternal Word came into the world, we are told that "the world" did not even recognize him who was its creator. The world failed to recognize themselves in his dazzling light. But the darkness shows itself even more trenchant when we consider that it was the very people God had chosen and formed over centuries who also rejected him (John 1:10–11). They, of all people, should have been able to discern the form and pattern of Christ! Here lies a terrible paradox of human existence: "religion" in its purest and loftiest form is found to belong to the area of darkness. Not those who are blind, but those who confidently claim to see are found to be in the realm of darkness. The question is for us, we who likewise confidently claim to know the word of the Bible, do we really know and recognize Jesus, who is the Word of God? Honestly ask yourself, "What would happen if Jesus turned up to our church one day? Would he be celebrated or crucified?"

As members of Western civilization, we are all children of the Enlightenment. The Enlightenment championed the role of reason and vetoed engagement with emotion. Western Christianity has been primarily about ideas. As a result, theological correctness and content quantity have become the obsessions in discipleship.

Yet the Bible speaks clearly to our content obsession and the limits of knowledge:

For this reason I bow my knees before the Father, from whom every family in heaven and on earth is named, that according to the riches of his glory he may grant you to be strengthened with power through his Spirit in your inner being, so that Christ may dwell in your hearts through faith—that you, being rooted and grounded in love, that you, may have strength to comprehend with all the saints what is the breadth and length and height and depth, and to know the love of Christ that surpasses knowledge, that you may be filled with all the fullness of God. (Eph. 3:14–19 ESV)

The love of God, in which we are to be rooted—an agriculture metaphor inviting us to sink our roots deep and be grounded and an architectural metaphor declaring our mystical union with God's love as essential and foundational—actually "surpasses knowledge."

Knowledge alone can't get you there, and it will never be enough.

Being filled with all the fullness of God, which is at the heart of the movement starfish, surpasses knowledge. In other words, having your theological furniture correctly arranged in your head is not the ultimate focus of the disciple-making journey. Rather, the Spirit-empowered, mysterious process of being filled with all the fullness of God affects the totality of our existence—not just the way we think but the way in which we live and move and have our being (Acts 17:28).

We have saved this ingredient for last because for most disciple-making in the West, content focus has been first and last. That is why it has failed so colossally. If the transfer of knowledge could have gotten the job done, it would have done so a long time ago.

Without an outcome focus on Spirit-empowered transformation, without habits to fuel the abiding that produces those outcomes, without the proper community to forge these outcomes and habits, and without the context of mission and risk, religious experience simply degrades to a data dump of doctrine.

What role, then, does content play? How does the ingredient of content flavored come properly into the mix of transformative and multiplicative disciple-making in an IDE?

Means to an End

Consider this statement of Jesus: "You will know the truth, and the truth will set you free" (John 8:32). Jesus places an exceptionally high value on the truth. But the truth is a means to an end—not the end itself. The end, or the purpose, of truth is freedom.

Brennan Manning, author of *The Ragamuffin Gospel* and vagabond evangelist, was known for asking people point-blank in one-on-one conversation, "Are you a free person?" Most would respond, "What do mean by free?" His response: "A free person wouldn't need to ask that question."

As the Spirit's empowerment and outcomes remain the focus of our disciple-making efforts, fueled by habits forged in community within the context of mission, we will see *genuine freedom* grow in people, not simply an accumulation of religious knowledge.

That doesn't mean content doesn't matter. Quite the opposite; the truth must flavor all IDEs. The key is to discover and define the "faith fractal," then let that flavor every IDE we create.

Faith Fractal

A fractal is the simplest possible repeating pattern in any system. You might also call this your DNA, or the minimum arrangement of core elements necessary to consider "whatever you are" to be "you."

Shell: Jitze Couperus/flickr, CC BY 2.0; Pinecone: jiyuhan01120/pixabay.com, CC0; Aloe: visualsumo/pixabay.com, CC0; Leaf: i5a/flickr, CC BY 2.0

In nature, fractals are ubiquitous. Look at a shell, a pine cone, or a leaf! Many flowers, fruits, and vegetables grow by fractal patterns. Take a close look at a pineapple! Every snowflake and ice crystal are a repeating fractal. Fractals also show up in the veins in your body and river deltas. Mother Nature has been called a "hell of a good designer," and fractals are the design principle she follows to put her most beautiful work together.[1]

A fractal design is a simple, repeating pattern.

If we hold tightly to a very small set of core, or fractal, values and beliefs, we don't have to intensively manage the complicated manifestations or extensions of the entire faith system. All great starfish movements have the capability to boil down their ideology into a fractal, an irreducible minimum that is easy to reproduce.

In *The Starfish and The Spider*, Ori notes the following: "Ideology is the glue that holds decentralized organizations together."[2] Consider the following examples: "The Apaches held the common belief that they belonged on the land and deserved to be self-governing. . . . Without that ideology, the Apaches wouldn't have had the motivation to remain decentralized," while resisting the Spaniards, Mexicans and Americans.[3] In fact, the destruction of the Apache movement began when a few Apaches walked away from this ideology by accepting the invitation to become farmers, thus domesticating themselves into oppression.

In our time, consider the twelve-step ideology of AA that has helped free countless people from addictions. Without any hierarchy and without bosses, AA has spawned thousands of mutual aid fellowships of men and woman from all walks of life whose bond is the shared belief and shared work of the Twelve Traditions.[4] Any variation from these beliefs is considered the first step back into addiction. The bar is high: people start with ninety meetings in ninety days. Why? The ideology must be set deep in the mind and lifestyle for freedom to become a reality in one life and then spread virally to another.

Movements always have a fractal.

Alan Hirsch: This is true: movements are comprised of fractals. To be clear, a fractal is a natural phenomenon, or a mathematic set, that exhibits a repeating pattern that recurs at every scale. It is also known as expanding or evolving symmetry—in other words, it repeats itself throughout the system. For instance, APEST (the function of apostles, prophets, evangelists, shepherds, and teachers) is a fractal built into the very life of the church. So are "Jesus is

Lord" and discipleship. These recur in the smallest unit and ought to be evident in the largest scale. Finding and naming fractal-like ideas that can be repeated throughout are an important key to organizing like a movement.

What is the irreducible minimum faith fractal of your disciple-making?

The church has unbelievably complex theological frameworks that have developed over two thousand years, since the time of Christ, resulting in tens of thousands of denominations within Christianity. More than thirty-three thousand according to the World Christian Encyclopedia![5] Over time, the complexity (and division!) has increased dramatically.

Jesus and Fractals

Yet if we return to the example of our Founder, we find him moving in the opposite direction, taking complexity and making it profoundly simple.

Jesus took the complexity of the entire Law and the Prophets, twenty-six books of the Old Testament,[6] and simplified it down to a fractal of two elements: love God and love your neighbor as yourself (Matt. 22:37–39). This fractal design for the Law and the Prophets, provided by Jesus, is a simple, repeating pattern that even a child can remember. Yet despite its simplicity and scalability, it still serves as the top of a rabbit hole by which one can go down into the depths as needed as the disciple matures on their journey.

If this is Jesus' primary fractal for the Old Testament, what was his fractal for his own message and teaching? How might the entire New Testament be summarized? What did the faith fractal of the early church sound and look like? As Jesus organized his teaching, he did it all through one—count it, one—predominant theme. What is the fractal Jesus taught?

After John was put in prison, Jesus went into Galilee, proclaiming the good news of God. "The time has come," he said. "The kingdom of God has come near. Repent and believe the good news!" (Mark 1:14–15)

Jesus went throughout Galilee, teaching in their synagogues, proclaiming the good news of the kingdom, and healing every disease and sickness among the people. (Matt. 4:23)

Jesus went through all the towns and villages, teaching in their synagogues, proclaiming the good news of the kingdom and healing every disease and sickness. (Matt. 9:35)

Jesus traveled about from one town and village to another, proclaiming the good news of the kingdom of God. (Luke 8:1)

When Jesus had called the Twelve together . . . he sent them out to proclaim the kingdom of God. (Luke 9:1–2)

The Lord appointed seventy-two others and sent them two by two ahead of him to every town and place where he was about to go. . . . "When you enter a town . . . tell them, 'The kingdom of God has come near to you.'" (Luke 10:1, 8–9)

Throughout his life, Jesus had one center for all his teaching.

Jesus repeatedly links the phrase "good news" with the kingdom of God. When you read the one hundred–plus passages where Jesus refers to the kingdom of God, you will quickly perceive that the kingdom of God is not just another topic for Jesus. It is not merely a volume of one possible topic on his proverbial bookshelf, somewhere between *Forgiveness* and *Money*. The kingdom of God *is the bookshelf* that holds all the other volumes. The kingdom of God is Jesus' paradigm, or fractal.[7] It is his framework. All other topics are simply descriptions of how to live and operate inside the kingdom of God within that specific area.

After rising from the dead, Jesus had forty short days with his followers. Pause and ask yourself, "If I had one month to live, what would I want to communicate to the people I love?" Bets are that it would be the irreducible minimum of all that you held to be sacred and immutable. If you want to know what Jesus' irreducible core is, look at this passage: "He appeared to them over a period of forty days and spoke about the kingdom of God" (Acts 1:3).

Indeed, this was the message the early church carried to the world. The last glimpse we have of the early church in the last verse in the last chapter of the book of Acts says it all. Paul is under house arrest in Rome. The summation of the apostle's life and ministry reads simply: "For two whole years Paul stayed there in his own rented house and welcomed all who came to see him. Boldly and without hindrance he preached the kingdom of God and taught about the Lord Jesus Christ" (Acts 28:30–31 NIV 1984).

Paul goes on to describe the gospel fractal in Romans 1:1–4: "Paul, a servant of Christ Jesus, called to be an apostle and set apart for the gospel of God—the gospel he promised beforehand through his prophets in the Holy Scriptures regarding his Son, who as to his earthly life was a descendant of David, and who through the Spirit of holiness was appointed the Son of God in power by his resurrection from the dead: Jesus Christ our Lord."

Disciple-making is all about adherence to Jesus and his lordship. It is always articulated over against all other competing claims for our attention, affection, and allegiance. In the context of the early church, their allegiance to Jesus was set against the claims of the false religious systems of their day and the demand for complete loyalty to Caesar. It was the refusal to submit to the claim of "Caesar as Lord" that got them into trouble.[8]

For Paul and the early followers of Jesus, the fractal came down to two things: the proclamation "Jesus is Lord" and the proclamation of the kingdom of God, which are essentially the same message.

Again, of the six elements that are the genetic coding of church as apostolic movement described in *The Forgotten Ways*, the first and most important is this: Jesus is Lord. At the center of every significant Jesus movement there exists a simple confession—the claim of the one God over every aspect of every life—and the response of his people to that claim (Deut. 6:4–6). In the New Testament this was expressed simply "Jesus is Lord!" On this, Alan explains,

> Apostolic movements spread like viruses. They are in a real sense caught and passed on, and they do so in a viral, epidemical way. Apostolic movements that reach the power curve of exponential impact are in a real sense, pay-it-forward movements. They transfer ideas exponentially, and these ideas are profound enough to lodge themselves in people's minds and change the way they think and act. For an idea to be spreadable, it needs to be simple enough for the audience to understand it. But to take root and transform the audience, it needs to be complex enough to carry a load of meaning. The rallying cry, "Jesus is Lord," and the gospel itself carry both of these aspects within it.[9]

To be content flavored, every IDE must repeatedly bring disciples back to the gospel fractal "Jesus is Lord" by repeating again and again, "How does the gospel inform all of life?"

Jesus and the good news of the kingdom are, and always will be, the fractal of the Christian faith. As his disciples, we trust completely in his finished work on the cross. Salvation is a gift of grace, by faith. We embrace a three-word worldview: Jesus is Lord. He is Master of the art of living. He is right about everything. Our lifelong journey is to move from unbelief to belief in Jesus in every area of life.

The proclamation "Jesus is Lord" functions for the church as the Shema did for Israel. In Hebrew tradition, the Shema is considered the faith fractal. It is difficult to overestimate the importance of this most basic confession of Israel's faith. The Shema was the centerpiece of the morning and evening prayer of God's people. The Shema encapsulates the oneness and presence of God, along with an invitation to a loving relationship: "Hear, O Israel: The LORD our God, the LORD *is* one! You shall love the LORD your God with all your heart, with all your soul, and with all your strength" (Deut. 6:4–5 NKJV).

Alan Hirsch: As with the Israelites, the faithful church is called to reorder its entire life around a central confession that defines everything. Theologians call the religion of the Bible by the drab term "monotheism," but there is nothing boring about monotheism at all. It involves an all-encompassing claim that leaves no aspect of life untouched. There can be no Sunday-Monday, sacred-secular disconnect. All of life must be brought under the sovereign claims of the one Lord.

Each day, a faithful Israelite asked and prayed again and again, "How does the Shema inform all of life?"

In the opening speeches of Deuteronomy, the words *listen* and *love* are inextricably woven together. The invitation "Listen, O Israel" isn't about the propagation of sound or the ear drum's capacity to receive it. Rather, *listen* is a deeper invitation to let this faith fractal saturate one's entire life, to let it sink in, and then activate change. In the Hebrew, hearing and doing are also inextricably woven together. What is the response being called for? Love your God with all your heart, all your being, and all your might. Love, in the context of the Hebrew Scriptures, is not primarily a warm, fuzzy feeling. Love is about action, loyalty, and faithfulness.

"Jesus is Lord" is not an invitation to add another box to your life labeled "religion" that you place alongside all the other boxes in your life (work, family, recreation, finances, friendships, and others). Many people are exhausted with religion for this very reason. If we see faith as a compartmentalized box we add to our life, it becomes a burden instead of an engine of transformation and an energy source at the center of being.

Gospel Language in the KC Underground

In the KC Underground, we have developed our own gospel dialect with the hope of framing the gospel in a wholistic and yet portable way. We describe it as the shift from saved souls to saved wholes.

Saved Souls Gospel = The Plan of Salvation

The plan of salvation is usually about forgiveness of sin and a place in heaven when we die. That's not incorrect; it's just radically incomplete. The gospel is much bigger!

Saved Wholes Gospel = Jesus Is Lord!

The saved wholes gospel includes three dimensions: the whole story, the whole expression, and the whole life.

The whole story. Jesus is the center of the story of God and all of history. All of creation, the story of Israel, and the Law and the Prophets find their fulfillment in Jesus. Jesus is the full and complete revelation of God. Jesus is the ultimate example of a human being fully alive. At his return, Jesus will bring about the consummation of God's plan to heal and redeem the entire creation. Through his saving work on the cross, all are invited to join Jesus' family, not based on their merits but by God's grace.

The whole expression. The gospel announcement "Jesus is Lord" includes a gospel presence (missionaries and microchurches), a gospel proclamation (verbal), and a gospel demonstration (service and signs).

The whole life. The gospel announcement "Jesus is Lord" is a three-word worldview. Being a disciple means moving from unbelief to belief in Jesus in every area of life. Jesus' way is our way.

For most of us, life already feels like a juggling act. Guess what? The overall box of life never increases in size. We still have only twenty-four hours in a day. The idea of squeezing in another box will only make life busier and more complex. The problem is, too often, this is what most churches offer the unengaged middle: "Please add some 'religious activity' to your life."

The gospel provides us a new operating system, a whole new framework for every area of life. We let the gospel provide a new center for all of life. In this way, every area of life relates to our faith fractal rather than competes with it.

Gospel Language and Tools

Let's get practical. To effectively mix the content-flavored ingredient into an IDE, an apostolic leader's role will be twofold:

1. **Provide gospel language** to describe the gospel in a clear, faithful, simple, and reproducible way.
2. **Provide gospel tools** to help disciples integrate the gospel into all of life, rather than merely giving intellectual assent.

Hearing a church leader teach the gospel, although vital, is not enough. The gospel language and tools practically equip disciples to let the gospel flavor their hearts, minds, and souls, shaping the deepest level of convictions, those that energize their worldview, attitudes, and actions.

Gospel Tools in the KC Underground

Disciples need tools to apply the gospel to all of life. Here is a sampling of a couple of tools, but we have many more!

Bible engagement built on discovery and obedience. Discovery is about asking the Spirit to highlight areas of unbelief as a disciple engages a passage of Scripture. Disciples are taught to write an "I believe . . ." statement to summarize what it means to trust Jesus based on what they read. Disciples then write an "I will . . ." statement to summarize how they will act into that way of believing. Finally, disciples ask, "Whom can I share this with?" Gospel proclamation becomes a daily habit, community is forged, and reproduction and multiplication become normative.

Gospel fluency. We use the tools Tim Chester developed and Jeff Vanderstelt further expanded on in his book *Gospel Fluency*. These tools include The Four Gs and Fruit to Root, Root to Fruit. The Four Gs tool equips a disciple to let the gospel heal their image of God, connecting his character with their soul's deepest needs. The Fruit to Root tool equips a disciple to start with the bad fruit in their life (fear, anxiety, pride, deception, etc.) and follow it down the trunk to the root lies that have infected their identity and image of God. Then Root to Fruit walks one back up the tree, through a repentance of unbelief in various areas of life.

The gospel fruit we see in people's lives through these tools alone is transformative and multiplicative!

According to Catholic philosopher Michael Novak, there are three levels of convictions or beliefs: public, private, and core convictions. John Ortberg picks up on these in his book *Faith and Doubt*.[10]

Public convictions. These are beliefs we want others to think we hold, even though we may not believe them ourselves. For example, we may want people to believe we are well-read in the Scriptures, even though we read the Bible only occasionally. A biblical example would be King Herod. He said to the Magi, "Go and look carefully for the child. When you find him, inform me so that I can go and worship him as well" (Matt. 2:7–8 NET). Was that Herod's true purpose? It may be hard to believe, but politicians in the ancient world would say anything to curry public favor. We all practice this Herodlike behavior on occasion.

Private convictions. These are things I sincerely think I believe, but it turns out I don't actually believe them at the deepest level of my being. Peter proclaimed to Jesus that he would never deny him: "Even if all fall away, I will not" (Mark 14:29). In that moment, he was sincere and convinced he believed it, but he soon found out that his belief was fickle. He denied Christ three times that very night.

Core convictions. You could call this the "mental map." Every one of us has "mental maps" about the way we think things really are and the way life really works. We will always live out those beliefs. Our behavior reveals our core beliefs.

The goal is to see the gospel flavor and marinate our core convictions. We can be amazingly self-deluded on what we actually believe, truly thinking our private religious convictions are running the show when we have core convictions that are actually pagan.

Paul had a word for this that we don't use much in our day: depravity. This is why, in Romans 1:21, 28, Paul described our gunked-up mental maps this way: "Although they knew God, they neither glorified him as God nor gave thanks to him, but their thinking became futile and their foolish hearts were darkened. . . . Furthermore, just as they did not think it worthwhile to retain the knowledge of God, so God gave them over to a depraved mind."

For a short period, through willpower we may be able to stave off the behavioral outcome of a misplaced core conviction. But eventually, we will snap back to the old behavior that is in alignment with our incorrect core conviction. To change your mental map, you have to learn the gospel; that's where gospel language comes in. But that's just the beginning. Secondly, you have to act your way into this new way of thinking through gospel tools, regular habits, and risky mission in community, all focused on the Spirit's outcomes in character and calling.

Before we proceed, we ask you, as a missional leader, to please pause and consider these questions:

- How content-codependent are our disciple-making efforts?
- How clear, simple, faithful, and reproducible is our gospel language? Do we have a gospel lexicon?
- Do we have gospel tools? How effective are they in helping disciples move from unbelief to belief in Jesus in every area of life?
- Pray and ask the Spirit to help you identify one next step.
- Write an "I will . . ." statement to summarize that step.
- Whom will you share your "I will . . ." statement with?

Conclusion

Along the way, we've asked you to reflect on some questions on each of the ingredients. An IDE contains the following five essential ingredients to create transformative and multiplicative ownership.

We challenge you, as a starfish leader, to grab a journal, walk slowly back through the questions in each section, pray, take notes, pray, jot down ideas, pray, and run your disciple-making, leadership-development, and team-building experiences, tools, and resources through these five filters. Are you creating intentional disciple-making environments? Which of these five ingredients are in the mix? Which are missing? How can you put the missing ingredients into the environment to create a greenhouse culture for multiplying disciples?

Figure 14.3

The Disciple-Making Ingredients Starfish: Creating Environments and Mixing Ingredients

Recently, one of my (Rob's) daughters decided on a whim to whip up some cookies. She was almost done when she realized we didn't have enough baking soda. Unfazed, she threw what little we had in the mix and went straight ahead.

Did we make cookies? Indeed. Were the cookies eaten? Not so much.

That missing ingredient makes a big difference.

With it, the cookies rise, the texture is wonderful, and the taste is delightful. Without it, they're flat as a pancake and as crispy as balsa wood. Expect the same results when it comes to IDEs. Without all the ingredients, you'll find things falling flat. Add all the ingredients and watch disciples rise to new levels of transformation and multiplication.

CHAPTER 15

The Disciple-Making Ecosystem Starfish

Balancing Elements and Cultivating an Ecosystem

A business ecosystem is just like the natural ecosystem; first, needs to be understood, then, needs to be well planned, and also needs to be thoughtfully renewed as well.

—Pearl Zhu, *Digital Maturity*

Sow with a view to righteousness,
Reap in accordance with kindness;
Break up your fallow ground,
For it is time to seek the LORD.

—Hosea 10:12 NASB

Figure 15.1

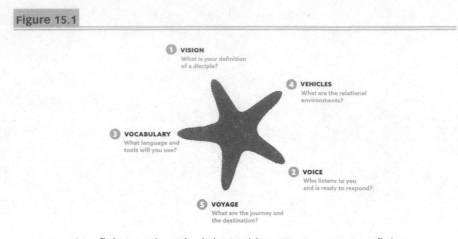

Starfish #6: The Disciple-Making Ecosystem Starfish

Purpose: The disciple-making ecosystem starfish provides a framework of five essential elements needed to design a disciple-making ecosystem that is transformative and multiplicative.

You won't find starfish nestled in the mountaintop crags of Mount McKinley. If you find a starfish buried in the sands of the Mojave Desert, someone must have dropped it! It certainly didn't crawl there.

Starfish inhabit the oceans of the world. Although you can find starfish on the deep-sea floor down to twenty thousand feet, the greatest number and diversity of the species occur in coastal areas and tidal pools, what is considered a shallow ocean ecosystem. They are considered the most important predator in that ecosystem. They are categorized as a "keystone species." This is a species that if negatively affected will have a "disproportionately greater effect on the whole ecosystem because they are the key component."[1]

Multiplying disciples are a keystone species. We need them to thrive and reproduce so the shalom of God can fill homes, neighborhoods, cities, states, and nations until "the earth will be filled with the knowledge of the glory of the LORD as the waters cover the sea" (Hab. 2:14).

Starfish survive and thrive only in the right ecosystem.

Ecosystems are communities of interacting organisms living together in their physical environment. The earth is filled with ecosystems like forests, grasslands, deserts, tundras, wetlands, prairies, rainforests, and mountains—each filled with plants, animals, and microorganisms in their natural environment. When ecosystems are healthy, the balance of energy and relationships sustains and reproduces life in all its various forms.

When wolves were reintroduced to their natural ecosystem in the world-famous Yellowstone National Park in 1995 after being eradicated in the 1920s, the returning wolves dramatically changed the park's rivers, forests, and even the landscape itself. They were brought in to manage the rising elk population, which were overgrazing. But scientists were shocked at the far-reaching ripple of direct and indirect consequences throughout the entire ecosystem. Everything from surging beaver populations to a massive recovery of willow tree stands by a factor of ten, from unbrowsed plants increasing by 84 percent to the number of songbirds, who find their habitat in those willow trees and plants, swelling.[2] Beavers build dams, which changed the course of rivers, creating new ponds and lakes, and the list goes on. One can't help but recall the scene in *The Lion, the Witch and the Wardrobe* where the curse is broken and Narnia springs forth with new life!

Doug Smith, a wildlife biologist in charge of the Yellowstone Wolf Project, describes it this way: "It is like kicking a pebble down a mountain slope where conditions were just right that a falling pebble could trigger an avalanche of change."[3]

Now consider that your faith community or organization has its own natural ecosystem. In a more general use, an ecosystem is any complex, interconnected system.

As demonstrated, small changes can yield dramatic change.

How can we make small strategic changes in our ecosystem so it will become become ripe for the flourishing of multiplying disciples, which will then unleash a ripple effect of a tsunami of shalom, filling everything every way with the fullness of Jesus?

This is where the disciple-making ecosystem starfish comes in.

This starfish provides a framework of five questions that pertain to essential dynamics or elements in a disciple-making ecosystem. I (Rob) was first introduced to these questions by my friends and partners Doug Paul and Dave Rhodes, both of whom have led significant movements of disciple-making (MDMs)—and I don't say that lightly. They've seen four generations or more on multiple strands, culminating into thousands of disciples. Over the years, we've worked together leading various learning communities and coaching initiatives where these concerns and questions were central. My conversations with them have profoundly shaped my thinking and practice.

In this chapter, we will first define each question. Please consider carefully your answers or lack of them. Each of these questions will trigger other questions in your mind. That's good. Keep a journal handy. Jot down answers and questions. Pray your way through. Use these as a guide for conversation with your team.

Figure 15.2

The Disciple-Making Ecosystem Starfish: Balancing Elements and Cultivating an Ecosystem

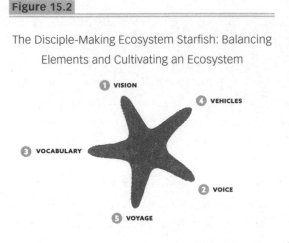

Once the question has been framed, I (Rob) will provide examples of how we are answering that question in the Kansas City Underground. These aren't "the right" answers per se. They are the right answers for *our* context. We believe there are hundreds of right answers to these questions, as each faith community must contextualize the ideas and practices for their own setting. Please know that our answers to these questions are evolving and always open to reformation.

May the Word and the Spirit reform us as we return to our deepest roots while simultaneously reinterpreting them for our time and space, our people and place.

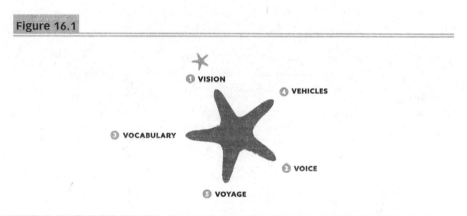

CHAPTER 16

Vision

Disciple-Making Ecosystem Element #1

Figure 16.1

Starfish #6: The Disciple-Making Ecosystem Starfish

Purpose: The disciple-making ecosystem starfish provides a framework of five essential elements needed to design a disciple-making ecosystem that is transformative and multiplicative.

What Is Your Definition of a Disciple?

Again, we return to this idea: Begin with the end in mind.

Imagine the CEO of Widgets International invites you to visit their premier factory. You're amazed by the sheer amount of activity in the factory, people buzzing back and forth like bees in a beehive. You have not yet seen, used, or purchased a widget, although you have heard of their fame. After a welcome from the CEO and his staff, along with a general look around, you excitedly ask the CEO, "May I see a widget? I have heard so much about them but have yet to experience one firsthand."

The CEO says, "Walk with me!" As you enter the vast factory floor, he pontificates on the necessity and importance of the widget in the American economy. You can barely keep up with his gesticulations and articulations as you tour the various departments, where teams are busily at work creating a plethora of products and programs. Hours later, in exhaustion, you are back at the front door. The CEO suddenly dismisses you, explaining, "The work of widget-making is never done! I must run!" As you walk back to the parking lot, you realize, *I still don't know what a widget is!*

Excuse the crass analogy, but we think you can see where this is going. Disciple-making "factories" should know with clarity and specificity what a disciple is. Our churches are filled with activities and programs that can all be generically labeled as "discipleship." But when everything is labeled "discipleship," then there's a chance nothing is discipleship.

If your faith community's ultimate purpose is to produce disciples—as that is the primary mission Jesus gave us in Matthew 28:19: "Go and make disciples"—then maybe we need to know what a disciple is. What is your vision for a fully devoted disciple?

That's the essence of the vision question: What is your definition of disciple?

Over the years, we have interacted with hundreds of church leaders on this very question. Typically, the answers fall into one of two categories.

The first is stunned silence, which turns into some stammering of religious catchphrases. From there, they pick up steam and start outlining all the various programs and departments of the church. Most of the folks who answer that way have never been asked that question so directly. It's discombobulating. We are often left thinking, "You have some great programs, groups, and people, a lot of activity, for sure, but I still don't know what you think a disciple is."

Alan Hirsch: This observation by Rob and Lance squares with my experience. The vast majority of church leaders I meet lack a clear idea or definition of what a disciple is and are even more muddy about how one might go about making disciples who can make disciples. After two thousand years of living under Jesus' command to go and make disciples, his people still don't have a clue! In fact, after the insight that we are perfectly designed to produce what we are currently producing, we can say the system is actually designed to exclude disciple-making! This is alarming. This must change if we are ever to become a movement again.

The second response is theological pontificating. These leaders will wind up like a major league pitcher and unleash a treatise. They often offer to share an immersive white paper on the topic that was the outcome of their dissertation or the summary findings of a multiyear committee they commissioned for this express purpose. Sincerely, their work and depth of insight impress us. But the response is so complex and nuanced that even a fraction of it couldn't be reproduced five minutes later. We are still left wondering, "What exactly is their definition of a disciple?"

Words matter. Definitions matter. We can't measure success in disciple-making if we don't know what our definition of one is.

Let us invite you to consider these qualifiers as you work on your definition or refine it.

1. **Is it biblical?** Is it firmly grounded in deep biblical convictions that have been tested over time and confirmed by the testimony of the church universal? What are your core theological convictions about disciple-making?
2. **Is it robust?** If someone lived into this definition, would they look like the disciples we see in the New Testament, who turned the world upside down? What are the irreducible minimums that have to be included for it to be robust?
3. **Is it simple?** Could you share it with a young teenager and have them understand it?
4. **Is it reproducible?** Could the average person easily remember it and share it with others?
5. **Is it compelling?** Does it make your heart beat fast when you share it with others? Does it remain compelling for people at various stages of spiritual maturity, beginners and sages alike? Does it remain compelling over a lifetime?

The first two questions ensure you are on firm foundation. The third and fourth questions allow your definition to scale so a movement can use it. The last question wins people's hearts and minds, yielding higher levels of participation and motivation.

The KC Underground Example

Our definition for a disciple is a double click.

Click One: Character × Calling = Impact

If you ask disciple-makers in our movement what it means to be a disciple, they will tell you, "Character × Calling = Impact!" You've already read what this means back in chapter 10. But let's unpack it through these qualifiers.

We feel this definition is simple, reproducible, and compelling. You can share it in three words! However, we also train our people to share this compelling invitation in a few minutes—something like this:

> Ever feel like you're not living, just existing? Jesus said in John 10:10 that he came that we might have life and have it to the full! Jesus invites us to live the fully-alive life. In other words, Jesus is the Master at the art of living. As the author of life, he can be our teacher to show us how to come alive in every area of life. If you accept Jesus as your teacher, there are two big areas in which you will experience transformation, character and calling. Character is becoming like Jesus: more love, more joy, more peace, more patience, more kindness, more goodness, more gentleness, and more self-control. Imagine that gap between who you are and who you want to be closing. Imagine how the quality of your relationships will go up. Calling is about making the unique contribution that God designed you for. As you grow in character, what the Bible calls fruit of the Spirit, and calling, what the Bible calls gifts of the Spirit, they have a multiplying effect. Impact increases both in you and through you! That's the transformation Jesus wants all of us to experience. Character × Calling = Impact.

Click Two: One-Sentence Definition

Disciple: A person who is apprenticed to Jesus in the fully-alive life, experiencing habit-fueled, ongoing transformation in character and calling while moving deeper into community and multiplying disciples.

This definition is a "behind the scenes" expanded version that we equip leaders to know. We believe this is both a biblical and robust definition of a disciple. Since we've already been through our disciple-making ingredients starfish, you've been down the rabbit hole with us and know our five foundational theological convictions that undergird our definition of a disciple. A disciple is . . .

- focused on the Spirit's outcomes.
- fueled by spiritual habits that Jesus embodied.
- forged by community that Jesus modeled.
- fixated on the mission of Jesus.
- flavored by the gospel of Jesus.

These theological convictions shape everything: our message, mediums, and methods. You may or may not agree with ours. You may or may not even like ours! That's okay. We offer it only as an example.

Based on what you just read, your lifelong theological reflections, and your personal embodiment of the life of Jesus, we urge you to consider the vision question through the lens of the five questions we've offered. Begin crafting or refining your definition of a disciple.

CHAPTER 17

Voice

Disciple-Making Ecosystem Element #2

Figure 17.1

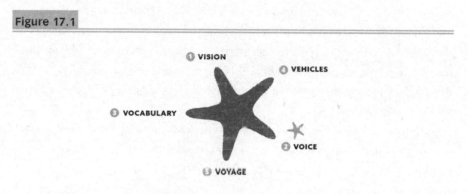

Starfish #6: The Disciple-Making Ecosystem Starfish

Purpose: The disciple-making ecosystem starfish provides a framework of five essential elements needed to design a disciple-making ecosystem that is transformative and multiplicative.

Who Listens to You and Is Ready to Respond?

Start right, stay right.

In 1979, Air New Zealand Flight 901, with 257 people on board, left Auckland for a sightseeing flight to Antarctica and back. What the pilots did not know, however, was that someone had modified the flight coordinates by a mere two degrees the night before. Extrapolated over their flight time, that error took them twenty-eight miles east of where the pilots assumed they would be.

Two degrees off in the beginning led to a twenty-eight-mile miss.

As they approached Antarctica, the pilots descended to a lower altitude to give the passengers a better look at the scenery. Because of cloud cover, they had no way of knowing that the incorrect coordinates had placed them directly in the path of Mount Erebus, an active volcano that rises from the frozen landscape to a height of more than twelve thousand feet. By the time the instruments sounded the warning that the ground was rising fast toward them, it was too late. The airplane crashed into the side of the volcano, killing everyone on board. It remains the deadliest accident in the history of Air New Zealand.[1]

The trajectory at the beginning of the journey sets the course for the final destination.

How people are invited into the discipleship journey matters profoundly. In many cases, the invitation to disciple-making is a "cattle call" from the platform to join a group or program. Or if we are more selective, we look for only the most competent people in the marketplace who "attend" our church. We target those we think have the most potential by the standards of our culture. For example, success in the marketplace is often considered an unwritten, nonnegotiable criteria for selection for most elder boards.

Furthermore, when we do invite personally, we want to ease people in by offering seeker-friendly easy access. Over the years, as Brian Phipps and I (Rob) have shared our IDEs with church leaders—some of which are ten-or twelve-month commitments—we've been surprised by how many pastors' first response is, "I could never get my people to commit to something like that. Maybe six weeks tops."

This response feels more than two degrees off from Jesus' answer to the voice question. In a healthy disciple-making ecosystem, it is important to have the right answer to the voice question, "Who listens to you and is ready to respond?"

How did Jesus use his voice to invite others? And whom did he invite? How can we do the same?

Jesus' Criteria for Devotion

Mike Breen, in his book *Building a Discipling Culture*, describes what he calls a high challenge or high invitation of Jesus.

- **High invitation:** Invitation has to do with a strong sense of grace, of being warmly welcomed and included, not for what you do but for who you are. It gives a sense of "I belong" and that the one who invites you is so glad to be with you. We can feel this type of invitation in our bodies; it slows our breathing, and a sense of rest comes over us.

- **High challenge:** Challenge has to do with being needed, having a valued contribution and a willingness to do hard things at great cost. It is like William Wallace's famous challenge in *Braveheart*: "Fight and you may die. Run and you will live at least awhile. And dying in your bed many years from now, would you be willing to trade all the days from this day to that for one chance, just one chance to come back here as young men and tell our enemies that they may take our lives but they will never take our freedom!"[2] The challenge rouses us from our slumber or trepidation and calls us to take up arms and run to the battle.

Sure, Jesus' friendship with Peter began with "Come . . .and you will see" (John 1:39), which is only invitational. But after a time of exploration, there was a clear starting line for intentional development to begin. At that point, Jesus' voice was clearly both high invitation and high challenge. He was simultaneously incredibly invitational and profoundly challenging. For example, consider Jesus' second invitation to Peter: "Follow me, and I will make you fishers of men" (Matt. 4:19 ESV). The first phrase is the invitation, and the second is the challenge.

Any coach will tell you that without a sense of challenge, players won't work hard on skills or try their best. The challenge is what makes training and winning matter. Without a sense of invitation, players won't put themselves out there, feeling safe enough to take a risk or willing to "take one for the team" versus being the glory hog. Both invitation and challenge are needed for the individuals to become a team, a family on mission. These are the essential elements in every great sports movie, from *Remember the Titans* to *Hoosiers*.

They're also key in the playbook of Coach Jesus.

Jesus' Criteria for Selection

- **Readiness:** Who listens to my voice and is ready to respond? Who is hungry? Who is responsive? Who is teachable? Who is willing to make themselves available? Who is willing to invest in others as I invest in them? (Luke 9:57–62)
- **Revelation:** Whom has the Father given me? Jesus spent extensive time in intentional prayer asking the Father to put a lightbulb over the heads of those he was to invite (Luke 6:12–13).

Jesus' Criteria for Invitation

- **Personal:** Jesus called them personally by name. No "cattle calls" or "sign-up lists." (Luke 6:13–16)
- **Limited:** Jesus invited only twelve disciples, with an inner core of three, whom he would invite to help him lead the Twelve. (Luke 6:14–16; 8:51; Mark 5:37; Matt. 17:1)

KC Underground Example

When it comes to inviting people into one of our IDEs like Followers Made, a six-month journey to become a disciple who can make disciples, we train the potential leader to begin a season of prayer as Jesus did. Think of those to whom you have said, "Come and see." Who are the people who listen to your voice and respond? You see they are hungry and responsive. Again, Followers Made's recommended grouping is twelve, with four triads within. Ask the Lord to show you your twelve.

Brian Phipps, by the Spirit's inspiration, came up with the following prayer request: "Lord, I'm slow, so please put a lightbulb over the right people's heads." Boy, do we have some amazing lightbulb stories—divine appointments that would give you the chills!

Then we invite the "lightbulb people" to read a book that pertains to the particular IDE we are inviting them to. For Followers Made, the book is *Not a Fan* by Kyle Idleman. We let them know, "I'm asking you to pray about going on a six-month journey with me. We will do life together at a different level, sharing our joys and burdens. We will do some hard things together. We will be different at the end of the journey. At that point, you should be ready to help others make the same journey. Read that book. In two weeks, I'm getting a group of around twelve people together who are also reading the book. We will discuss what the Lord is teaching us and look at the commitments of this journey."

Then the leader checks in on them. If they haven't finished reading the book, the leader politely lets the person know, "We can get together another time if and when you finish the book."

At the meeting, which is only for those who have finished the book, the book is discussed. The commitments of daily engagement in spiritual habits, missionary formation, calling discovery, and so forth are listed out in writing. People know exactly what they are committing to. This meeting is now known as the information huddle. At the end, the potential disciples are asked, "Is Jesus calling you to go on this journey? That's what you need to know. If so, sign that commitment. If you're not sure, take one more week to pray." Most people sign up that night. Our drop-out rate on Followers Made is less than 5 percent, and our reproduction rate is 30 percent—those who go through the program and go on to make disciples.

Start right, stay right. Again, this is not the only right way, just our best efforts to honor the devotion, selection, and invitation criteria of our King Jesus.

CONSIDER THE FOLLOWING VOICE QUESTIONS:

- **Devotion:** What level of commitment do you ask of those you are inviting to the intentional disciple-making journey? Is it both high invitational and high challenge?
- **Selection:** What criteria do you use to select those you develop as disciples? Do they align with those of Jesus? He didn't look for the best and brightest. He looked for those who were hungry, humble, and willing to hustle. Whom is the Holy Spirit revealing to you?
- **Invitation:** How many people do you invest in at a time, and how do you invite them? Jesus had twelve with an inner circle of three. Do you have twelve with a triad within it? Surely, we must agree that we can't improve on the methods of Jesus. Therefore, who are your twelve? Who are your three? Have you personally invited them to the journey?

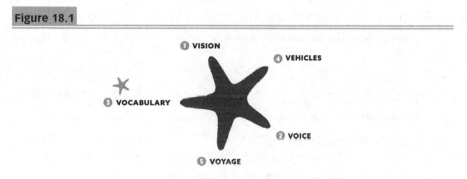

CHAPTER 18

Vocabulary

Disciple-Making Ecosystem Element #3

Figure 18.1

Starfish #6: The Disciple-Making Ecosystem Starfish

Purpose: The disciple-making ecosystem starfish provides a framework of five essential elements needed to design a disciple-making ecosystem that is transformative and multiplicative.

What Language and Tools Will You Use?

For a healthy disciple-making ecosystem, it is important to use the right vocabulary, so we recommend asking yourself the vocabulary question: What language and tools will you use?

Language is critical because it brings order from chaos. The power of language begins in the first chapter of the Bible, in Genesis 1. From the beginning, we see words have tremendous power. When God speaks, he doesn't just convey information but creates new realities.

There is a pattern to God's Word, as scholar Pete Enns notes.[1]

What he forms on day one (separation of light and dark), he fills with the sun, moon, and stars on day four. The night and the day he fills with the sun and the moon. The sky he forms, he fills with birds. That's day five. The sea and the land he forms, he fills with living creatures. That's day six. This pattern is the way our Father works words.

First his words form, and then they fill.

Through his words, Jesus turned the chaos into a cosmos. Furthermore, as cocreators—ask any anthropologist—we use language to create culture. In any area of expertise or apprenticeship, there is a vocabulary one must learn to ply that trade.

Tools then amplify and enhance our ability to create and realize what our words describe. Entire ages of human civilization have been defined by the available tools—stone, bronze, and iron—which emphasizes the profound importance tools play in the advancement of any human endeavor. Better tools yield new possibilities.

Alan Hirsch: In design thinking, we tend to talk about grappling with what appears to be an unresolvable mystery, coming up with a working theory that attempts to make sense of it and interprets it. This then leads to developing algorithms—repeatable patterns and formulas that enable us to live out the theory in ways that make sense. Tools we use are one aspect of the algorithms. Every tool delivers an idea, a core value, or an important function. Most people are changed simply by using the tools. Doubt this? Then consider how the tool of the printing press changed history. Or how the tool of social media has shaped behaviors of whole societies. Formulating the right tools is a critical key to movement thinking.

Of course, in any given trade, the tools and language must be carefully selected and complimentary for the given project at hand. The teacher must help the student know what the terms mean and how the tools work.

Grant me (Rob) grace to return to my ineptness with mechanics. I'm the guy in the garage who asks, "What's that thing-a-ma-bobby?" And when a friend with know-how asks, "Can you hand me the $3/8$" ratchet with a 24mm socket?" I'll need to pull out my phone and hit up Google to know what he's talking about. But if I spent a summer working on the car with him, I'd know what he meant and even be able to make the repair myself.

In the trade of disciple-making, the right language and tools are essential as well. If we spend time with someone who's further down the road in their apprenticeship, anyone can learn this trade and move forward. Since Jesus is a disciple-maker, his language and tools are still ours to use today. He is still taking apprentices!

Jesus' Language

Jesus was the master at turning a phrase and seeding language with meaning that worked on people's souls like a slow-release pill. Ponder Jesus' lengthy list of "mic-drop" statements that still burn themselves into our minds some two thousand years later. To demonstrate, let's consider just a handful of examples. We bet you can finish every one of these.

I have come that they may have _____, and have it to the _____ (John 10:10).
The Son of Man did not come to be _____, but to _____ (Matt. 20:28).
Repent and _____! (Mark 1:15).
Love your _____ and pray for those who persecute you (Matt. 5:44).
Many who are first will be last, and many who are _____ (Matt. 19:30).
Whoever wants to save their life will _____, but whoever loses their life for me will _____ (Luke 9:24).
Let any one of you who is without sin be the first to throw _____ (John 8:7).

Jesus worked with words as an artist works with paints. His words of art are breathtaking and beautiful beyond compare.

Jesus' Tools

Jesus also had tools he used. Although he was a carpenter by trade, his disciple-making tool kit is far more impressive than whatever he had in his workshop in Nazareth. What were some of Jesus' disciple-making tools? Again, this is not an exhaustive list, as every dimension of Jesus' life is an example to us. For our purposes, we consider three categories of tools Jesus used: practices, parables, and procedures.

Practices: In chapter 11, we explored more than a dozen practices Jesus embodied, such as Scripture engagement, various forms of prayer, fasting, Sabbath rhythms, a particular way of ordering his relational world, gospel proclamation in stories and messages, gospel demonstration in signs and service, intentionality with meals and parties, and the list goes on.

Parables: Each parable is first a picture that you look at and are captivated with. Then it becomes a mirror you can see yourself in. Finally, it becomes a window you look through to frame your world with new meaning.

Procedures: Jesus had established training procedures, which organized the way he used his tools. These procedures were a series of oscillating actions that he repeatedly used personally and with his disciples. For example, one procedure was that of engagement, then retreat. After intensive times of engagement in mission, he would retreat to solitude alone or with his disciples for refreshment and renewal. We ignore this procedure to the peril of our own souls. Another procedure Jesus used was action, then reflection. He would thrust his disciples on mission to the cliffs of poverty, sickness, and need, involving them in miracles and service among the marginalized. Then he would invite them to reflection in conversation, leading to both correction and celebration. Another procedure Jesus employed was teaching, then debriefing. After a public teaching, he would debrief his disciples, where he would often discover they didn't have a clue or had totally missed the point. Overall, each of these procedures is an expression of the same metaprocedure that is the synthesis of contemplation and action, which Jesus saw as essential.

KC Underground Example of Language

Of course, the KC Underground seeks to make our first language that of the Scriptures. Yet each faith community has its own dialect. A dialect is a particular form of a language that is peculiar to a specific social group. Our faith communities have their own dialect, for good or for ill. Either our language helps us make disciples or hinders us.

I've been in many church buildings that have the words *worship center* above the doors of the auditorium. This may appear harmless, but the implicit message is, "This is the center of our worship." Does our worship really center in this building a few hours a week? Romans 12 invites us to use our entire lives as worship, all day, every day.

In the opening weeks of the COVID-19 pandemic, as thousands of churches moved their Sunday services online, my Facebook feed was flooded with invitations from these congregations with advertisements that cheerfully proclaimed, "You can still go to church online!" Really? How do you go to something you are? Church is not a location or activity, but an identity. Maybe you're thinking, "Oh, come on. Aren't you being a little overzealous? Are we supposed to audit our language?" Our language creates a culture. The celebrated repetition of the phrase *go to church* affirms a radically reduced ecclesiology.

Recently, we put together the first draft of our lexicon, the phrases and language we use repeatedly to reinforce what we hope will be a robust disciple-making ecosystem. This isn't an exhaustive list, just some examples.

The way of Jesus is our way.

We exist to fill our city with the beauty, justice, and good news of Jesus.

Church is an extended spiritual family.

A missionary on every street and a microchurch in every neighborhood or network of relationships.

Character × Calling = Impact

God is great, so we don't have to be in control.

God is glorious, so we don't have to be afraid.

God is good, so we don't have to look elsewhere.

God is gracious, so we don't have to earn it.

We are moving from unbelief to belief in Jesus, in every area of life.

Extraordinary prayer and fasting.

Live like a missionary.

Plant the gospel.

Look for the person of peace.

Multiply disciples, leaders, microchurches, hubs, and networks.

Flourishing souls.

Sacrificial faith.

We are generous people.

Church is an identity, not an activity.

We don't go to church; be the church. You can't go to something you are.

On mission where we live, work, learn, and play.

We don't convert anyone; we bless everyone.

Breathe and BLESS.

Write an "I will . . ." statement.

We share stories of mission.

You are the voice of the Underground.

We love to party. Our tables are open.

How many churches are there in our city? One.

Every people and every nation.

We are sent.

Discover, obey, and share the Bible.

Everyone is an artist, and every context is unique.

We won't stand for injustice. Put us in the fight.

We work from a place of rest.

Reproduce at every level.

KC Underground Example of Tools

Our tools are organized on a continuum from informal to formal.

Table 18.1

INFORMAL		FORMAL
Discovery Bible Study	Shapes & Symbols	IDEs
Breathe and BLESS	Story Diamond–Scripture	GPS Calling
	Identity Triangle–Identity	Assessment
	Impact Equation–Transformation	Followers Made
	Kairos Circle–Obedience	Leaders Made
	Semicircle–Rest	Missionaries Made
	Prayer Circles–Prayer	Microchurch LC
	Spheres of Influence–Relationships	
	Leadership Square–Reproduction	
	2 Out x 2 Up x 2 In–Community	
	Practice Wheel	
"From the harvest into the church"		"From the church into the harvest"

The informal tools are those we use in the harvest to help others move toward Jesus and his church. These include the Breathe and BLESS rhythms described in chapter 11. As a person lives faithfully into those missionary rhythms among the same network of people, they begin to have meaningful and then spiritual conversations. At that point, we begin to share the story of how Jesus has changed us and how the gospel changes everything. Then that missionary will invite that spiritually curious person to join them in a Discovery Bible Study (DBS).

Discovery Bible Studies are simple and reproducible groups that consist of spiritually interested people who read a Bible passage together, discover what it says through a set of simple, open-ended questions that focus on the character of God and the invitation to obey him. The members are encouraged to immediately experiment with living out what they have learned and to share with someone else what they have discovered. It's a simple way for them to discover for themselves, firsthand, what the Bible says about God, people, and what it means to follow Jesus. The emphasis is not on teaching but on facilitation and discovery and the immediate application and sharing of what you've learned with others outside the group. It's simple and reproducible.

As I mentioned earlier, one of our microchurch leaders brought DBS into the jail system in one of the counties of Kansas City. The DBSs quickly multiplied to every single pod in the entire jail, leading to a massive spiritual awakening and numerous salvations. We've seen DBS work across multiple contexts, from the suburbs to the jail cells. When the pandemic hit, a number of our missionaries who had been living the BLESS rhythms heard the Spirit say, "Now is the time," and invited those they had been living among to join them in an online DBS. The number and frequency of DBSs doubled during the pandemic. We've seen four microchurches emerge in new contexts during that two-month period. For example, John and Heather typed out an invitation to the online DBS and taped it to the front doors of the homes of those in their immediate neighborhood. Six families engaged. A couple of weeks in, John was taking the garbage to the curb and ran into the person of peace in their neighborhood, who has lived there thirty years and knows everyone. She asked, "You still doing that Bible study online for the neighborhood? I meant to try that." John assured her they were. She showed up the next week with six additional families from their neighborhood that she invited! You can see what an adaptive and powerful form of gospel planting DBS can be.

In the middle of the continuum, between informal and formal, you'll see a category called Shapes and Symbols. We have eleven of these in all, which function as our visual parables for a visual culture. Each symbol or shape is built around a key area of life and is highly instructive on how to follow Jesus in that area. Each of these shapes or symbols can be shared in a few moments on a napkin or over coffee for an hour. Or we've developed a series of DBSs for each one that ranges from three to six weeks.

> **Alan Hirsch:** This idea of lacing the Christian life with sets of algorithms and tools is as old as Scripture itself. Consider the role of the Shema (Deut. 6:4–9) in the life of Israel. It is repeated three times a day in the set prayers. It is also posted on the lintels on the entry to every Jewish house. This is called a *mezuzah*, and upon entry and exit to the house—their going out and coming in—the faithful Jew kisses the *mezuzah* and thus acknowledges the rule of God in their lives and over the house. The Shema is also contained in the phylacteries (*tefillin*) that the religious Jew wraps around his right arm and puts on his forehead at least once a day. The Shema thus infuses its reality into every nook and cranny of Jewish life. The Catholic use of signing the cross over head, heart, mouth, and hands has a similar effect.

As you can see, the Shapes and Symbols are a bit more formal. The Shapes and Symbols could function as almost a yearlong discipleship journey. Our set of shapes and tools includes a few that 3DM developed. Go to https://www.kcunderground .org/missionary-tools to explore a sample of three of our shapes and symbols, including overview videos and training PDFs.

Finally, at the far right of the continuum, you'll see the formal category where our IDEs and GPS sit. This suite of comprehensive disciple-making experiences is designed to bring real transformation to followers of Jesus. Modeled after Jesus' disciple-making rhythms, these experiences teach spiritual habits, build genuine community, encourage high investment, multiply leaders, and unleash people to become missionaries where they live, work, learn, and play. All our experiences are outcome focused: Our app helps leaders track both individual and community spiritual growth. Followers Made reorients church consumers to become contributors to Jesus' mission. Missionaries Made equips disciples to become everyday missionaries where they live, work, learn, and play. These are great places to start. Leaders Made empowers servant leaders to guide and influence communities on mission. The Microchurch Learning Community equips everyday missionaries to lead extended spiritual families in their neighborhoods or networks. These two are more advanced. Our GPS assessment process helps people discover their unique, personal calling. GPS is baked into all four experiences. You can learn more about these at https://disciplesmade.com.

Again, our goal is not for anyone to cut and paste our language or tool kit.

Our language and tools are the overflow of decades of learning, experiments, many iterations, failures, grace, and grit—the shared work of many leaders bringing their best to the table.

Also notice, we have language and tools to mobilize both directions: from the harvest to the church and from the church to harvest. We have a vision to see DMMs catalyzing new disciples from lostness through regeneration, four generations deep on multiple strands. We also envision MDMs catalyzing new disciples from believers through personal revival, four generations deep on multiple stands.

CONSIDER THE FOLLOWING VOCABULARY QUESTIONS:

- What would we discover if we audited our language?
- What words and phrases do we want to seed into our disciple-making ecosystem?
- What words and phrases do we want to remove?
- What tools do we currently employ? How effective are they?
- What tools need to be retired? What tools would we like to introduce?
- How do we organize our tools? How do people know when to use what tool?

CHAPTER 19

Vehicles

Disciple-Making Ecosystem Element #4

Figure 19.1

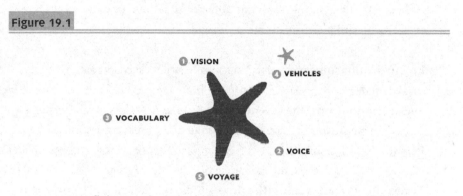

Starfish #6: The Disciple-Making Ecosystem Starfish

Purpose: The disciple-making ecosystem starfish provides a framework of five essential elements needed to design a disciple-making ecosystem that is transformative and multiplicative.

What Are the Relational Environments?

"Come, follow me" (Matt. 4:19). This was first an invitation to relationship. Jesus didn't gather his disciples for lattes at the synagogue once per week and conclude, "Make sure to fill out your Torah study. See you back here Sunday night at six." His discipleship wasn't compartmentalized into classroom settings or weekly small group meetings. Mark 3:14–15 tells us that he chose the Twelve "that they might be with him and that he might send them out to preach and to have authority to drive out demons."

Dave Ferguson, in his book *Hero Maker: Five Essential Practices for Leaders to Multiply Leaders* points out, "The word for 'spend time' in the Greek is pronounced 'dia-tree-bo' (and transliterated diatribe). Dia means 'against' and tribo means 'to rub.' So, diatribe literally means 'to rub against' or 'to rub off.'"[1] Jesus spent a significant percentage of time with his disciples, and he most certainly rubbed off on them.

Fundamentally, the church is a family. We were broken in a family. We will be healed only in a new family, Jesus' family, where he can rub off on us, in and through his people.

In chapter 12, we identified five key relationships where discipleship happens in our lives. In each relational environment, we need to understand how discipleship occurs, and we need to set appropriate expectations for each context. This is how Jesus made disciples and how disciples were formed in the early church. Each of the relational environments is necessary at different times and in different ways as a person grows toward maturity in Christ:

Public relationships (crowds): The church gathering corporately for worship.

Social relationships (the seventy-two): Smaller networks of relationships where we engage in mission and live out our faith in community.

Personal relationships (the Twelve): Small groups of six to sixteen people where we challenge and encourage one another regularly.

Transparent relationships (the three): Close relationships of three to four where we share intimate details of our lives for accountability.

The Divine relationship: Our relationship with Jesus Christ where we grow through the empowering presence of the Holy Spirit.

KC Underground Relational Environments

Public Relationships
Collective Gatherings

A collective is a network of four to six microchurches in a geographic region or affinity group. A collective gathering is for all the members of those microchurches and are open to all.

Social, Personal, and Transparent Relationships
Hub Equipping Gathering (Social Space)

An equipping gathering is designed for the missionaries and

microchurch leaders of the Underground. These gatherings are comprised of vision, storytelling, worship, prayer, and equipping in missionary skills. It's a gathering for the renewal and strengthening of leaders.

Microchurches

An extended spiritual family that lives in everyday gospel community, led by ordinary people, and owning the mission of Jesus in a network of relationships. Most will find that the transparent (the three), the personal (the Twelve), and, in many microchurches, the social space (the seventy-two) are experienced as they grow and throw parties in their context.

Missional Teams

A group of missionaries who come together for a common mission in a particular context, working and praying together to see disciples made and a microchurch emerge.

Discovery Bible Studies (DBS)

A group of people discovering Scripture together and learning to be obedient to Jesus. This is an expression of the personal relationships.

Intentional Disciple-Making Environments

Followers Made, Leaders Made, Missionaries Made, Microchurch Learning Community. These are designed for groups of twelve (personal) with triads (transparent) as subgroups.

Divine Space

Time Alone with Jesus

Disciples are encouraged and equipped to spend time alone with Jesus each day.

Over time, a person can experience all five of these spaces, overlapping and integrating, in one network or neighborhood, as people who "nest" their community within their microchurch, collective, and hub connection within their section of the city.

As we mentioned earlier, this way of life is radically countercultural. It usually takes a disciple months or years to begin to overlap and deepen their relational world. In this way, rather than running

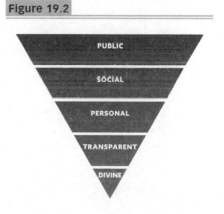

Figure 19.2

among multiple networks of relationship, where community is a mile wide and an inch deep, they can plant their relational roots deep, in one network or neighborhood. In so doing, relationships are deep and wide. The pace of life can slow down, as much of our living happens in one or two contexts, not five or six, as is common sense in many places in America and is the source of much of our busyness and ensuing isolation.

Again, this is how the KC Underground answers the vehicles question. We love our answer; we think it's the best way to live. But now it's your turn. What is the Word and the Spirit saying to your community?

CONSIDER THE FOLLOWING VEHICLES QUESTIONS:

- To what degree is our disciple-making organized and programmatic versus organic and relational?
- What are our relational environments? List them. Then evaluate the following.
- To what degree do those vehicles move people toward living in spiritual extended families that practice the "one anothers" as a way of life?
- To what degree do they cover and integrate all five social spaces?
- What relational environments do we have that are stagnant or toxic? Why? Should those vehicles be retired? How can those relational environments be restored to health?
- What new relational environments do we need?

CHAPTER 20

Voyage

Disciple-Making Ecosystem Element #5

Figure 20.1

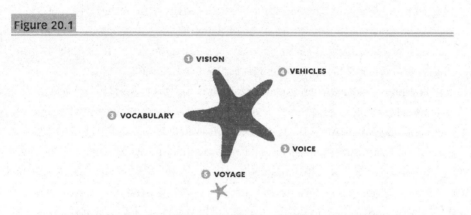

Starfish #6: The Disciple-Making Ecosystem Starfish

Purpose: The disciple-making ecosystem starfish provides a framework of five essential elements needed to design a disciple-making ecosystem that is transformative and multiplicative.

What Is the Direction of the Journey and the Destination?

When I (Rob) was in middle school, I had an early existential crisis. I didn't know it at the time, but I was a very unhealthy three on the enneagram. If you're not familiar with the enneagram, you must have had your head in the sand for the last few years. The enneagram is a system of personality typing that describes patterns in how people see the world and manage their emotions and relationships. Each type has a dark side. The three is the achiever. When a three is unhealthy, we slide toward the dark side of the nine, which you could affectionally call the chameleon.

As a young teenager, I was the chameleon. I could flow with any of the various cliques—athletes, band kids, smart kids, stoners—because I knew how to pretend. I had a whole backpack of masks I would wear through various moments of the day to entertain and impress whomever I was with. As with millions of other teenagers in American Lit, when I read *Catcher in the Rye*, I realized, *I'm a phony!* I did indeed feel like an empty suit. The emptiness eventually led to a desperate prayer in the solitude of my bedroom: "God, can you help me? I don't know who I am. I'm tired of all the masks and pretending."

A few days later, I was tagging along with my sister, who was hanging at her best friend's house. My sister's best friend had an older sister, who was cool. She had a *huge* LP collection and was cranking some sweet tunes from the basement. I was playing bumper pool and nodding my head, enjoying the guitar licks. Then I noticed that this rock vocalist was singing about . . . Jesus. I shouted out loud, "What? Is he singing about Jesus? Rock music and Jesus? Can you do that?"

This pretty, older woman explained that, indeed, this is possible and acceptable. I wasn't going to disagree with her. The next day, I saw her at Sunday service, and she sought me out in the hallway. Did I mention she was an older woman? Like nineteen! She said, "Rob, I made something for you," and pulled a mixtape out of her purse. The older woman gave me a mixtape! Up to that point, this was the single greatest moment of my life. After I got home, I ran upstairs and turned it up. The shredding guitar burst out of the speakers and "melted my face." I loved it. But as the song continued, my heart sunk.

The song, by Petra, was titled "Chameleon," and it was my story. The lyrics said, "Chameleon, you blend with your surroundings. Chameleon, no one knows where you come from." The song was a prophetic punch in the face, bemoaning the phoniness and pretending we pursue to impress others. The song ended with a call to find identity in Christ.

I knew God was speaking to me, that somehow he was answering my prayer. I prayed again, "Whatever this means, God, please show me."

The next Sunday, we had a big announcement in the service: "We have a new pastor! He is here to serve the youth." He got up and said, "If you're a teenager, I'd love to meet you. If you have questions about God and what it means to know him, I'd love to talk. I'm having a cookout at my house tonight. Come on over."

My heart was beating fast. I knew God was telling me, "You'll find your answer with that man."

That man, Dan, led me to Jesus, and then he took me on a journey that changed the rest of my life. Not long after I started finally owning my faith and following Jesus, Dan explained to me and some other students, "Jesus had a plan. Many people read the Gospels and think Jesus was some kind of hippie floating here and there. Jesus was more deliberate than any general has been with his armies. He had a plan for his disciples. Some of them were probably just a little older than you. Jesus wants to work the same plan with you."

Then Dan hauled out a whiteboard and started a drawing with four sections. "First, he would win people, and they would become disciples. Then, he would build them up in their faith so they could experience all Jesus had for them. Next, he would equip them to win and build others. Finally, the fourth phase was to multiply. Now those disciples would win, build, equip, and multiply others, who would do the same. That's what we are going to do. Jesus has won you; now it's time to build and equip so you can multiply."

You read the story about that youth ministry in the opening pages of this book. It worked! He led me on a journey to a destination with Jesus. That framework was called the Son Life Strategy. Later, I read *The Master Plan of Evangelism*, which opened up me and millions of others to the Master's plan, the journey and the destination of Jesus. Since then, I've read hundreds of books that tease out the strategies of Jesus. His genius is inexhaustible!

Do you reflect your best understanding of Jesus' strategy in how he trained and developed others? What does the journey and destination look like? The destination continues on into eternity with God, where we will never fully arrive but will continue exploring his glories forever. But there is a clear direction toward that never-arrived-at destination. There are, indeed, stages in the journey.

For a healthy ecosystem for disciple-making to exist, we must also ask the voyage question: What is the direction of the journey and the destination?

The Bible provides a number of frameworks for the stages of the journey. Here are a few that have been distilled.

- A Summary of Stages of Growth by Jim Putman:
  - Stage 1: Spiritually Dead
  - Stage 2: Spiritual Infant
  - Stage 3: Spiritual Child
  - Stage 4: Young Adult
  - Stage 5: Parents

- Peter's Life as a Prototype by Brian Phipps:
  - Come and See (Explore)
  - Come and Follow (Develop)
  - Feed My Sheep (Lead and Multiply)
- A Summary of the Master's Plan by Robert Coleman:
  - 1. Selection
  - 2. Association
  - 3. Consecration
  - 4. Impartation
  - 5. Demonstration
  - 6. Delegation
  - 7. Supervision
  - 8. Reproduction
- The Four Chair Discipling Model by Dan Spader:
  - Win
  - Build
  - Equip
  - Multiply
- T4T, a training tool for church planters, uses the Four Fields as the major stages of the journey:
  - Field 1–Engaging the Lost
  - Field 2–Sharing the Gospel
  - Field 3–Making Disciples
  - Field 4–Church Formation
  - Multiplying Leaders

Alan Hirsch: I've always appreciated the Engel Scale because it highlights the aspect of journey toward God, not just the time from conversion onward. This is important because missional approaches to discipleship recognize that discipleship begins preconversion and continues postconversion (with some change in emphasis in the switch. The Engel Scale can be represented like this:

+5 Stewardship

+4 Communion with God

+3 Conceptual and behavioral growth

+2 Incorporation into Body

+1 Postdecision evaluation

New birth

-1 Repentance and faith in Christ

-2 Decision to act

-3 Personal problem recognition

-4 Positive attitude toward gospel

-5 Grasp implications of gospel

-6 Awareness of fundamentals of gospel

-7 Initial awareness of gospel

-8 Awareness of supreme being, no knowledge of gospel

Kansas City Underground Example

In the Underground, we have multiple answers to the voyage question, offering what we hope are clear maps for the journey.

Example #1: The Missionary Pathway

Since we are a mission agency that exists to prepare missionaries and disciple-makers, our primary journey is what we call the missionary pathway. As we study the movement of the church in the New Testament and even modern-day movements, we see a pattern. The following phases describe a journey that a disciple goes on in a new missionary endeavor in a new context.

Phase 1: Extraordinary prayer and fasting. If you don't know where you are, start here. Even if you're in phase 3, just keep working on this phase. Always. This is the most important phase. Remember, whatever your prayer rhythms are right now, add one thing. That one thing is extra. You just moved into extraordinary prayer. Add to that the focus that comes through fasting. Extraordinary prayer and fasting remain the undercurrent in all phases. Pray for the ones you are sent to. Pray for laborers to be raised up in the harvest. Pray for people of peace. Ask the Lord, "Where are you at work? How can I join you?"

Phase 2: Live as missionaries. We first identify a missional focus: To what people and place have I been sent? Each person needs to identify their primary mission context. Then we identify a person of peace (Luke 10) and live the BLESS rhythms. We have been blessed to be a blessing (Gen. 12). Begin in prayer. Learn the story

Figure 20.2

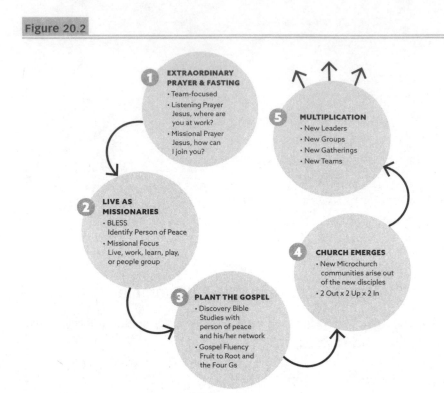

of the people and places where you live, work, learn, or play. Eat with them. Serve them. Then ask, what would be a meaningful engagement with the gospel for those people?

Phase 3: Plant the gospel. Here we speak the gospel to ourselves and the people to whom Jesus has sent us. If we lead in prayer and know the people well, we will always discover ways to communicate good news—which also means we must be fluent in the gospel. So learn to speak good news to your own soul every day. Plant the gospel by helping others engage the Scriptures in a way that facilitates self-discovery, immediate obedience, and sharing with others.

Alan Hirsch: Planting the gospel is a better way to talk about church planting. The problem of using the term *church planting* is that we think we know exactly what a church is, what it looks like, and how it should operate. That's the problem. Maybe we don't really know. The following is ascribed to philosopher Epictetus: "It is impossible to teach a man what he thinks he already knows."

Touché! When we use the term *church* in America, well, everyone *knows* what that is, don't they? By planting the gospel, we acknowledge that it is Jesus' task to grow the church. And the reality is that it ought to look different in differing contexts.

Phase 4: Church emerges. As we communicate the gospel and multiply disciples, the church will emerge. The church is an identity, not an action. It's who we are, not what we do. The church is an extended spiritual family, led by ordinary people, owning the mission of Jesus in a network of relationships.

Phase 5: Multiplication. The church that emerges out of true discipleship is a church with multiplication in its DNA. As the church emerges from disciple-making, multiplication will arise as well. We must reproduce at every level: disciples, leaders, microchurches, teams, gatherings, and networks.

We use the missionary pathway to organize our training and tools. The missionary pathway is the annual liturgy for our equipping gathering, which serves the missionaries and microchurch leaders.

Example #2: The IDE Journey

Jesus spent about three years making his disciples. So do we. If you move through all four intentional disciple-making experiences, it is a three-year journey of discipleship, with the following destination: the equipping of ordinary people with the disciple-making and leadership skills to lead an extended spiritual family on mission. Followers Made and Missionaries Made function as the beginning point; often people will proceed from one to the next. Leaders Made and Microchurch Learning Community function as the next level up, participants often proceeding from one to the next. You can see how these four experiences create a road map for a spiritual journey, as a disciple is ready for the next leg of the journey.

Example #3 Harvest to the Church, Church to the Harvest

As was explained with the informal to formal tools continuum, and in chapter 18, we are always pushing the church toward the harvest field, while we are inviting those in the harvest toward the church. It's a cyclical motion that never ends. In a subversive but not overt way, the win, build, equip, multiply framework, buried so deep in me, informs our informal to formal tool continuum. Our informal tools like BLESS and DBS are in the win phase. The shapes and symbols are mostly in the build phase, with a few shapes in the equip phase. The formal tools are about equipping and multiplying, which takes us back to the harvest, where the multiplication happens.

Finally, one more time, our answers aren't "the right answers" for the voyage question. It is our best answer for our faith community at this time, under the guidance of the Word and the Spirit, as best as we can discern it. We offer it to you, with prayers that it may help you as your community enters the same process of discernment.

CONSIDER THE FOLLOWING VOYAGE QUESTIONS:

- How would you describe the journey and the destination of your disciple-making ecosystem?
- What are the stages and the phases?
- How clearly do you think those you are inviting into the journey understand those various phases? Is there a clear map for the journey?
- How well have the Scriptures and the testimony of the church in her best hours informed your journey?

As we finish this portion of the book, we move from a focus on the cultivation of environments and ecosystems for disciple-making multiplication to the cultivation of environments and ecosystems for leadership development and multiplication. Everything rises and falls on our disciple-making systems. In fact, disciple-making and leadership development are two sides of the same coin. If your disciples and leaders are healthy, you'll end up producing healthy, multiplying microchurches, hubs, and networks. Then you'll have a movement on your hands! Let's explore finally how to bring the collective genius of a decentralized network together for the best decision-making and the brightest future.

CHAPTER 21

The Collective Intelligence Starfish

Embedding Simple Processes and Becoming a Learning System

The complexity of systems requires that we engage everybody just so we can harvest the intelligence that exists throughout the organization.

—Margaret Wheatley, *Finding Our Way*

Figure 21.1

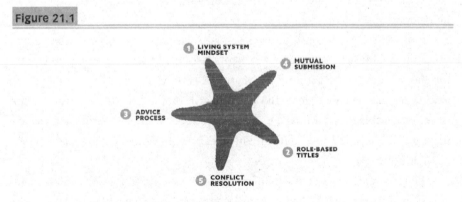

Starfish #7: The Collective Intelligence Starfish

Purpose: The collective intelligence starfish helps us unlock the shared intelligence of every member of our living system for the purpose of better decision-making and constant improvement through implementing five simple processes.

The earth functions as an ecosystem of ecosystems designed by the Spirit of God. It embodies unmatched beauty and intricacy that are both fragile and resilient. It adjusts, renews, and sustains itself as a living system, emerging from its own cells and organisms. The ecology of the earth provides some wonderful clues for developing movemental organizations.

The first time I (Lance) went white-water rafting, within thirty seconds I thought I was going to die because I couldn't breathe. I was at the front of the raft and a huge splash of ice-cold water had plastered my entire body. For what seemed like several minutes, I gasped desperately for air. If you have ever gone white-water rafting, you know the thrill, the fear, the shocking cold, and the overall exhilaration of going with the biggest of flows.

Movements are like rivers. They gush and flow by the power of the Spirit, shallow in some places and deep in others. Ripples and splashes at the top are full of fast action. They appear impressive. But the currents underneath the surface are where the real power resides.

The rocky spots cause the most noise and create the greatest points of energy. Similarly, the processes and the learning systems we place into our networks of disciples, leaders, microchurches, congregations, and hubs create "hot spots" that determine movemental power flow and successful mission objectives.

What does a hot spot, created by a simple process, look like, and how does a living system collectively learn?

In *Radical Inclusion*, Ori shares the story of Jasper, a high-school dropout and Vietnam veteran who worked transporting patients between rooms and emptying the trash at the Albert Einstein Medical Center in Philadelphia. The hospital was urgently trying to dissipate the spread of MRSA, the antibiotic-resistant staph infection that plagues many hospitals. For over a century, health professionals have known that washing hands and regularly wearing gloves and gowns is effective in preventing MRSA.

The hospital's head of infection control gathered a select group of staff members drawn from all ranks and responsibilities, from surgeons to janitors, to work on heading off the rate of infection. It was during this session that Jasper would do something that would literally save lives. He shared that he had noticed that the garbage cans in a wing with many MRSA infections were always mostly empty and had no used gloves in them. The group went to that wing to try to figure out why the nurses weren't using gloves. Strangely enough, it just so happened that all the nurses in the wing had very small hands. The hospital stocked equal numbers of each glove size. This wing used many more extra-small gloves, which would always run out before the others. Larger gloves were too unwieldy, making simple tasks awkward, so the nurses seldom used gloves at all.

The head of infection control asked the nurses if they would wear gloves if their size were continually stocked. The nurses said, "Of course we would." Jasper wrote down his direct phone number and gave it to the nurse's station so that if the wing was running low on extra-small gloves, they just needed to call him, and Jasper would refill the stock within minutes.

Within a year the patient mortality rate had been reduced by 70 percent.

Jasper represents a cell in the body. In the midst of a crisis, the information he contained was priceless, and, although appearances might hide this truth, his voice was the most important one in the room. He was not a medical expert and had no medical training to speak of. Yet the simple process of asking the people closest to the situation to share their observations and ideas created a hot spot of learning, where Jasper's astute observation unleashed an intervention that saved lives. This is a shining example of the collective intelligence starfish at work.

Process #1: Living System Mindset

Every organization is a network of relationships. We either ignore or forget this fact to our own loss. The central nervous system is the people themselves. It has the capacity to receive outside and inside information, process it, and act accordingly. It is what makes a body work. When disconnections, such as a spinal cord injury, come about, the CNS loses its ability to function properly, and there is a risk of loss of movement or death. How the system is regulated, maintained, and opened or closed determines the effectiveness of our systems. This is a matter of processes. The right practices draw from present relationships and deepen them as well. Margaret Wheatley writes, "We've lost confidence in our great human capabilities, partly because mechanistic organizational processes have separated and divided us and made us fearful and distrusting of one another. We need processes to help us reweave connections, to discover shared interests, to listen to one another's stories and dreams. We need processes that take advantage of our natural ability to network, to communicate when something is meaningful to us."[1]

Alan Hirsch: To be able to learn something new, whether it is related to God or to other forms of learning, we need to be willing to let go of obsolete ideas and open our eyes and our hearts to being willing to grow, mature, and get back on the road of discipleship and learn again. The learner needs to venture out of fixed paths into the unknown, not allowing mere routine to stunt their heart and head—this is especially true of religious routine. I would even suggest that new breakthroughs are gained only by those who break out of the arbitrary boundaries that have been set by mere convention—that's why they're called breakthroughs.

While on staff at a large church led by the hierarchy of a senior and executive pastor, I (Lance) received a harsh phone call from the senior pastor after I had sent an email to the executive pastor taking issue with the Christmas weekend staff schedule. The schedule had been announced without any input from staff members. It meant the entire staff would be working on both Christmas Eve and Christmas Day, which was unnecessary. I had offered an alternative solution and had an idea about how to make it happen. The senior pastor called me and asked if I had been "polling" other staff members. He warned me that if I had, it would be grounds for serious discipline.

Two individuals had made a unilateral decision, affecting every staff member, their immediate families, and their extended families, without any input from a large team of creative and smart men and women.

In Ephesians 4:16 (ESV), the apostle Paul wrote, "The whole body, joined and held together by every joint with which it is equipped, when each part is working properly, makes the body grow so that it builds itself up in love." Where a trusting community culture exists, creativity and responsibility course through the life of the body. There is collective ownership of the vision by the community of saints when we operate under the Spirit's design. One or a few higher-ups do not regulate, dominate, or commandeer the accomplishment of the vision. Teams begin to form, and life explodes through the collective gifts and talents of the men and women God has called together.

Those who leave pyramid forms of leadership behind must develop new processes and practices to fill the void left by managers and bosses. Who decides the where, what, when, and how issues of strategic initiatives, schedules, programming, and production? How are conflicts resolved? How are salaries decided on? Since leadership is about power, a commitment away from hierarchal leadership means we must work to develop a new power grid for our organization. What might that look like?

A typical GM factory in the 1980s evoked every stereotype we have of an assembly line. Each worker was responsible for a single task, and the hierarchy was rigid and clear. The system was producing cars that were at best okay. If an employee made a mistake or detected a problem, he could stop the line, whereupon a loud alarm would sound. Get ready to be critiqued! You're a problem.

The Toyota assembly line was drastically different. Employees were regarded as members of a team, and each team member was considered an important contributor and given a high level of autonomy. What happened if an employee stopped the line? A pleasant "ding-dong" would sound, and teams would carefully study what was going on in an effort to continually improve the process. Line workers were constantly encouraged to make suggestions.

Take a moment and imagine you're the head of Toyota. How many worker suggestions would you implement? Assuming most suggestions are well meaning but wouldn't work, 15 percent? Playing the odds that half the suggestions are likely to be helpful, 50 percent? Try 100 percent. Like Wikipedia edits—but thankfully more accurate—each suggestion made by a Toyota line worker was implemented. In decentralized fashion, teams functioned like a circle, and whatever ideas employees had for innovation were put into practice. And in Wikipedia fashion, if someone's suggestion proved counterproductive, another employee would inevitably make a suggestion to undo the previous suggestion. This was an entirely different way of dealing with employees. Rather than regarding line workers as drones who had to follow directions and be kept in line, Toyota viewed its employees as key assets. Imagine the line workers' feeling of empowerment. Their opinions mattered. But Toyota didn't stop there. It also flattened its management hierarchy and equalized the pay scale. Now everyone was in it together.

GM proposed, almost in a dare, that the Japanese take over management of its Fremont, California, auto plant, one of the company's lowest-producing plants. They could run the plant as they saw fit, but they had to use the same union force. The results were staggering. Within three years, it was one of GM's most efficient plants. Their productivity was 60 percent higher than other comparable GM plants![2]

One hundred percent inclusion of input. A new power grid indeed! That's a living system, even in a factory. With the implementation of a proper *advice process*, which we will discuss ahead, the wisdom of the team emerges apart from the weaknesses of consensus.

In *Radical Inclusion*, Ori wrote, "[It is] the leader's responsibility to harvest the knowledge that exists throughout the organization and to build a broader understanding of the ways the team's abilities can be aligned to solve the problem. Rather than the leader bearing the immense responsibility of discovering solutions unilaterally or alone, solving the problem becomes a matter of narrowing down a diverse list of creative solutions proposed by the team."[3]

The dominant leadership theory of our time is based primarily on persuasion— how to influence and manipulate others—rather than biology and physics—how life, growth, and interconnectivity happen and do so in an orderly way.

In *A Failure of Nerve*, Edwin Friedman wrote,

> Recent findings about the brain-body connection have the potential to revolutionize our concept of hierarchy. For they suggest that to a large extent we have a liquid nervous system. The brain turns out to function like a gland. It is the largest organ of secretion, communicating simultaneously with various parts of the body, both near and far, through the reciprocal transmission of substances known as neurotransmitters. In other words, the head is *present* in the body![4]

To this day, scientists can't exactly figure out how starfish move. They have no central brain, yet somehow when one arm moves, the other arms know to move with it. The head is present in the body.

For the church, the body of Christ, Jesus is the *head*. He is the only head. Neither a senior pastor nor any other human is the head of any local church. Calling oneself head pastor is not only theologically incorrect, it is usurping the authority of Christ himself and circumventing the flow of his wisdom and understanding through the rest of the body of Christ.

Committing to a living system of collective intelligence frees in our organizations the secondary intelligences of:

Emotional Intelligence

Daniel Goleman spread the concepts of emotional intelligence and points to five keys that compile it—self-awareness, self-regulation, motivation, empathy, and social skills.

Relational Intelligence

    Relational intelligence is the ability to learn, understand, and comprehend knowledge as it relates to interpersonal dynamics. The more relationally intelligent we become, the more we will demonstrate increased love, respect, and trust in every relationship in our lives, which will inevitably elevate our influence.[5]

Strategic Intelligence

    Strategic intelligence is what helps organizations look beyond themselves by providing its members any and all information available to make informed decisions.

Daniel Cable writes,

Most neuroscientists agree that one of the most basic emotional systems pertains to a functionally identifiable neural circuit that depends on dopamine, and that emotional system might be called interest, anticipation, or seeking. This means that the seeking system is a real place in the brain: a neural network that runs between the prefrontal cortex and the ventral striatum. When the seeking system is activated, we experience persistent feelings of interest, curiosity, sensation seeking, and in the presence of a sufficiently complex cortex, the search for higher meaning.[6]

The life-giving force of a free-flowing seeking system supplies joy in everyday life as well as the workplace!

Process #2: Role-Based Titles

In the early 1900s there was an exceptional pitcher in Major League Baseball with a career earned run average of 2.28 that still ranks in the top fifteen of all time. His win/loss record was 94–46, and he led his league in shutouts in 1916 and was in the top five for strikeouts in two of his five seasons as a pitcher. This dominant hurler's name was Babe Ruth. Most nominal sports fans know who Babe Ruth was, but even many dedicated baseball fans are unaware he was a great pitcher. So why did he pitch for only five seasons if he was so great? Because he was an even better hitter, and the wise decision was made to let him focus on his skills with the bat. However, Ruth was used as a pitcher a handful of times later in his career when his team was shorthanded in that position. To just call him a great pitcher or a great hitter would fall short. No, Babe Ruth was a great *baseball player*. Without question, his team prospered because of his greatness as a hitter, and if he had never pitched in another game, his magnitude spoke for itself. But using him, even sparingly, as fill-in pitcher was an added bonus that made the overall team even better.

When we pigeonhole people in singular titles, chances are, we take others or ourselves out of consideration for filling in during times of need or change. Or we occupy a position that another, better player could fill.

In the arena of church planting, an oft-repeated cycle takes place to the determent of the development of the church. Someone with an apostolic gifting usually starts a given church plant. These people are the *innovators* within Everett Rogers's Diffusion of Innovations scale, and they represent around 3 percent of an organization's populace. Innovators have a magnetic presence and ability to influence. They attract other innovators and those Rogers termed *early adopters*. These are the folks who see a new idea, quickly assess it, and are some of the first to buy in. Early adopters represent about 14 percent of a group.

Figure 21.2

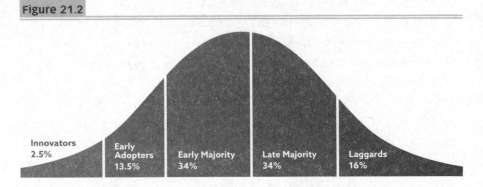

| Innovators 2.5% | Early Adopters 13.5% | Early Majority 34% | Late Majority 34% | Laggards 16% |

As a young church gets started, it is typically the innovators and a few others who jump on board the earliest. As it begins to grow and develop, two other types— which Rogers called *early majority* and *late majority*—join up. Often the person with the innovative or apostolic gifting does not possess strong shepherd or pastor skills. Two issues frequently come into play as the church adds people. They need what a pastor brings, but all they have is an apostle. And he or she is likely occupied and passionate about future steps, dreaming of the next hill to take. Many church plants plateau at this point unless a team develops. Some organizational theorists call this the *founder's trap*.

On rare occasions the innovator or apostle transitions into the role of shepherd or pastor, or unsuccessfully attempts to do so. Frustration mounts when an apostolic or innovator type tries to fill the shepherd role because a void exists in that role. More often than not, leaders who attempt this aren't even aware they are trying to fill a different role. They are just trying to help the people in their fellowship.

Alan Hirsch: Here is one of the big flaws in the prevailing, inherited understandings of ministry: we have reduced ministry down from the much more vigorous and comprehensive APEST typology in the New Testament to a more limited one of the *S* and *T* alone. This means many who now call themselves "pastor" (shepherd) are not vocationally gifted to be shepherds. Likewise, pastors—whatever their particular vocational APEST wiring—are also now required to do *all* the functions represented in the APEST typology. So they have to be healthy expressions of all five! This is an impossible task. Ministry was never intended to be done by one person but by the entire body of Christ! Deep repentance is needed here if we are to correct this inherent dysfunction in the system.

As a young church planter, I (Lance) experienced this exact scenario. My innovative gifts are fairly strong. My pastoral gifts? Uh, em, not so much. The problem was that from the beginning of the church plant, my title was senior *pastor*. So everyone, including myself, expected me to be the expert pastor. As the church grew, all of us were frustrated! I felt inadequate and like a failing leader. It wasn't until we began to bring on others with pastoring skills that we moved past a stage of growth stall.

Churches that move past the founder's trap usually develop a team with other roles (prophetic, evangelistic) represented. We have come to believe that churches should be started with teams with as many roles of the five types mentioned in Ephesians 4:11–12 (ESV) as possible: "[Jesus] gave the *apostles*, the *prophets*, the *evangelists*, the *shepherds* and *teachers*, to equip the saints for the work of ministry, for building up the body of Christ" (emphases ours).

We are more convinced than ever that for the church in North America to experience a genuine disciple-making and church-planting movement, we must implement a disciple-making and leadership-development pipeline that focuses on covocational APEST teams as the new normal, where the living system of Ephesians

4 is honored as Jesus' original design. Currently, the prevailing model still works on the template of the "lead planter," who recruits a core team of helpers. At that point, the codependency and hierarchy has already been set into the foundation before it has begun.

As we launched the KC Underground, we refused to have any titles among the leaders, seeking rather to build on the Ephesians 4 APEST typology and Ephesians 2 assessment of each person's calling. At times, people wonder, "Who's in charge?" With no cynicism and with deadly earnestness, we reply, "Jesus. He is the head. Together, those who have emerged as elders and equippers discern in prayer, conversation, and consultation what the Spirit is saying to the KC Underground." Ruth Haley Barton's book *Pursuing the Will of God Together: A Discernment Practice for Leadership Groups* is a phenomenal and practical treatise on how this can be done.

Earlier in the book, we covered the reasons for moving beyond rank-based titles that underscore status. But if we drop titles altogether, how are we to identify who does what and who to contact regarding the what? Many of the leaders and organizations we have learned from and researched for this book have found wisdom—and, yes, fun—in creating role-based titles that describe what a person does.

One company, HolocracyOne, uses the term *lead link* for the role of a department leader. The term *link* promotes a connecting catalytic and coworking ethos rather than a rank or status culture. Lead link titles are fun and based on the actual role or function of the position. For instance, the lead link role for social media outreach is named social media butterfly, with a purpose to "pollinate the web with Holocracy." We propose taking it further and losing the term *lead*, instead preferring something along the lines of catalyzer or provocateur.

Our friend J. R. Woodward has developed some wonderfully imaginative and helpful role-based titles for the five giftings mentioned in the Ephesians text mentioned before:

Apostles = Dream Awakeners
Prophets = Heart Revealers
Evangelists = Story Tellers
Pastors = Soul Healers
Teachers = Light Givers

A change to role-based titles takes the edge off hierarchy emphasis, especially when we leave behind status predescriptors such as "senior _____" and "executive _____." Within the KC Underground, we exclusively use role-based titles in our operations team. For example, the person who leads the start-up coaching equipping team is simply called the director of start-up coaching. The person who leads financial services is the director of financial services. None of the titles communicate hierarchy, just role. Within a board of directors, we have a small, efficient hierarchy of the traditional offices: president, secretary, and treasurer, who work with the board members. The governance of the board is high level: strategy, oversight, accountability.

As another example, the Make-A-Wish foundation implemented a policy that allowed its people to create their own role-based titles. Then-CEO Susan Fenters came up with "fairy godmother of wishes" for her role. Other titles included "Minister of Dollars and Sense," "Duchess of Data" "Heralder of Happy News"[7]

Process #3: Advice Process

In the spirit of mutual submission, a multitude of organizations in our research were found to use some form of "advice process." This process is not complex.

1. Anyone in any department or domain can make a decision, but prior to doing so *must* seek advice from all affected parties and people with expertise on the matter.[8]
2. The person weighing a decision is not beholden to incorporate every piece of advice in order to create consensus or compromise.
3. The point is to take wise counsel seriously into consideration and to thoughtfully evaluate how the decision will affect others within the organization, both positively and negatively.

We believe decisions are typically made in one of two ways: The boss decides (hierarchy), or a vote is taken (consensus). An advice process exceeds both of these options. Those who will be affected or who have a vested interest are heard, and the people closest to an issue have the power to move beyond bureaucracy and the slow and frustrating course of consensus in order to make a speedier and informed decision.

Dennis Bakke underscores the paybacks of a good advice process:

- It draws people whose advice is sought into the issue and proposition at hand. They become informed of the subjects and become conversant censors or supporters. The sharing of information reinforces the feeling of community and perpetuates a feeling of honor and value.

- The act of seeking advice is an act of humility. Often a senior leader (elder) may hesitate to seek advice from other less experienced team members out of concern that his "all knowing" reputation or responsibility will be tarnished. What if the worker thinks, "Shouldn't he know what to do? Why is he asking me?" When an advice process is common practice, this concern goes out the window.
- It is educational. It creates peer-to-peer learning opportunities and mines the knowledge nuggets of those in the field.
- The odds for the best decision are greatly enhanced versus a top-down approach. The one making the decision is closest to the issue and will be held accountable by those who gave advice for the consequences of the decision.
- The process is plain fun. It is a team-making activity that stimulates creativity and camaraderie.[9]

It is important to clarify that seeking to eschew unilateral decisions with a good advice process is not *consensus*. On the surface, consensus sounds generous, but functionally it can bog down progress through the paralysis of analysis and perpetuate ego trips, hurt feelings, and quasifilibusters. When consensus is incorporated, it mitigates accountability. No one is ultimately held responsible because the majority voted to go a particular way. Frederic Laloux suggests, "With the advice process, the ownership for the decision stays clearly with one person: the decision maker. Convinced that she made the best possible decision, she sees things through with great enthusiasm, trying to prove to advice givers that their trust was well placed or their objections immaterial. While consensus drains energy out of organizations, the advice process boosts motivation and initiative."[10]

Process #4: Mutual Submission

Be subject . . . to every fellow worker and laborer. (1 Cor. 16:16 ESV)

Submit to one another out of reverence for Christ. (Eph. 5:21)

In the book *Unleader*, I (Lance) wrote of how mutual submission is seen in a local church setting. When I visited with my friend David Fitch, professor at Northern

Seminary and the founding pastor of Life on the Vine Christian Community, he began by saying that as a person with strong apostolic gifting, he does in fact come up with a lot of ideas. He is a prototypical innovator, a forward thinker with a heavy dose of entrepreneurial overtones. David said, "When I have an idea, concern, or opinion on an issue, I bring it to the other members of the team of fivefold [Eph. 4:11–12] elders and say, 'I have something I want to submit to you.'" At that point, David stopped and said, "Do you see that? I say, 'I want to *submit* this to you.'" David mentioned the use of submissive language to season the conversation in grace and humility and to emphasize the mutual submission he and the others were committed to. He then told me how the ideas he lays on the table are handled.

If all the other elders are in agreement, the idea will then be submitted in prayer, set on the proverbial altar before the Lord for a time, and revisited to see if God had spoken anything different to any team members in the meantime. The same scenario is played out if there is disagreement from any or all the other elders. The idea or issue is submitted to the Lord in prayer and revisited later. If there is still not complete agreement on how to move forward, the issue is left on the prayer altar indefinitely.

David then grabbed a napkin and sketched out three points that he has subsequently blogged on: posture, process, and pnuematocracy.

Posture

Anyone in a recognized role of leadership is called to maintain the posture of submission to Jesus Christ as Lord of the church and to model the posture of mutual submission to all others who are in the sphere of leadership. From this position, one can expect to witness God's truth revealed for the fellowship.

Making Sure All Voices Are Heard

Once you've assessed everyone on your team for their APEST profile, Steve Cockram, coauthor of *5 Voices: How to Communicate Effectively with Everyone You Lead*, recommends trying these rules of engagement so that everyone can be heard and leveraged for the greatest collective genius. This little shift in practice in the KC Underground leadership team has unleashed so much wisdom into our decision-making! Remember, the apostolic guy is writing this, which means I've had to get used to going last. So hard, at first. Now I love it.

In a group discussion, make sure . . .

Shepherds go first:

- Because they don't like to disagree with what's already been said.
- But they represent 43 percent of the people in the organization!
- Promise not to critique them right off the bat.

Prophets go next:

- Let them think outside the box and take risks.
- Don't judge them right off.
- Ask them clarifying questions.

Teachers go third:

- Encourage them to ask the difficult questions and show where the group is making mistakes.
- Let them do due diligence.

Evangelists go fourth:

- They sell it for all it's worth, and make us cry if needed.
- When they challenge, don't take it personally.

Apostles go last:

- They need to listen first while everyone else talks, even though that's probably hard for them!
- Careful critique is vital so that it's not too sharp.
- They help us dream and see the future!

Process

Jesus lays out a detailed process in Matthew 18 that provides fundamental steps for navigating disputable matters or issues that arise among his followers. The binding and loosing terminology open this process for application beyond sin issues among individuals.

Fitch writes,

We go to one another and in humility discuss the issue. If we believe someone is in sin, we say that and then submit ourselves to that person, being careful to listen as to why we might be wrong. If agreement cannot be reached, if insubordination is detected, we then bring in a third person. At the point where an issue simply cannot be agreed upon (and these issues are rare and outside the creedal orthodoxies that guide a given church), then we take it to the elders, then to the community to study and pray over the issue (Acts 15:28). The Holy Spirit at work in the community drives the issues that will determine the direction of the church, not the single chosen leader who shall determine what shall be discerned, what shall be tolerated, and what shall [not be] allowed.[11]

Pnuematocracy

Pnuematocracy has its roots in the word *pneuma* (spirit), and Spirit-driven leadership is what we all should be searching for. In terms of governance or leadership, the idea of pneumatocracy speaks of a collective voice derived from apostles, prophets, teachers, evangelists, and pastors whom the faith community recognize. "Each one must be given authority for what gifts God has given them. Yet they must exercise that gift in grace and humility (Romans 12:3–4)."[12]

> **Alan Hirsch:** In seeking to remain true to the calling and purpose of the church, we together must seek to look, act, and sound like Jesus. To do this, we have to learn to think like Jesus. In the words of Scripture, this means to seek the mind of Christ in and through the Spirit of Christ (1 Cor. 2:6–16). It is through the Spirit of God that we, together and as individuals, can access the inner rationality of Christ. This is not just access to a theo-logic as if it involved some abstract rational process, but rather is thinking through the lens of Christo-logic, the thought processes of the very Person who rules the universe. This is part of the treasure that the church has access to in Christ (Col. 2:1–5).

Process #5: Conflict Resolution

With a fleet of 200 trucks and 3 processing plants, Morning Star produces 40 percent of diced tomatoes and tomato paste consumed in the United States. Depending on the season, between 400 and 2,400 people work at Morning Star at any given time. But there are no management positions, and there is no HR department. How does this large company deal with conflict that is certain to come about from time to time in a company of this size?

Accountability Process

We have found it uncanny that a multitude of large corporations (over one hundred employees) have developed a dismissal process that virtually mirrors the way Jesus taught conflict resolution in Matthew 18. At Morning Star, for example, should circumstances deem it necessary for someone to leave the company, the accountability process comes into play:

1. Have a direct conversation with the person. No gossiping. No backbiting allowed. Anyone noticing a coworker with performance or integrity issues in conflict with the company's values is required to discuss the issue directly with their coworker. If a person is unwilling to initiate a discussion along these lines, then they just have to live with it.

2. If the one-on-one conversation does not bring resolve, then another person is brought into the discussion as a mediator. This person must be trusted by both colleagues, listen to both parties, clarify what they have heard, and share their thoughts on points made by both coworkers. The mediator is not an arbiter who decides. The power and resolution continue to be in the hands of the two coworkers. The mediator is important to keep the conversation on track and to facilitate mutual understanding. Some differences of opinion don't result in a resolution, especially if one colleague asks another to terminate his or her own employment.

3. If differences of opinion among coworkers can't be resolved, a panel of three colleagues are convened to listen to both sides and pursue the conversation until resolution. Doug Kirkpatrick writes, "If the panel became deadlocked, the company owner participates in the deliberations and renders a final decision. At some point, all disputes must come to an end."[13]

Dismissal Process (via an Accountability Process)

A process such as this eliminates the impetuousness of unilateral firings by one or two higher-ups and follows a Jesusy way of treating others. An important aspect of this sort of dismissal process is that it provides a great opportunity for a team member who is experiencing performance issues to move to a role that better fits his giftings, talents, and skills. Sometimes a person simply does not fit in an organization. Dismissal via an accountability process often helps a person discover this on their own.

Fit, Split, Contend, Transcend

In *The Permanent Revolution*,* Alan and his coauthor, Tim Catchim, offer up a **Model for Creatively Managing Conflict** by riffing off Richard Pascale's thoughts on moving between the dialectical poles of fit and split, contend and transcend:

Having more viewpoints around the table heightens the likelihood of conflict. Nevertheless, well-handled conflict can be highly creative.

- *Fit* refers to a team's affirming of the characteristics that hold them together: their love and respect for each other, their love for God's church and his mission through it, and their commitment to the city, for example. In many ways, this correlates to Paul's teaching in Ephesians 4:1–6, where we are called to strive for the unity of the Spirit in the bond of peace and to base our faith in the one God, faith, or church.

- *Split* is Pascale's term for intentionally legitimizing, acknowledging, and allowing for great diversity of expression in the team. Here the team acknowledges that people are all different and that God has given each their particular calling. This corresponds to Ephesians 4:7–11, where we are told that the church's ministry is expressed in fivefold diversity.

- *Contend* is what Pascale tells us happens when everyone steps into their distinctive roles and contributes what they think. It requires permitting, even encouraging, disagreement, debate, and dialogue around the core tasks of the organization. This corresponds to Ephesians 4:15, where we are encouraged to speak the truth in love, giving each other respect based on our APEST distinctives.

- *Transcend* means that all collectively agree to overcome disagreement to find new solutions. The group is committed to finding the mind of Christ through the unity and diversity he has given his people. Transcend happens when we creatively manage contend. In Ephesians 4:12–16, we eventually are enabled to reach unity in the faith and the knowledge of the Son of God and become mature, to the measure of the full stature of Christ. We are told we must grow up in every way into Christ.

* Alan Hirsch and Tim Catchim, *The Permanent Revolution: Apostolic Imagination and Practice for the 21st Century Church* (New York: Jossey-Bass, 2012), 89–90, 209.

Problem Solving

When broad problems or issues needing decisions arise in aggressive organizational cultures dominated by extroverts or highly dominant personalities, aka type A and high D people, the sway of decision-making often comes from the quickest-to-speak, fast-paced person(s) in the room.

There are ways for resolving conflicts in a spirit of humility and nonaggression whereby every personality type has an equal voice:

1. Circle Up

Consider the majority of social media conflict (which seems to be the bulk of its content). People predominantly yell via keyboard, argue their position, don't practice seeking to understand the other person, and so on. Few people become convinced of an opinion they previously disagreed with. It is an overall aggressive platform for disagreement. Many face-to-face disagreements carry these same aspects of aggression to one degree or another.

Let's go back to the circle—which we spent a good time considering earlier in the book. The circle is a form of equality. No one is at the head of the table. Facing one another, we lay down our personal agendas and demonstrate that we are willing to listen so hard that we are prepared to risk forgetting what we hoped to say.

The circle helps settle our emotions because it reminds us that we will have a chance to be heard, while reminding us that it is important to hear our coworker's points of view. It stirs curiosity and awakens our imagination.

The circle session begins by drawing everyone in by hearing everyone's voice.

Everyone in the circle is asked to answer these questions, and colleagues are encouraged to hear one another's heart.

Circle questions:

How does this issue relate to your personal experiences?
How will the decision on this issue affect you moving forward?
What outcome are you hoping for when we leave the circle today?

2. Practice Appreciative Inquiry

At this stage we begin to discuss the issue at hand. In doing so, we ask questions of those who have differing opinions in regard to the proper solution for the given issue. The posture, tone, and respect we show to one another is to genuinely seek to understand the points of argument by the other person(s).

Circle question:

What am I hearing that makes sense and could provide a better answer than I currently have?

3. Assemble the Discoveries

Through humble listening, at this stage, some key points of knowledge, wisdom, and mutual understanding have most likely surfaced. This is when we may choose to pull out the flip charts and whiteboard to begin collecting what we have learned.

Checking the vitals of our circle, we ask:

- *Who is missing from this conversation?*
- *What did we just see or hear?*
- *Have we been honest and open?*
- *Who are we right now?*

4. Decide

At this point we have practiced what we have said we believe and value. We are one body, a family, where everyone has an equal voice and value. We have demonstrated faith in believing that our collective presence contains the wisdom, knowledge, and skill from God's Spirit to take us where we need to go. This is where we propose our refined solutions, the answers that have been processed (refined) through the gifts and wisdom of those we have become one with.

Every human being represents the *imago Dei*, which means every person is infused with infinite value and unimaginable God-given potential. Furthermore, the Spirit of God is in his people—the very same Spirit that raised Jesus from the dead. When we come together under the headship of Jesus, wonderful, even miraculous, things can and do happen in our midst. Jesus said we would do even greater things than he did, as hard as that is to imagine. Laying down the reigns of hierarchical leadership and picking up the towel and basin of servantship is essential if we are to see that lofty vision realized.

Long live the collective intelligence starfish. May it unleash the genius of the mind of Christ and the power of the Spirit expressed in all members of his body!

The Starfish Journey

This book has been organized into three sections: "Reimagining Church," "A Culture for Multiplying Leaders," and "A Culture for Multiplying Disciples." While this categorical organization has been helpful for the structure of this book, it does not reflect the actual starfish journey a leader and faith community will make toward missional movement. Now we will share with you a map of the starfish journey, which is about natural sequence and stages of the expedition. Let's quickly review the seven starfish.

Starfish #1: The Movement Starfish: Reimagining the Church as a Missional Movement

Purpose: The movement starfish helps us reimagine the church as a decentralized network of multiplying disciples, leaders, houses, hubs, and networks that fill a city or region with the fullness of Jesus.

Starfish #2: The Light-Load Leader Starfish: Equipping Others and Distributing the Weight

Purpose: The light-load leader starfish helps us equip others in a fivefold fashion (Eph. 4:11–13) with five postures, distributing the weight of leadership throughout the entire body rather than on the shoulders of a few.

Starfish #3: The Structure Starfish: Thinking outside Pyramids and Creating Circles

Purpose: The structure starfish helps us structure around organic systems by repeating five patterns in every cell of the body.

Starfish #4: The Self-Management Starfish:
Unleashing Freedom and Facilitating Order

Purpose: The self-management starfish helps us create a culture of empowerment and self-management through activating five potentials in every leader and team.

Starfish #5: The Disciple-Making Ingredients Starfish:
Creating Environments and Mixing Ingredients

Purpose: The disciple-making ingredients starfish helps us discover the five essential ingredients required for creating intentional disciple-making environments (IDEs) that are transformative and multiplicative.

Starfish #6: The Disciple-Making Ecosystem Starfish:
Balancing Elements and Cultivating an Ecosystem

Purpose: The disciple-making ecosystem starfish provides a framework of five essential elements needed to design a disciple-making ecosystem that is transformative and multiplicative.

Starfish #7: The Collective Intelligence Starfish: Embedding
Simple Processes and Becoming a Learning System

Purpose: The collective intelligence starfish helps us unlock the shared intelligence of every member of our living system for the purpose of better decision-making and constant improvement through implementing five simple processes.

The Stages of the Starfish Journey

There are five stages in the starfish journey. **Stage One:** The starfish journey begins with the **movement starfish**. The **mDNA**, or genetic coding of church as movement, are the paradigmatic, interconnected elements that must combine for a movement starfish to emerge. Apostolic leaders are fascinated with these ideas. They hear the Spirit say, "Look up!" These leaders open their hearts, minds, and souls to reimagine the church as a missional movement. They begin to pray regularly and desperately, "Lord, help me perceive the new thing you want to do." They decide the movement

The Map of the Starfish Journey

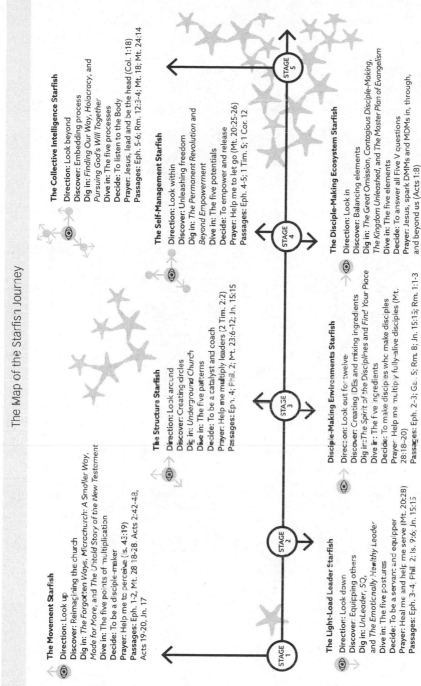

The Movement Starfish

Direction: Look up
Discover: Reimagining the church
Dig in: *The Forgotten Ways, Microchurch: A Smaller Way, Made for More,* and *The Untold Story of the New Testament*
Dive in: The five points of multiplication
Decide: To be a disciple-maker
Prayer: Help me to perceive (Is. 43:19)
Passages: Eph. 1–2, Mt. 28:18–28; Acts 2:42–48, Acts 19–20, Jn. 17

The Structure Starfish

Direction: Look around
Discover: Creating circles
Dig in: *Underground Church*
Dive in: The five patterns
Decide: To be a catalyst and coach
Prayer: Help me multiply leaders (2 Tim. 2:2)
Passages: Eph. 4; Phil. 2; Mt. 23:6–12; Jn. 15:15

The Collective Intelligence Starfish

Direction: Look beyond
Discover: Embedding process
Dig in: *Finding Our Way, Holacracy,* and *Pursuing God's Will Together*
Dive in: The five processes
Decide: To listen to the Body
Prayer: Jesus, lead and be the head (Col. 1:18)
Passages: Eph. 5–6; Rm. 12:3–4; Mt. 18; Mt. 24:14

The Self-Management Starfish

Direction: Look within
Discover: Unleashing freedom
Dig in: *The Permanent Revolution and Beyond Empowerment*
Dive in: The five potentials
Decide: To empower and release
Prayer: Help me to let go (Mt. 20:25–26)
Passages: Eph. 4–5; 1 Tim. 5; 1 Cor. 12

The Light-Load Leader Starfish

Direction: Look down
Discover: Equipping others
Dig in: *UnLeader, 5Q,* and *The Emotionally Healthy Leader*
Dive in: The five postures
Decide: To be a servant and equipper
Prayer: Heal me and help me serve (Mt. 20:28)
Passages: Eph. 3–4, Phil. 2; Is. 9:6, Jn. 15:15

Disciple-Making Environments Starfish

Direction: Look out for twelve
Discover: Creating DEs and mixing ingredients
Dig in: *The Spirit of the Disciplines* and *Find Your Pace*
Dive in: The five ingredients
Decide: To make disciples who make disciples
Prayer: Help me multiply fully-alive disciples (Mt. 28:18–20)
Passages: Eph. 2–3; Ga. 5; Rm. 8; Jn. 15:15; Rm. 1:1–3

The Disciple-Making Ecosystem Starfish

Direction: Look in
Discover: Balancing elements
Dig in: *The Great Omission, Contagious Disciple-Making, The Kingdom Unleashed,* and *The Master Plan of Evangelism*
Dive in: The five elements
Decide: To answer all Five V questions
Prayer: Jesus, spark DMMs and MDMs in, through, and beyond us (Acts 1:8)
Passages: The Gospels chronologically in parallel

The Motion of the Starfish Journey

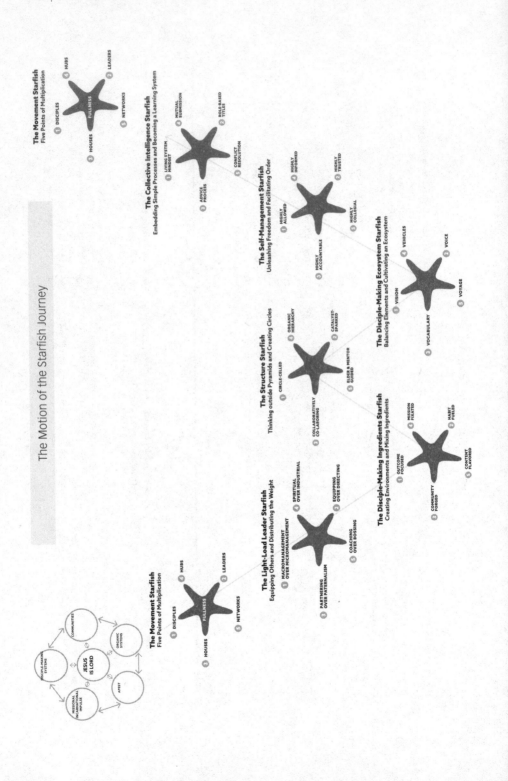

must start with them, and they commit to being a disciple-maker. They dive in to the five points of multiplication—disciples, leaders, houses, hubs, and networks. They meditate on passages like Ephesians 1–2, Matthew 28:18–20, Acts 2; 19–20, and John 17. They read books like *The Forgotten Ways*, *Microchurch: A Smaller Way*, *The Untold Story of the New Testament*, *Pagan Christianity*, *Miraculous Movements*, *Movements that Change the World* and lead their team through the *Made for More Resource Kit*.

Stage Two: The second stage is learning the way of the **light-load leader starfish**. As soon as a leader hears, "Look up," almost immediately they hear the Spirit also say, "Look down." The leader joins Jesus in his Philippians 2 pattern of downward mobility. *Kenosis*, which describes Jesus' practice of self-emptying, becomes the way of this leader as they empty themselves of the idolatrous attachments of the false self. They find themselves on their knees, praying, "Lord, heal me and help me to serve," and tend to their souls like never before. They dive in and begin to practice the five postures of a starfish light-load leader. They kneel down and wash others' feet by focusing their best energy on equipping others for *their* maximum healing, influence, and impact. They meditate on passages like Ephesians 3–4, Philippians 2, Isaiah 9, and John 15. You'll find them reading books like *UnLeader*, *5Q: Reactivating the Original Intelligence and Capacity of the Body of Christ*, *Hero Maker*, and *The Emotionally Healthy Leader*.

Stage Three: In the third stage, the leader begins to cultivate intentional disciple-making environments by way of the **disciple-making ingredients starfish**. As Jesus did, in prayer, they hear the Father speaking names to them: "Look for the twelve." They decide to make disciples who can make disciples. Therefore, they dive into the five ingredients needed to create IDEs, which are a greenhouse for flourishing and multiplying disciples. They keep mixing and stirring the ingredients while praying, "Lord, help me multiply fully-alive disciples!" They meditate on passages like Ephesians 2–3, Galatians 5, Romans 8, John 15, and Romans 1:1–3. They read books like *The Spirit of the Disciplines*, *Soul Custody*, *Emotionally Healthy Spirituality*, *Discipleship that Fits*, *Faith of the Leap*, *Gospel Fluency*, and *Find Your Place*.

At this point, because disciple-making is the root for the fruit of leadership development, new leaders are emerging, springing up from those who have been discipled! Leaders are those who have successfully made other disciples and disciple-makers. The Spirit says to this leader, "Look around, it's time to create more circles." The leader has had their own circle, but it's time to multiply circles of disciples and leaders. Now the move from addition to multiplication has begun.

It is the time to explore the **structure starfish**, diving into the five patterns that will create an organic structure that can scale infinitely and adapt in real time to challenges and opportunities. Every day they pray, "Lord, multiply the gospel, disciples, leaders, and circles!" They meditate on passages like Ephesians 4, Philippians 2, Matthew 23:6–12, and 2 Timothy 2:2. You'll find them reading books like *Underground Church: A Living Example of the Church in Its Most Potent Form*, *On the Verge: A Journey Into the Apostolic Future of the Church*, *Spent Matches*, and *Reinventing Organizations*.

Stage Four: In this stage, the leader continues to keep their eye on the ball of disciple-making. They know the possibility of the movement starfish coming to life rises and falls on a thriving disciple-making ecosystem. They have learned much about multiplying disciples and leaders. Now begins the process of creating systems for this to be simple and reproducible. The Spirit says to them, "Look in. What have you learned?" The leader begins to see a burgeoning movement and realizes it is an ecosystem that must be balanced and stewarded. They dive into the five elements of the **disciple-making ecosystem starfish**. They open dialogue and conversation with other leaders, whom they perceive as peers and co-laborers, discerning together how their faith community will answers the five V questions. They engage in a parallel reading of the Gospels in chronological order, moving right through Acts, in an effort to see how Jesus kick-started a disciple-making movement that changed the world. They read books like *The Great Omission*, *Contagious Disciple Making: Leading Others on a Journey of Discovery*, *The Kingdom Unleashed*, and *The Master Plan of Evangelism*. Every day they pray, "Jesus, spark DMMs and MDMs in, through, and beyond us" (see Acts 1:8).

Now that multiplication is kicking in, disciples, leaders, microchurches, hubs, and even networks are beginning to emerge. The Spirit is saying, "Look within all these new disciples, leaders, and microchurches, and realize there is unlimited potential! In every seed there is the potential for a forest!" The leader knows, more than ever, that it's time to empower and release. They are determined to set God's people free and at the same time facilitate order and accountability. It's time for the **self-management starfish** and a deep dive into the five potentials being unlocked in all God's people. They meditate on passages like Ephesians 4–5, 1 Timothy 5, and 1 Corinthians 12–14. You'll find them reading books like *The Permanent Revolution*, *Beyond Empowerment*, *A Theology of Church Leadership*, *Church 3.0*, and *Dry Bones Can Live Again*. Even though multiplication is happening, and a movement is brewing, you won't find this leader bragging or taking credit. Instead, you'll find them daily facedown, humbled and hidden, praying, "Help me to let go, Lord. These people are yours. Everything is yours. You must increase; I must decrease."

Stage Five: In this stage, the Spirit is whispering, "Look beyond!" No matter what we know of Jesus, he is always more. The vision of gospel saturation, of Jesus filling everything every way through his people manifesting his fullness, is being realized in that movement's context. Multiplying disciples, leaders, houses, hubs, and networks are beginning to fill the city or region. But the Spirit wants us to look to spread the gospel to every corner of culture. Every sphere of society. Every tribe. Every tongue. Every nation. The Great Commission is designed to become the Great Completion. At this point, the leader is aware of their need for the headship of Jesus and the collective intelligence starfish. The wisdom needed is radically beyond the capacity of a single leader or even a great leadership team. The leaders must dive into five processes of the **collective intelligence starfish.** In so doing, they can listen and learn from the entire Body. They seek to grow up into the headship and leadership of the Lord Jesus Christ. Daily they pray, "Jesus, lead on. You alone are the Head." You'll find apostolic leadership teams interacting and co-laboring together across a city, region, and even nations. They meditate on the entire book of Ephesians as the constitution for the church. You'll find them reading books like *Pursuing the Will of God Together: A Discernment Practice for Leadership Groups,* *Holocracy,* and *Finding Our Way: Leadership for an Uncertain Time.*

The Conclusion of the Matter

In your relationships with one another, have the same mindset as Christ Jesus:

> Who, being *in very nature God,*
>> did not consider equality with God something to be used to his own advantage;
> rather, he made himself nothing
>> by taking the *very nature of a servant,*
>> being made in human likeness. (Phil. 2:5–7, emphasis ours)

Jesus, *being in very nature God.* Jesus is the King of Kings. The Lord of Lords. The first and the last, the Alpha and Omega, the apex of all that is. Jesus is the centerpiece and the Sun of God's Universe. Jesus isn't just the middle or the margins; he is the whole show and the whole point of history. The entire heavenly realm—the Father, the Holy

Spirit, and the angelic hosts—is occupied with one person: Jesus. The entire universe was created by Jesus, through Jesus, and for Jesus. He is the Creator and Sustainer—everything in all creation is held together in him. Jesus is the key that unlocks the entire canon of Scripture. Every passage in every book, both Old Testament and New Testament, is ultimately occupied with one person—Jesus. All Scripture proclaims him. The Father exalts him. The Spirit magnifies him. The angels worship him. The church exists to follow him. He is Almighty God, Sovereign and Supreme. May our eyes be opened to see his greatness! Because Jesus trumps everything.[1]

When we drop to our feet to worship Jesus with awe and wonder, fear and trembling, we are astounded beyond words to find him bowing down at our feet, washing them with a basin and a towel: "[Jesus] got up from the meal, took off his outer clothing, and wrapped a towel around his waist. After that, he poured water into a basin and began to wash his disciples' feet, drying them with the towel that was wrapped around him" (John 13:4–5).

The room must have grown very quiet as the status-seeking disciples quietly watched the creator of the world, the King of Kings, the Lord of Lords bend down to wash their dirty, smelly feet. A task reserved for the lowest of servants, the washing of feet was regarded as so lowly, so demeaning, that even Jewish slaves did not have to do it. Ancient stories tell us that in the Jewish world, if at all possible, this job was reserved for gentile slaves.[2] You know what you can't find in history prior to Jesus? There had never before been a story of anyone of a higher status washing the feet of someone of lower status. That never happened until this night. Jesus is the origin of starfish leadership.

Jesus, *taking the very nature of a servant.*

Do you know what greatness looks like in God's eyes? Washing feet. Jesus took on the "very nature" of a servant. Service and generosity were the pervasive worldview of Jesus. Service isn't something you do; it's who you are: a servant. It becomes part of every area of our lives. Service is not just an activity but an identity. Service isn't about an outward performance but an inner posture. "Now that I, your Lord and Teacher, have washed your feet, you also should wash one another's feet. I have set you an example that you should do as I have done for you. Very truly I tell you, no servant is greater than his master, nor is a messenger greater than the one who sent him. Now that you know these things, you will be blessed if you do them" (John 13:14–17).

If it were possible, dear reader, at this point, we would love to remove your shoes, bow down, and wash your feet. If we did, however, we would find that Jesus had already beaten us to it.

This book, as flawed and humble as it may be, is our alabaster jar that we have broken at the feet of Jesus. It's our costly gift to him, that in many ways is the sum of our life's work, and it is here for his pleasure.

That is enough.

It is our sincere prayer that you, the beloved of God, have rediscovered truths that have awakened again the wild holy rumpus in you. In the name of Jesus, we pray you will carry these starfish with you and see them unleash the freedom of God, the genius of his body, the fullness of Jesus, and a movement of multiplying disciples, leaders, houses, hubs, and networks until the good things of God run wild!

If you desire further help or training for your church or organization, please visit https://disciplesmade.com/ to learn more about IDEs, calling discovery and deployment, development of disciple-making ecosystems, and starfish coaching. Feel free to contact us at starfish@disciplesmade.com. We'd love to hear your starfish stories.

Long live the starfish!

Acknowledgments

This book has been quite the journey. Without our decades of experiences—including highs, lows, bumps, bruises, triumphs, and tragedies—in the field of church leadership, and the myriad colleagues and friends entailed therein, we would not have been able to take on this task. There is no way we can include all the names of those who have shaped us and our insights on this point in our journeys. We believe you know who you are, and we are forever thankful for your influence.

We certainly want to honor our friend Ori Brafman for his arduous counsel throughout the years long process of developing this work. Ori not only suggested the title but also pushed us deeper into particular areas of research and the spheres we were inclined to cover. Ori's friendship and faith in our purpose have been a strength and encouragement from the very beginning of this work.

Many of our friends in leadership have encouraged us along the way through personal words, notes, and their own work—Mark Labberton, Brian Sanders, Doug Paul, Dave Ferguson, Michael Frost, Brad Brisco, Brian Phipps, Doug Paul, Peter Block—and shared important insights to the final text.

We are extremely thankful for our agent, Mark Sweeney, who believed in and fought for this book by finding the perfect publishing partner with Zondervan and executive editor Ryan Pazdur. Ryan championed the book from the beginning and stayed with us through a series of roadblocks that easily could have doomed the book from seeing ink. Finally, thanks to Kyle Rohane and Kim Tanner. Your editing skills are amazing. Our book is miles and miles better because of your hard work and vision for the aim of this work.

Notes

Chapter 1: Arachnophobia and Spider Bites

1. Inspired by a talk given by my friend John Mark Comer at Exponential 2019 on Ephesians 6. Used by his permission.
2. We understand this is a significant claim. Alan doesn't claim to have "discovered" something "new," but rather sees himself as the custodian of something given to him by grace through the study of Scripture and historical apostolic movements. He further suggests that while apostolic movements might have "more than the six elements, they never will have less than the six elements." Alan Hirsch and Dave Ferguson, *On the Verge: A Journey into the Apostolic Future of the Church* (Grand Rapids: Zondervan, 2011), 84. Based on our experience in India and our own research, we wholeheartedly agree.
3. Rob Wegner and Jack Magruder, *Missional Moves: 15 Tectonic Shifts that Transform Churches, Communities, and the World* (Grand Rapids: Zondervan, 2012), 220–21.
4. Alan Hirsch and Tim Catchim, *The Permanent Revolution: Apostolic Imagination and Practice for the 21st Century Church* (San Francisco: Jossey-Bass, 2012), loc. 829 and 5755 of 8049, Kindle.
5. Bachrach and Baratz suggested that to fully understand power, researchers should also consider decisions that are not made—nondecisions. A primary function of nondecision-making is to maintain a *mobilization of bias*. Mobilization of bias represents a dominant set of beliefs, values, and institutional processes and procedures that work to privilege some groups in relation to others. Peter Bachrach and Morton S. Baratz, *Power and Poverty: Theory and Practice* (New York: Oxford University Press, 1970).

Chapter 2: Good Things Running Wild

1. Alan Hirsch and Dave Ferguson, *On the Verge: A Journey into the Apostolic Future of the Church* (Grand Rapids: Zondervan, 2011), 130.

2. Richard J. Krejcir, "Statistics on Pastors," Into Thy Word, 2007, http://www .intothyword.org/apps/articles/?articleid=36562; and Tod Bolsinger, *Canoeing the Mountains: Christian Leadership in Uncharted Territory* (Downers Grove, IL: InterVarsity Press, 2018), 229.

3. Alan Hirsch, *The Forgotten Ways: Reactivating Apostolic Movements* (Grand Rapids: Brazos, 2016), 139.

4. Thom S. Rainer, "Seven Trends in Worship Service Times," Church Answers, May 25, 2015, http://thomrainer.com/2015/05/seven-trends-in-worship -service-times/.

5. Hirsch, *The Forgotten Ways*, 199–200.

6. Ori Brafman and Rod A. Beckstrom, *The Starfish and the Spider: The Unstoppable Power of Leaderless Organizations* (New York: Penguin, 2007), 35.

7. Thom S. Rainer, "Declining, Plateaued, and Growing Churches from Exponential and LifeWay Research," Church Answers, March 6, 2019, https://churchanswers.com/blog/major-new-research-on-declining-plateaued -and-growing-churches-from-exponential-and-lifeway-research/.

8. Rainer, "Declining, Plateaued, and Growing Churches."

9. Rainer, "Declining, Plateaued, and Growing Churches."

10. Todd Wilson, *Multipliers: Leading Beyond Addition* (Centreville, VA: Exponential, 2019). A summary of Kindle location 247–303.

11. Life.Church, led by Craig Groeschel, is widely considered the most successful multisite model, with more than thirty-four locations gathering in ten states. Life.Church has had a huge kingdom impact with the development of such resources as YouVersion and Open, a website where they offer thousands of free sermons, small group materials, and other training resources to the church. Those are starfish contributions!

12. Jeremy Heimans and Henry Timms, "Understanding 'New Power'," *Harvard Business Review*, December 2014, https://hbr.org/2014/12/understanding -new-power.

13. Heimans and Timms, "Understanding 'New Power'."

14. Heimans and Timms, "Understanding 'New Power'."

15. Moisés Naim, *The End of Power: From Boardrooms to Battlefields and Churches to States, Why Being In Charge Isn't What It Used to Be* (New York: Basic Books, 2013), 52.

16. Naim, *The End of Power*, 52.

17. Alan Hirsch and Tim Catchim, *The Permanent Revolution: Apostolic Imagination and Practice for the 21st Century Church* (San Francisco: Jossey-Bass, 2012), loc. 5759 of 8049, Kindle.

18. Hirsch, *The Forgotten Ways*, 117.

19. Darin H. Land, *The Diffusion of Ecclesiastical Authority: Sociological Dimensions of Leadership in the Book of Acts* (Eugene, OR: Pickwick, 2008), 229–30.

Chapter 3: The Movement Starfish: Reimagining the Church as a Missional Movement

1. Modified version of a definition of gospel saturation sourced from Christ Together, Gospel Saturation. Free resource at https://christtogether.org /resources/.

2. David Chudwin, *I Was a Teenage Space Reporter: From Apollo 11 to Our Future in Space* (London: LID Publishing), loc. 2726 of 2896, Kindle.

3. Ki Mae Meussner, "The 12 Moonwalkers: Where Are They Now?," ABC News, July 15, 2009, https://abcnews.go.com/Technology/Apollo11MoonLanding /12-moonwalkers-now-apollo-11-anniversary/story?id=8094239.

4. "A Pale Blue Dot," The Planetary Society, https://www.planetary.org/explore /space-topics/earth/pale-blue-dot.html, accessed September 15, 2020.

5. Alan Hirsch and Tim Catchim, *The Permanent Revolution: Apostolic Imagination and Practice for the 21st Century Church* (San Francisco: Jossey-Bass, 2012), loc. 631 of 8049, Kindle.

6. Cornelius Plantinga Jr., *Not the Way It's Supposed to Be: A Breviary of Sin* (Grand Rapids: Eerdmans, 1995), 10.

7. Alan Hirsch, *The Forgotten Ways: Reactivating Apostolic Movements* (Grand Rapids: Brazos, 2016), 64.

8. Hirsch, *The Forgotten Ways*, 65.

9. Robert E. Coleman, *The Master Plan of Evangelism* (Grand Rapids: Revell, 1993), 89.

Chapter 4: The Movement Starfish: Five Points of Multiplication

1. Rodney Stark, *The Rise of Christianity: How the Obscure, Marginal Jesus Movement Became the Dominant Religious Force in the Western World in a Few Centuries* (San Francisco: HarperSanFrancisco, 1997).

2. Michael Green, *Evangelism in the Early Church* (Grand Rapids: Eerdmans, 2004), loc. 3637–639 of 5531, Kindle.

3. Dan White Jr., *Subterranean: Why the Future of the Church Is Rootedness* (Eugene, OR: Cascade, 2015), loc. 117 of 3710, Kindle.

4. "The groupings indicate at least five different house churches in Rome (vv 5, 10, 11, 14, 15; e.g., Minear, *Obedience*, 7), and is more likely than Zahn's

suggestion that those mentioned in vv 5–13 were all members of the home church of Prisca and Aquila, which would imply a double greeting on Paul's part (v 5a, vv 5–13)." James D. G. Dunn, *Romans 9–16*, Vol. 38b of Word Biblical Commentary (Grand Rapids: Zondervan, 2014), 891.

5. Alan Hirsch, *The Forgotten Ways: Reactivating Apostolic Movements* (Grand Rapids: Brazos, 2016), 102.

6. Gene Edwards, *Revolution: The Story of the Early Church* (Jacksonville, FL: Seedsowers, 1974), 31.

7. "When Paul left Antioch to discuss the gospel with the Jerusalem leaders, he took Titus with him (Gal 2:1–3); acceptance of Titus (a Gentile) as a Christian without circumcision vindicated Paul's stand there (Gal 2:3–5). Presumably Titus, who is not referred to in Acts (but is mentioned 13 times in the rest of the NT), worked with Paul at Ephesus during his third missionary journey." Introduction to Titus, *NIV Study Bible*, Fully Revised Edition (Grand Rapids: Zondervan, 2020), 2139.

8. Acts 15:19–20; 16:1–4; 1 Timothy 1:1–3

9. Acts 20:4; Acts 19:29

10. Acts 20:4

11. Acts 20:4

12. Acts 20:4

13. Acts 20:4

14. Acts 20:4

15. "According to the Western Text, Paul had use of the building for these hours. Further, the hours between 11 a.m. and 4 p.m. are when public affairs such as schooling and judicial activities come to a halt in all Greco-Roman cities." Frank Viola, *The Untold Story of the New Testament Church: An Extraordinary Guide to Understanding the New Testament* (Shippensburg, PA: Destiny Image, 2004), 136.

16. Viola, *The Untold Story*, 115–16.

17. Patrick O'Connell, "The Missing Element of the Jesus Mission: The Three GREATS of the Jesus Mission," Medium, April 6, 2019, https://medium.com/@patjamoco/the-missing-element-of-the-jesus-mission-5ebadd7954e.

18. Dave Ferguson and Patrick O'Connell, *Together: The Great Collaboration* (Centreville, VA: Exponential, 2020), 34.

19. NewThing 2019 Annual Report, https://static1.squarespace.com/static/5464e9d9e4b0bb89e3fdf5f6/t/5e25dd33c1003e671f30a116/1579539809709/2019_NT_Annual_Report_-_final.pdf.

20. Download *Together* at https://exponential.org/resource-ebooks/together/.

21. The house and hubs language framework is borrowed from the Microchurch Learning Community; Hugh Halter, Brian Johnson, and Rob Wegner; copyright Disciples Made.

22. Rodney Stark, *The Triumph of Christianity: How the Jesus Movement Became the World's Largest Religion* (New York: HarperOne, 2011), 114–19.

Chapter 5: The Movement Starfish: What Makes a Movement and How Do We Measure It?

1. David Garrison, *Church Planting Movements: How God Is Redeeming a Lost World* (Monument, CO: WIGTake Resources, 2004), Kindle.

2. Justin Long, "24:14 Movement Dashboard," 2414, May 2020, https://www
.2414now.net/wp-content/uploads/2414-Movement-Data-Dashboard
_05-05-20.pdf.

3. Noah Kaye, "10 Characteristics of Church Planting Movements," Noah Kaye (blog), May 11, 2012, http://noahkaye.com/blog/10-characteristics-of
-church-planting-movements.

4. Roy Moran, "Disciple Making Movements—A History and a Definition," Discipleship.org, https://discipleship.org/bobbys-blog/disciple-making
-movements-part-1/

5. 24:14 is a global coalition praying and working together to start kingdom movements in every unreached people and place by 2025.

6. Alan Hirsch and Tim Catchim, *The Permanent Revolution: Apostolic Imagination and Practice for the 21st Century Church* (San Francisco: Jossey-Bass, 2012), 132–33.

7. Hirsch and Catchim, *The Permanent Revolution*, 123, Location 3704, Kindle.

8. Hirsch and Catchim, *The Permanent Revolution*, loc. 3898 of 8049, Kindle.

9. We were introduced to Grant LeMarquand's reading of Matthew 15 in Brian D. McLaren, *Everything Must Change: Jesus, Global Crises, and a Revolution of Hope* (Nashville: Thomas Nelson, 2007), 154–59. LeMarquand's work on this passage is available at tesm.edu/articles/lemarquand-canaanite-woman

10. Grant LeMarquand, *One God, One People, One Future: Essays in Honor of N. T. Wright* (Minneapolis: Fortress , 2019), 245–47.

11. Justin Long, director of global research at Beyond, in discussion with author, July 2020. Publicly available report from March 2020, https://2414now.net/wp
-content/uploads/2020/09/2414_Movement_Data_Dashboard_06-01-20.pdf.

Section 2: A Culture for Multiplying Leaders

1. "Repentance" in *Holman Treasury of Key Bible Words: 200 Greek And 200 Hebrew Words Defined and Explained*, eds. E. E. Carpenter and P. W. Comfort (Nashville: Broadman and Holman, 2000), 153. In addition, Rob Bell's sermon on T'Shuva from episode 77 of the *RobCast* unpacks the idea of teshuva as the return home from exile, the return to wholeness from the place of sin, which shatters and scars the original blessing of the *imago Dei*. The message can be heard at https://www.youtube.com/watch?v=JgrtYEkbh2Y.

2. Dante, "The Inferno: Canto 1," *The Divine Comedy*.

3. Kate Shellnutt and Morgan Lee, "Mark Driscoll Resigns from Mars Hill," *Christianity Today*, October 14, 2014, https://www.christianitytoday.com/ct /2014/october-web-only/mark-driscoll-resigns-from-mars-hill.html.

4. Bob Smietana, "Billy Hybels Resigns from Willow Creek," Christianity Today, April 10, 2018, https://www.christianitytoday.com/news/2018/april/bill -hybels-resigns-willow-creek-misconduct-allegations.html.

5. Daniel M. Cable, *Alive at Work: The Neuroscience of Helping Your People Love What They Do* (Boston: Harvard Business Review Press, 2018), 124.

6. Jeffrey S. Nielson, *The Myth of Leadership*: *Creating Leaderless Organizations* (Boston: Davies-Black, 2004), 6.

Chapter 6: The Light-Load Leader Starfish: Equipping Others and Distributing the Weight

1. Alan Hirsch, *The Forgotten Ways: Reactivating Apostolic Movements* (Grand Rapids: Brazos, 2016), 93.

2. Pastor Eugene Cho's Resignation Letter, June 3, 2018, http://seattlequest.org /wp-content/uploads/2018/06/Pastor-Eugene-Chos-Resignation-Letter -6.3.18.pdf.

3. Hirsch, *The Forgotten Ways*, 184.

4. Hirsch, *The Forgotten Ways*, 159.

5. Alan Hirsch is the leading author and working theologian on the restoration of the fivefold giftings in Ephesians 4. Because he is a personal mentor and spiritual father to me (Rob), this section is the synthesis and overflow of many conversations and his books: *The Forgotten Ways*, *The Permanent Revolution*, and *5Q*.

6. Alan Hirsch and Tim Catchim, *The Permanent Revolution: Apostolic Imagination and Practice for the 21st Century Church* (San Francisco: Jossey-Bass, 2012), 16–17.

7. Rob Wegner and Brian Phipps, *Find Your Place: Locating Your Calling through Your Gifts, Passions, and Story* (Grand Rapids: Zondervan, 2019), 123–24.

8. Hirsch, *The Forgotten Ways*, 163.

9. Margaret J. Wheatley, *Finding Our Way: Leadership for an Uncertain Time* (San Francisco: Berrett-Koehler, 2007), 32.

10. From the back cover of Doug Kirkpatrick's *Beyond Empowerment: The Age of the Self-Managed Organization* (Scotts Valley, CA: CreateSpace, 2011).

11. Franciscan Ecological Wisdom, May 18, 2020, https://cac.org/pope-francis -and-st-francis-of-assisi-2020-05-18/.

12. Skye Jethani deserves credit for what he termed the "evangelical industrial complex." Skye Jethani, "The Evangelical Industrial Complex and the Rise of Celebrity Pastors (Pt. 1)," *Christianity Today*, February 20, 2012, https://www .christianitytoday.com/pastors/2012/february-online-only/evangelical -industrial-complex-rise-of-celebrity-pastors.html.

13. Dan White Jr., "Church as Movement, Not Industrial Complex," V3 Movement, http://thev3movement.org/2016/08/08/church-as-movement-not-industrial -complex/, accessed September 16, 2020.

14. Hirsch, *The Forgotten Ways*, 180.

15. Kirkpatrick, *Beyond Empowerment*, 39.

16. Daniel M. Cable, *Alive at Work: The Neuroscience of Helping Your People Love What They Do* (Boston: Harvard Business Review Press, 2018), 6.

17. Quoted in Michael Bungay Stanier, "How to Coach in 10 Minutes or Less," Soymicoach, April 1, 2016, https://rutinaspositivas.wordpress.com/2016/04 /01/how-to-coach-in-10-minutes-or-less/.

18. Lance Ford, *UnLeader: Reimagining Leadership . . . and Why We Must* (Kansas City: Beacon Hill, 2012), 94–95.

19. Wheatley, *Finding Our Way*, 178.

20. Brian J. Robertson, *Holacracy: The New Management System for a Rapidly Changing World* (New York: Holt, 2015), 26.

Chapter 7: The Structure Starfish: Thinking outside Pyramids and Creating Circles

1. Peter Block, *Stewardship: Choosing Service over Self-Interest* (San Francisco: Berrett-Koehler, 1993), 17.

2. Christina Baldwin and Ann Linea, *The Circle Way: A Leader in Every Chair* (San Francisco: Berrett-Koehler, 2010), xvi.

3. Fr. Richard Rohr, "A Circle Dance," Center for Action and Contemplation, February 27, 2017, https://cac.org/a-circle-dance-2017-02-27/.

4. Alan Hirsch and Tim Catchim, *The Permanent Revolution: Apostolic Imagination and Practice for the 21st Century Church* (San Francisco: Jossey-Bass, 2012), loc. 5876 of 8049, Kindle.

5. Alan Hirsch, *The Forgotten Ways: Reactivating Apostolic Movements* (Grand Rapids: Brazos, 2016), 253.

6. Peter Block, *Community: The Structure of Belonging* (San Francisco: Berrett-Koehler, 2008), 152–54.

7. Freederic Laloux, *Reinventing Organizations: A Guide to Creating Organizations Inspired by the Next Stage of Human Consciousness* (Brussels, Belgium: Nelson Parker, 2014), 45.

8. Lance Ford, *UnLeader: Reimagining Leadership . . . and Why We Must* (New York: Beacon Hill, 2012), 62.

9. Ori Brafman and Rod A. Beckstrom, *The Starfish and the Spider: The Unstoppable Power of Leaderless Organizations* (London: Portfolio, 2006), 129.

10. Brafman and Beckstrom, *The Starfish and the Spider*, 93.

11. Jeffrey S. Nielson, *The Myth of Leadership: Creating Leaderless Organizations* (Boston: Davies-Black, 2004), 101.

12. Brafman and Beckstrom, *The Starfish and the Spider*, 92.

13. Brafman and Beckstrom, *The Starfish and the Spider*, 93.

14. Dictionary.com, s.v. "peering," https://www.dictionary.com/browse/peering.

15. Sinonimos-Oneline, s.v. "squint," https://sinonimos-online.com/english/squint.html.

16. Merriam-Webster, s.v. "peer," https://www.merriam-webster.com/dictionary/peer.

17. Nielson, *The Myth of Leadership*, 151.

18. Laloux, *Reinventing Organizations*, 68–69.

19. Laloux, *Reinventing Organizations*, 68–69.

20. Margaret J. Wheatley, *Finding Our Way: Leadership for an Uncertain Time* (San Francisco: Berrett-Koehler, 2007), 92.

21. Francisco Varela quoted in Wheatley, *Finding Our Way*, 92.

22. Paul D. Stanley and J. Robert Clinton, *Connecting: The Mentoring Relationships You Need to Succeed in Life* (Colorado Springs: NavPress, 1992), 18.

23. Frank Viola, "Rethinking Leadership in the New Testament," Beyond Evangelical, https://frankviola.org/2014/01/15/rethinkingleadership/.

24. Robert K. Greenleaf, *Servant Leadership: A Journey into the Nature of Legitimate Power and Greatness*, 25th Anniversary Edition (New York: Paulist, 1977), 63.

Chapter 8: The Self-Management Starfish: Unleashing Freedom and Facilitating Order

1. Margaret J. Wheatley, *Finding Our Way: Leadership for an Uncertain Time* (San Francisco: Berrett-Koehler, 2007), 64.

2. Alan Hirsch and Tim Catchim, *The Permanent Revolution: Apostolic Imagination and Practice for the 21st Century Church* (San Francisco: Jossey-Bass, 2012), loc. 5790 of 8049, Kindle.

3. Mike Bonem and Roger Patterson, *Leading from the Second Chair: Serving Your Church, Fulfilling Your Role, and Realizing Your Dreams* (San Francisco: Jossey-Bass, 2005), 1, 3.

4. Lance Ford, *UnLeader: Reimagining Leadership . . . and Why We Must* (New York: Beacon Hill, 2012), 144–45.

5. Rob Lebow and Randy Spitzer, *Accountability: Freedom and Responsibility without Control* (San Francisco: Berrett-Koehler, 2002), 90.

6. Lebow and Spitzer, *Accountability*, 19.

7. Peter Block, *Stewardship: Choosing Service over Self-Interest* (San Francisco: Berrett-Koehler, 1993), 8.

8. Brian Zehr quoted in Todd Wilson, "Beyond Addition to Multiplication: What Does It Take to Lead a Kingdom-Advancing Level 5 Culture Shift in You and Your Church?," Exponential, 2017, https://exponential.org/beyond-addition-to-multiplication/.

9. Wilson, "Beyond Addition to Multiplication."

10. Hirsch and Catchim, *The Permanent Revolution*, 209.

11. Kim Field, "Willie Mays," May 6, 2019, http://www.kimfield.com/blog/2019/5/6/willie-mays.

12. Max De Pree, *Leading without Power: Finding Hope in Serving Community* (San Francisco: Jossey-Bass, 2003), 125–26.

13. Jeffrey S. Nielson, *The Myth of Leadership: Creating Leaderless Organizations* (Boston: Davies-Black, 2004), 109.

14. Doug Kirkpatrick, *Beyond Empowerment: The Age of the Self-Managed Organization* (Scotts Valley, CA: Createspace, 2011), 51.

15. Ori Brafman and Rod A. Beckstrom, *The Starfish and the Spider: The Unstoppable Power of Leaderless Organizations* (London: Portfolio, 2006), 39–40.

16. Frédéric Laloux, *Reinventing Organizations: A Guide to Creating Organizations Inspired by the Next Stage of Human Consciousness* (Brussels, Belgium: Nelson Parker, 2014), 111.

17. Kirkpatrick, *Beyond Empowerment*, 72.

18. Bill Easum, *Leadership on the Other Side* (Nashville: Abingdon, 2000).
19. Hirsch and Catchim, *The Permanent Revolution*, loc. 829 of 8049, Kindle.

Section 3: A Culture for Multiplying Disciples

1. Alan Hirsch, *The Forgotten Ways: Reactivating Apostolic Movements* (Grand Rapids: Brazos, 2016), 103.
2. Dallas Willard, *The Great Omission: Reactivating Jesus's Essential Teachings on Discipleship* (New York: HarperOne, 2014).

Chapter 9: The Disciple-Making Ingredients Starfish: Creating Environments and Mixing Ingredients

1. "Why Are So Many Starfish Dying?" video, National Geographic, https://www.nationalgeographic.com/animals/invertebrates/group/starfish/.
2. Aylin Woodward, "Marine Researchers Say Recent Sea Star Wasting Disease Epidemic Defies Prediction," UC Santa Cruz, March 20, 2018, https://news.ucsc.edu/2018/03/sea-stars.html.
3. "Why Are So Many Starfish Dying?" National Geographic.
4. Fred Edwords, "Faith and Faithlessness by Generation: The Decline and Rise Are Real," *Humanist*, August 21, 2018, https://thehumanist.com/magazine/september-october-2018/features/faith-and-faithlessness-by-generation-the-decline-and-rise-are-real.
5. Edwords, "Faith and Faithlessness by Generation."
6. Betsy Cooper et al., "Exodus: Why Americans Are Leaving Religion—And Why They're Unlikely to Come Back," PRRI, September 22, 2016, https://www.prri.org/research/prri-rns-poll-nones-atheist-leaving-religion/.
7. Cooper et al., "Exodus: Why Americans Are Leaving Religion—And Why They're Unlikely to Come Back."
8. The General Social Survey, 2018, University of Chicago, http://gss.norc.org.
9. The General Social Survey, 2018, University of Chicago, http://gss.norc.org.
10. Alan Hirsch and Debra Hirsch, *Untamed: Reactivating a Missional Form of Discipleship* (Grand Rapids: Baker, 2010), loc. 2662–665 of 2699, Kindle.
11. Justin Long, "Advancing through Persecution," 110 Mini L4, Case Studies, 2414.

Chapter 10: Outcome Focused: Disciple-Making Ingredient #1

1. Sheldon Vanauken, *A Severe Mercy: A Story of Faith, Tragedy, and Triumph* (New York: HarperOne, 1987), 85.
2. A paraphrase of Alan Hirsch, *The Forgotten Ways: Reactivating Apostolic Movements* (Grand Rapids: Brazos, 2016), 114.

3. Thomas Keating, *Fruits and Gifts of the Spirit* (New York: Lantern, 2007), 3.
4. Ken Wilber, *One Taste: Daily Reflections on Integral Spirituality* (Boulder, CO: Shambhala, 2000), 25–26.
5. These five points are adapted from E. Stanley Jones, *Christ's Alternative to Communism: And All Other "Isms" Today* (New York: Abingdon, 1935), 41–42.

Chapter 11: Habit Fueled: Disciple-Making Ingredient #2

1. Curt Thompson, "Spirituality, Neuroplasticity, and Personal Growth–Curt Thompson (Full Interview)," Biola University Center for Christian Thought, March 7, 2013, https://cct.biola.edu/spirituality-neuroplasticity-and-personal -growth-curt-thompson-full-interview/.
2. Alan Hirsch, *The Forgotten Ways: Reactivating Apostolic Movements* (Grand Rapids: Brazos, 2016), 113.

Chapter 12: Community Forged: Disciple-Making Ingredient #3

1. Abraham Joshua Heschel, *The Sabbath: Its Meaning for Modern Man* (New York: Farrar, Straus and Young, 1951), 6.
2. Michael Frost and Alan Hirsch, *The Faith of Leap: Embracing a Theology of Risk, Adventure & Courage* (Grand Rapids: Baker, 2011), 53–54.
3. Frost and Hirsch, *The Faith of Leap*, 54.
4. Matt. 4:25; 7:28; 8:1; 9:36; 13:2; 15:30; 19:2
5. Luke 10
6. Mark 3:13–19
7. Matt. 17:1; Mark 5:37; 9:2; 14:33
8. George Friedman, *The Storm Before the Calm: America's Discord, the Coming Crisis of the 2020s, and the Triumph Beyond* (New York: Knopf Doubleday, 2020), 217–18, 221.
9. Friedman, *The Storm Before the Calm*, 220.
10. Friedman, *The Storm Before the Calm*, 221.
11. Lesslie Newbigin, *The Gospel in a Pluralist Society* (Grand Rapids: Eerdmans, 1989), 227.

Chapter 13: Mission Fixated: Disciple-Making Ingredient #4

1. Alan Hirsch, *The Forgotten Ways: Reactivating Apostolic Movements* (Grand Rapids: Brazos, 2016), 82.
2. John I. Durham, *Exodus*, Word Biblical Commentary 3 (Dallas: Word, 1987), 260.
3. Hirsch, *The Forgotten Ways*, 128.
4. Mark Greenbaum, "Lincoln's Do-Nothing Generals," *New York Times*,

November 27, 2011, https://opinionator.blogs.nytimes.com/2011/11/27
/lincolns-do-nothing-generals/.
5. Greenbaum, "Lincoln's Do-Nothing Generals."

Chapter 14: Content Flavored: Disciple-Making Ingredient #5

1. Shea Gunther, "14 Amazing Fractals Found in Nature," Mother Nature Network, April 24, 2013, https://www.mnn.com/earth-matters/wilderness -resources/blogs/14-amazing-fractals-found-in-nature.
2. Ori Brafman and Rod A. Beckstrom, *The Starfish and the Spider: The Unstoppable Power of Leaderless Organizations* (London: Portfolio, 2006), 95.
3. Brafman and Beckstrom, *The Starfish and the Spider*, 95.
4. AA Grapevine (15 May 2013), AA Preamble (PDF), AA General Service Office, retrieved May 13, 2017.
5. David Barrett, George Kurian, and Todd Johnson, *World Christian Encyclopedia*, vol. 1 (New York: Oxford University Press, 2001), 16.
6. What Jesus considered the Law and Prophets was different from the modern reckoning and would have included twenty-six books. David Regan, "Law and the Prophets," Learn the Bible, http://www.learnthebible.org/law-and-the -prophets.html, accessed September 16, 2020.
7. Content adapted from Rob Wegner and Jack Magruder, *Missional Moves: 15 Tectonic Shifts that Transform Churches, Communities, and the World* (Grand Rapids: Zondervan, 2012), 32.
8. Paraphrase of Alan Hirsch, *The Forgotten Ways: Reactivating Apostolic Movements* (Grand Rapids: Brazos, 2016), 106.
9. Alan Hirsch and Tim Catchim, *The Permanent Revolution: Apostolic Imagination and Practice for the 21st Century Church* (San Francisco: Jossey-Bass, 2012), loc. 5835 of 8049, Kindle.
10. John Ortberg, *Faith and Doubt* (Grand Rapids: Zondervan, 2008), 42.

Chapter 15: The Disciple-Making Ecosystem Starfish: Balancing Elements and Cultivating an Ecosystem

1. Dr. Miles Lamare, "Role of Starfish in the Ecosystem," Science Learning Hub, September 17, 2009, https://www.sciencelearn.org.nz/videos/41-role-of -starfish-in-the-ecosystem.
2. Brodie Farquhar, "Wolf Reintroduction Changes Ecosystem in Yellowstone," Yellowstone Park, July 3, 2019, https://www.yellowstonepark.com/things -to-do/wolf-reintroduction-changes-ecosystem.
3. Farquhar, "Wolf Reintroduction Changes Ecosystem in Yellowstone."

Chapter 17: Voice: Disciple-Making Ecosystem Element #2

1. "Mount Erebus Disaster," Wikipedia, https://en.wikipedia.org/wiki/Mount _Erebus_disaster, accessed September 16, 2020.
2. *Braveheart*, directed by Mel Gibson (Paramount Pictures, 1995).

Chapter 18: Vocabulary: Disciple-Making Ecosystem Element #3

1. Peter Enns and Jared Byas, *Genesis for Normal People: A Guide to the Most Controversial, Misunderstood, and Abused Book of the Bible* (Study Guide Edition) (Denver: Patheos, 2019), 314–18.

Chapter 19: Vehicles: Disciple-Making Ecosystem Element #4

1. Dave Ferguson, *Hero Maker: Five Essential Practices for Leaders to Multiply Leaders* (Grand Rapids: Zondervan, 2018), 115.

Chapter 21: The Collective Intelligence Starfish: Embedding Simple Processes and Becoming a Learning System

1. Margaret J. Wheatley, *Finding Our Way: Leadership for an Uncertain Time* (San Francisco: Berrett-Koehler, 2007), 106.
2. Ori Brafman and Rod A. Beckstrom, *The Starfish and the Spider: The Unstoppable Power of Leaderless Organizations* (London: Portfolio, 2006), 185–86.
3. Martin Dempsey and Ori Brafman, *Radical Inclusion: What the Post-9/11 World Should Have Taught Us about Leadership* (Missionday, 2018), 125.
4. Edwin H. Friedman, *A Failure of Nerve: Leadership in the Age of the Quick Fix*, eds. Margaret M. Treadwell and Edward W. Beal (New York: Seabury, 2007), 16–17.
5. Saga Briggs, "Student Learning and Relational Intelligence," informED, October 25, 2019, https://www.opencolleges.edu.au/informed/features /student-learning-relational-intelligence/.
6. Daniel M. Cable, *Alive at Work: The Neuroscience of Helping Your People Love What They Do* (Boston: Harvard Business Review Press, 2018), 18.
7. Brian J. Robertson, *Holocracy: The New Management System for a Rapidly Changing World* (New York: Holt, 2015), 68.
8. Frédéric Laloux, *Reinventing Organizations: A Guide to Creating Organizations Inspired by the Next Stage of Human Consciousness* (Brussels, Belgium: Nelson Parker, 2014), 100.
9. Dennis W. Bakke, *Joy at Work: A Revolutionary Approach to Fun on the Job* (Seattle: PVG, 2005), 98–99.

10. Laloux, *Reinventing Organizations*, 103.

11. David Fitch, "On How Flat Leadership Works for Mission: The Three P's," *Reclaiming the Mission*, June 15, 2010, http://www.reclaimingthemission.com /on-how-flat-leadership-works-for-mission-the-three-p-'s/.

12. Fitch, "On How Flat Leadership Works."

13. Doug Kirkpatrick, *Beyond Empowerment: The Age of the Self-Managed Organization* (Scotts Valley, CA: Createspace, 2011), 31.

Conclusion: The Starfish Journey

1. Inspired by portions of Leonard Sweet and Frank Viola, *Jesus Manifesto: Restoring the Supremacy and Sovereignty of Jesus Christ* (Nashville: Thomas Nelson, 2016). This is a must-read!

2. John Ortberg, *Who Is This Man? The Unpredictable Impact of the Inescapable Jesus* (Grand Rapids: Zondervan, 2012), 80.

**EXPONENTIAL
RESOURCES**

About the Exponential Series

The interest in church planting has grown significantly in recent years. The need for new churches has never been greater. At the same time, the number of models and approaches is expanding. To address the unique opportunities of churches in this landscape, Exponential Network, in partnership with Leadership Network and Zondervan, launched the Exponential Series in 2010.

Books in this series:

- Tell the reproducing church story.
- Celebrate the diversity of models and approaches God is using to reproduce healthy congregations.
- Highlight the innovative and pioneering practices of healthy reproducing churches.
- Equip, inspire, and challenge kingdom-minded leaders with the tools they need in their journey of becoming reproducing church leaders.

Exponential exists to attract, inspire, and equip kingdom-minded leaders to engage in a movement of high-impact, reproducing churches. We provide a national voice for this movement through the Exponential Conference, the Exponential Initiative, Exponential Venture, and the Exponential Series.

Leadership Network exists to accelerate the impact of 100X leaders. Believing that meaningful conversations and strategic connections can change the world, we seek to help leaders navigate the future by exploring new ideas and finding application for each unique context.

For more information about the Exponential Series, go to
https://churchsource.com/collections/exponential-series.